Modernising Super-Exploitation

Modernising Super-Exploitation

Restructuring South African Agriculture

Tessa Marcus

Zed Books Ltd.
London and New Jersey

Modernising Super-Exploitation was first published in 1989 by
Zed Books Ltd., 57 Caledonian Road, London N1 9BU, UK, and
171 First Avenue, Atlantic Highlands, New Jersey 07716, USA.

Copyright © Tessa Marcus, 1989.

Cover designed by Andrew Corbett.
Typeset by Anne Field.
Map by Reuben Ruff.
Printed and bound in the United Kingdom
at Bookcraft (Bath) Ltd., Midsomer Norton.

British Library Cataloguing in Publication Data

Marcus, Tessa
 Modernising Super-Exploitation: Restructuring
South African Agriculture.
 1. South Africa. Agricultural Industries
 I. Title

 338. 1′0968

 ISBN 0-86232-844-6
 ISBN 0-86232-845-4 (pbk.)

Library of Congress Cataloging-in-Publication Data

Marcus, Tessa
 Modernising Super-Exploitation: Restructuring South African Agriculture
      p.   cm.
 Bibliography: p.
 Includes index.
 ISBN 0-86232-844-6. -- ISBN 0-86232-845-4 (pbk.)
 1. Agricultural laborers -- South Africa. 2. Farm tenancy -- South Africa. 3. Agriculture
-- Economic Aspects -- South Africa. I. Title.
 HD1518 .S6 M37   1989
 3381 ′0968--dc20   89-5835
                                                                      CIP

Contents

Tables

Acknowledgement

Many people and organisations have contributed to making this book possible. In particular, I am indebted to the Govan Mbeki Fund of the University of Amsterdam, the AABN, the KZA and Werkgroep-Kairos in the Netherlands, the Polski Komitet Solidarnosci z Narodami z Azji i Afriki and the University of Lodz in Poland. Professors Gerd Junne, Jolanta Kulpinska, Norman Long, Dr Peter Geschiere and Dr. Maria van Diepen have all played a vital part in helping me realise this project. I also want to thank my editors, John Daniel and Mike Kirkwood, and all those at Zed responsible for the essential technical aspects of production.

This work would not have been possible without the people of South Africa and the African National Congress, the revolutionary vanguard of the South African national liberation movement. It is the clarity of vision and the revolutionary sacrifice, embodied in all the men and women — some of whom have died, others who are in jail, underground or in exile — who have led and continue to lead our struggle, that has provided me with an understanding of the South African social formation and the means by which to go about changing it. Nor would this book have been possible without the vision and support of the members of my family, to whom this book is dedicated.

Preface

This book makes an important contribution to the analysis of patterns of agrarian development in South Africa. By concentrating on the commercial sector, rather than on the bantustans or on the problems of peasant agriculture, it fills a significant gap in our understanding of the dynamics of capitalist expansion in the rural sector of the South African economy. It adopts an historical approach to the study of agricultural development, plotting out successive stages in the confrontation of capital and labour, although at the same time it demonstrates convincingly that agricultural development does not follow any fixed linear model. There is instead a subtle phasing of development that reflects the pattern of changing strategies adopted by the state for subsidising white-controlled agriculture — replacing labour by mechanisation, suppressing labour tenancy arrangements at certain times whilst at others devising new forms of labour participation through the use of migrant and 'part-time' labour. The study also reveals important differences in the timing and structuring of agrarian change between regions and branches of the commercialised rural sector.

A notable feature of the book is the way in which it cracks the code of official statistics and questions the conclusions of existing local studies to expose certain features of socio-economic exploitation, ones which would go missing if existing ideological categories were simply accepted as scientifically valid. This is illustrated by the concealment in official documents of the high degree of participation of female and child labour in substitution for males, and of the use of various types of 'part-time' employment. Although based entirely on secondary data, the analysis is remarkable, too, for the extent to which it brings to light the views, interpretations and forms of social consciousness expressed by black workers, in opposition to the stereotypes promoted by government spokesmen and official investigators. In this way, Tessa Marcus has injected a vital human content into the many statistics she has assembled.

These issues are of major importance for comprehending the types of restructuring processes that have been developing in South African commercial agriculture over the last three or more decades. Although Marcus argues that changes in the social position and living and working conditions of workers are directly related to changes in the position and conditions of capital in the commercial sector, her analysis challenges existing orthodoxies which imply that mechanisation simply expels labour, leading to ever more capital-intensive forms of production. She argues that there is no real contradiction between the move towards capital-intensive production and the intensive exploitation of labour. The latter simultaneously involves the stabilisation of a reduced number of on-farm permanent workers, combined with the creation of a relocated seasonal labour force, forced labour by prisoners, and casual work provided by the families of 'full-time' workers. A further central theme of the book is the need to take full account of the coercive measures (political and ideological) deployed by the state in order to implement these changes.

Within the broader context of theoretical debates concerning capital penetration and agrarian development, it might seem that the commercial sector of South Africa is an unusual model of agricultural development, being based as it is upon racial as well as class domination. However, Marcus's study raises critical analytical issues relating to the increasing marginalisation of labour in the face of technological and bio-chemical change and concerning the role of authoritarian state apparatuses in managing such patterns of development, suggesting by implication that coercive forces are much more widespread than we often appreciate. It also stimulates questions concerning the significance of 'labour aristocracies' in agriculture and of the re-emergence of migrant and casual labour in contemporary Third World rural economies, of which Chile and Brazil provide parallel examples. Moreover, given the preponderance of women among these new types of agricultural workers, her book leads one to consider how this affects women's consciousness of and ability to resist such exploitative practices.

This book, then, offers much food for thought on issues of agrarian transformation and the role of the state. It also portrays vividly the continuing struggles by agricultural labourers against capitalist and racist oppression. This work will, I believe, be read widely by all those interested in the analysis of the dilemmas of agrarian and political change in South Africa.

Norman Long
The Agricultural University
Wageningen

May 1989

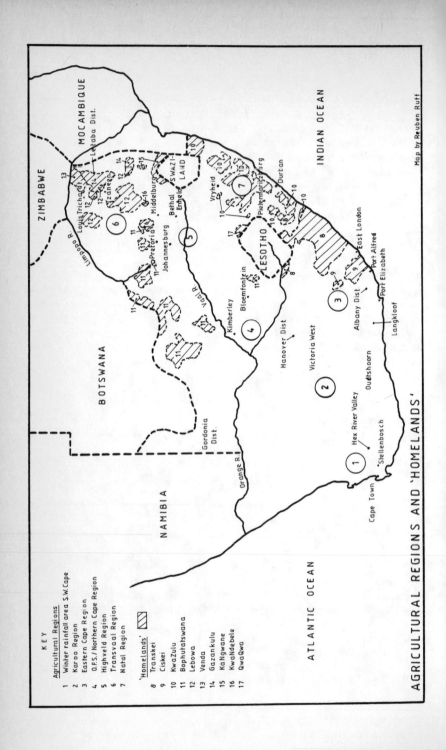

KEY

Agricultural Regions
1 Winter rainfall area S.W.Cape
2 Karoo Region
3 Eastern Cape Region
4 O.F.S./Northern Cape Region
5 Highveld Region
6 Transvaal Region
7 Natal Region

'Homelands'
8 Transkei
9 Ciskei
10 KwaZulu
11 Bophuthatswana
12 Lebowa
13 Venda
14 Gazankulu
15 KaNgwane
16 KwaNdebele
17 QwaQwa

AGRICULTURAL REGIONS AND 'HOMELANDS'

Map by Reuben Ruff

ZIMBABWE

MOCAMBIQUE

INDIAN OCEAN

BOTSWANA

NAMIBIA

ATLANTIC OCEAN

LESOTHO

SWAZI-LAND

Limpopo R

Vaal R

Orange R

Letaba Dist.
Louis Trichardt
Tzaneen
Pietersburg
Middelburg
Bethal
Ermelo
Vryheid
Pietermaritzburg
Durban
Pretoria
Johannesburg
Kimberley
Bloemfontein
Hanover Dist.
Victoria West
Gordonia Dist.
East London
Port Alfred
Port Elizabeth
Albany Dist.
Langkloof
Oudtshoorn
Hex River Valley
Stellenbosch
Cape Town

Introduction

This study is an attempt to understand how the position and conditions of farm workers in commercial agriculture in South Africa have been affected by what is known as the restructuring process. By restructuring is meant a process of reorganisation of relations of production and distribution by the ruling or dominant classes in an attempt to make the existing social system more functional and more efficient. It has three major characteristics:

- First, it does not alter the essential relations of the existing social system. Instead, it reorganises these social relations, adjusting them in response to changes occurring in the production process and to the shifts in the balance of class relations in the society. There is no fundamental transformation of these relations, which is why Hobart Houghton's description of the restructuring of South African commercial agriculture as a 'major agricultural revolution' (1964:62) is wrong and misleading.

- Second, it is a process which occurs at many levels, moving from the global scale of the world capitalist system, through regional relations between different nation states, to the specifics of national economies, extending right down to the particularities of sectoral relations within these economies. At each of these levels, the restructuring process has both general and specific features which influence, and are influenced by, changes at the same or other levels. Thus, the changes in South African commercial agriculture, which this study reveals, are inseparable from such developments as the rise to predominance of manufacturing in the South African economy and the balkanisation or 'bantustanisation' process carried out by the ruling white minority in response to African decolonisation, an economic, social and political reorganisation at the national level which has also been accompanied by a reorganisation of relations within the region.

- Third, restructuring is not just about technology, or even more narrowly put, mechanisation. While involving mechanisation and technological innovation, in the context of South African agriculture the process has been much more complex and extensive, involving the concentration of land, the concentration and centralisation of capital, and the reduction, differentiation and casualisation of the labour force. Each of these aspects of the process has occurred with active state intervention.

This study focuses on the third of these characteristics and will trace the development of the process through the two distinct phases or periods into which it falls. The first runs from the late 1930s/early 1940s until the mid-1960s, while the second began in the mid-1960s and was still ongoing in the late 1970s. During the first phase, farm production was still labour-intensive. However, the growing capitalisation and expansion of agricultural production was intensifying the demand for farm labour. Simultaneously, the concomitant rapid growth of secondary industry in South Africa created its own demand for labour and emerged as a more attractive alternative to work on the farms. There was thus something of an exodus from the land and during this period farmers and the state acted to counter the exodus and to immobilise black workers in commercial agriculture. In the second phase, production in commercial agriculture had changed from labour- to capital-intensive a shift with far-reaching consequences for the organisation of the labour force. These included a drastic decline in the number of farm workers and a shift in the social composition of the agricultural workforce, with a proportionate growth in the use of migrant and female, child and prison labour.

To pose the problem of the impact of restructuring in South African commercial agriculture on farm workers, one immediately confronts an apparent disparity in the existing literature, thinking and common wisdom on the subject. It is expressed in two seemingly unrelated bodies of knowledge on this question. The one focuses on the materially evident, extensive reorganisation of capital in the agricultural sector. It emphasises the facts of mechanisation and technological innovation, the rationalisation of production, the concentration of land, production and ownership, etc. This is the orthodoxy which pervades most people's assumptions regardless of the differing perspectives they may have. It is articulated in the dominant ideology and crystallised in the thinking of members of the South African Agricultural Union (SAAU) and all the ministers of agriculture since 1910. The orthodoxy even contends that the process is 'progressive' and 'modern', whatever these terms may mean.

The other set of information or body of knowledge, which is equally pervasive, emphasises the continued intense oppression and exploitation of black farm workers. It is expressed, for example, in the papers presented to the pioneering 1976 Farm Labour Conference organised by the University of Cape Town and to the 1984 Carnegie Conference on Rural Poverty in South Africa, as well as in the five-volume report produced by the Surplus People's Project (1983), the documents of the Association for Rural Advancement (AFRA) in Natal, and the Transvaal Rural Action Committee (TRAC). The collective evidence reaffirms the proposition that relations in this, the most backward sector of the South African political economy, continue to rest extensively on forced and super-cheap labour. My own view is that these sets of information are not incongruous and that the disjuncture between so-called modern farming and forced, cheap labour falls away as they express different sides of the same relation — the relation of capital and labour in conditions of national and social oppression.

Following from the above, this study takes the view that it is not possible to talk about capital restructuring without anticipating that the process will have consequences for workers and without examining what those consequences are. Certain key questions have to be examined: why, in conditions where labour is so cheap, should it be profitable (the main ideological content behind such notions as 'modern' and 'progressive') to substitute capital for labour? what is the relation of cheap labour to the restructuring process? is it really 'not a factor', as the dominant ideology of capitalism contends, or is it the central, material force in the process of reorganising production relations on South Africa's white-owned farms?

This study will take the latter view and go further to show both that it was only possible to keep labour so cheap by changing the position and conditions of workers in the sector and that this was also necessary for capital's continuing profitability.

This study is ground-breaking in several important ways:

● First, unlike the main body of literature on social relations in South African commercial agriculture, it treats capital and labour as a relation, two sides of the same coin. In this way, all the available information on the topic can be brought together and analysed.

● Second, it treats race and national oppression as significant social relations which operate in close interplay with class. That all but a few farmers are white and all farm workers black — and the overwhelming majority African — is not incidental to relations in the sector. However, neither is it adequate nor sufficient to explain these racial and national divisions by recourse to such descriptive categories as 'physical and cultural differences', which is the most usual way they are treated in the South African literature and everyday orthodoxy. The approach of this study is to regard African national oppression as organically integrated into relations of social exploitation in the South African social formation. Thus, in exploring the implications of restructuring for capital and labour on farms, it is necessary to consider simultaneously how the relation of national domination relates to and is affected by restructuring. By establishing the way race and national oppression are integral to one another, it is possible to reach a better understanding of social relations on white-owned farms. This approach also has consequences for the way the social formation as a whole is conceptualised, a matter to which I shall return in the conclusion.

● Third, it focuses on the oppression of women in agriculture, and shows how that relates to the oppression of women in general. Without an understanding of the specific form and function of women's oppression in conditions of national domination and social exploitation, it is not possible to understand the implications of restructuring for labour. With few exceptions, the existing literature seems to have considerable difficulty in coming to grips with the manner in which the sexual division of labour and gender oppression form part of the exploitation inherent in South African commercial agriculture. Mostly, the problem is ignored altogether. When it is not, it is usually presented as a *fait accompli*, either without exploring its context and implications, or by simply repeating all the orthodox social presumptions and prejudices about black working women.

The key analytic tool in this study is the notion of labour forms, because it enables us to understand the position of workers on the farms as a relation of production. The features which characterise farm workers in South Africa are more than descriptive categories about the social characteristics of the workforce. The notion or concept of labour forms provides us with the means to understand the relation of labour to capital, of black to white, of men to women, not only at a specific point in time but also over time. It enables us to understand how the social characteristics of workers in the sector, which have a direct and material bearing on the labour forms, are integral to the process of production. This makes them both constant and changing at the same time. It means that it is necessary to explore beneath form to look for content.

This approach becomes a challenge to the language of apartheid. While some writers have questioned some terms and concepts, they have often tended to confine themselves to the more obvious expressions and manifestations of white minority domination such as the bantustans, 'black spots', etc. Rarely, however, do these writers explore beneath the assumptions underlying these terms and concepts. These assumptions extend to the very notion of commercial agriculture itself, and the meaning of work in the sector expressed in such terms as 'white farming', 'casual labour', 'migrant labour', the 'permanent workforce', etc. The point is that in the context of South Africa nothing can be assumed; words can never be taken at face value simply because they often do not mean what they appear to mean. The commonplace vocabulary used when discussing work and workers on South African farms has to be treated with caution, explained or changed. This is not easy to do without overloading the text or obscuring the primary line of argument altogether. Thus, when I have been unable to use more suitable alternative terms, I have used inverted commas to draw attention to the problem of taking these words at face value.

This work is not a presentation of new empirical evidence. The material I have drawn on is essentially secondary, the most important of which is the still small, but growing body of work produced by researchers in the past ten to fifteen years. The purpose of bringing this information together is to contribute to a more precise interpretation of the empirical evidence. That evidence does not 'speak for itself' and, very often, the theoretical framework in which it is presented is an inadequate or incorrect explanation of the social relations in South African commercial agriculture.

The few worthy analyses, such as those by Seleoane (1984), De Klerk (1983, 1984, 1984a) and Levatan (1984), have come out of local and specific case studies. Here I propose to develop some of these themes at a more general level, placing the discussion of developments in the agricultural sector in the context of the society as a whole.

Inevitably, this study is only a partial answer to my main question, i.e., what impact restructuring has had on the position and conditions of farm workers. Naturally what is occurring within commercial agriculture is integrally linked to broader processes in the South African political economy as a whole. Structural unemployment and deteriorating conditions in the reserves, the fusing of industrial, mining and commercial capital, the social, economic and political crises of apartheid all have a bearing on the significance and implications of restructuring within agriculture.

Furthermore, I have confined my argument in this work to the problems of workers in commercial agriculture proper. This means that the position of non-agricultural workers on the farms — particularly domestic workers — has not been looked at. These women and children form part of the working class employed in the sector and a knowledge of the social relations under which they work is essential to a fuller understanding of it. To date, however, their position and conditions have not been studied. The only information we have is periodic reports over the years in the press which record violence and abuse meted out to domestic workers; a common wisdom amongst the oppressed which is expressed as a hatred of domestic work on the farms, and of farm work in general, and which comes out of the experience of those who have worked on the farms; and lastly, from the agricultural censuses which only record, and then imprecisely, the number of domestic workers in the sector.

It has also not been possible to deal with all aspects of the impact of restructuring on workers in agricultural employment. This has meant that important details of the restructuring process as they have affected general social conditions have not been examined. Particularly, I am referring to the interrelated questions of control, violence and physical abuse, health and safety at work and organisation and resistance. The question of health and safety, like domestic work on farms, has never been studied. The situation is slightly better when it comes to the problem of control and violence. In addition to Ruth First's (1959) pioneering exposure of conditions in the Eastern Transvaal, the problem has been highlighted by Ombudsman Roelofse's investigation in the late 1970s and most recently in papers given at the Second Carnegie Conference, e.g., Seleoane's small study of eight Middelburg farms, as well as in periodic press reports. Work on organisation and resistance is also limited, although important advances have been made in historical research in particular. In short, essential research into each of these aspects still has to be done. Much of the information that exists has yet to be explored and made coherent. However, although this study omits these important questions, it is still able to bring out the main forces at work governing relations in the sector. It presents a framework and provides the analytic tools to systematise and analyse the material evidence as it is uncovered.

This approach makes it possible to proceed from abstract questions to a very concrete analysis of material conditions. It allows us to explore the very depths of exploitation in the South African countryside and to uncover relations that are shocking in the extent and intensity of the oppression they make possible. It reveals the real content of the notion of super-exploitation, not simply as an adjective to describe exploitation, but as an expression of a specific set of relations where capitalism functions in colonial or colonial-like conditions.

My purpose has not just been to expose and shock but to lead us beyond that condition to an understanding of the forces which produce such scandalous conditions. With such an understanding it is possible to identify what has to change and to look for ways to bring about this change. This has been my goal. My work is offered as a contribution to the continuing and bitter mass popular and workers' struggle to end exploitation and oppression in South Africa and to bring about a just social order.

1.   The Restructuring of
Commercial Agriculture

Over the past 50 years, and particularly since World War Two, commercial agricultural production in South Africa has undergone considerable restructuring. Whilst the focus of this essay is on the implications of this restructuring process for workers in agriculture, it is necessary, albeit briefly, to look at some of the most important processes which have brought about this transformation. It must be stated at the outset, however, that the course of this restructuring — its stages, directions and contradictions; its relation to developments in the potential economy as a whole; its relation to the international capitalist system etc., — has yet to be systematically analysed, so that this account is, at best, preliminary, and intends only to look at some general indicators and to raise some questions.

All too often, the restructuring of commercial agricultural production (termed by Hobart Houghton 'the major agricultural revolution', 1964:62) has been characterised predominantly, if not exclusively as 'mechanisation'. But, on its own, mechanisation is insufficient to account for the transformation process. This is true even if it is given a broad interpretation to include technological changes ranging from the use of tractors and machines to the application of chemistry and biology in plant and animal husbandry. Rather, 'mechanisation' is one of at least four primary and interrelated processes which have brought about this restructuring. These are i) the concentration of land; ii) the concentration of capital; iii) mechanisation and technological innovation; iv) the promotion and subsidising of these processes by the state. Each of these will be looked at in turn.

The concentration of land

Land is a central and indispensable necessity in agricultural production. In South Africa, it is concentrated, generally speaking, in the hands of the ruling white minority and, as such, it is a key feature of their national domination.[1] In this sense, therefore, the process of land (and capital) concentration began with the appropriation of more than 87 per cent of the land by the white minority for its exclusive exploitation and occupation.

The total area available for agricultural production (including forestry) outside the reserves has remained virtually constant over the past half century, rising from 83 million ha in 1930 to only 85.7 million ha in 1976. In this period, there have been two interrelated sources of 'new territory' for white agricultural capital. One has derived from the dispossession of African- and mission-owned African-farmed land lying outside the reserves which has been transferred to white and state hands in terms of the so-called 'blackspot' clearance policy. Since 1960, this policy is estimated to have affected some 610,000 people, with a further 1,530,000 Africans under threat of eviction.[2] While attention has focused naturally on the human dimension of suffering caused by this process of land dispossession, the fact that a considerable amount of African-owned land has also been appropriated has been somewhat overlooked. In actuality, it has amounted to some 106,305 ha (SAAU, Annual Report 1978:71), much of which was used for agricultural purposes — a manifestation of the centuries-old continuing dispossession of the African majority.

The second source of 'new' land has been the reserves themselves. In 1972, state policy regarding private white access to land and non-mineral resources in the reserves changed, and it was decided to "invite white-owned and operated companies to undertake major crop production in the 'homelands',"[3] thereby opening up, at least theoretically, some 15 million ha[4] to white agricultural capital. The decision drew warm approval from big business, whose support derived more from an eye for potential profit than any philanthropic concerns like 'development'.[5] Another effect of this change in policy was to ensure that land purchased from white farmers under 'homeland consolidation' measures (i.e., the purchase of land by the state to create more physically complete entities out of the various reserve patchworks) did not entail any loss of land for 'white' agriculture.[6]

Taken together, these two measures increased the land surface area available to (white) commercial agricultural exploitation to at least 100 million ha.

Census statistics show that on land outside the bantustans there has been a steady decrease in the number of farm units and a concomitant growth in farm size. In other words, fewer farmers are farming larger units. Table 1.1. shows that the number of farm units began to decline after 1950 with the most dramatic reduction occurring in the period after 1969.

Table 1.1
Decline in the number of farm units — 1937-1984

Year	Number of Units	Number +/−(%)
1937	104 554	—
1950	116 848	12 294 + (11.74)
1960	105 859	10 989 − (9.41)
1969	91 885	13 974− (13.20)
1976	75 562	16 323 − (17.77)
1984*f*	70 000	5 562 − (7.36)

(*f* = estimate)
Source: Abstract of Agricultural Census, 1980 and RSA Yearbook, 1984.

Simultaneously, as the number of units declined, their average size increased. Nationally, (excluding the reserves), average farm unit size rose in physical terms from 736.5 ha in 1951 to 978.8 ha in 1970 and to 1 134.4 ha in 1976. The extent of this land concentration was even greater when account is taken of the differences between regions and farming types. For example, in the extensive bushveld farming regions in the Transvaal in 1972, the average farm covered 3,000 ha grazing 340 head of large stock. By 1978, it measured 3,800 ha with 430 head of cattle, and in 1983 it had grown to 5,000 ha with 500 stock units.

The significance of physical size for the concentration of wealth and production warrants some consideration. Whilst land ownership is an immediate indicator of wealth, the ownership of large tracts of land does not in itself mean a relatively greater concentration of capital, since land size is not the only or primary indicator of production concentration. Other variables need to be taken into consideration including the quality of the soil, climatic conditions, the type of agricultural activity, the intensity with which the land can be and is used, etc. Also, and equally importantly, the growth in physical unit size has to be assessed against a rise in the cost of production. This has meant the increase in size has been accompanied by a concomitant tendency for the physical threshold of farm unit economic viability to rise. Thus, in 1960, the Du Toit Commission Report (1960, para.265,4) stated that:

> ... a farmer and his family can only earn a decent livelihood on a farm of less than 100 morgen (85,7 ha) under the following conditions:
> a) where intensive farming is possible in areas with a high rainfall or under irrigation, as in the Western Province fruit area, the closer settlements or private irrigation schemes;
> b) where subtropical fruit, vegetables and sugar can be grown as in the lowveld areas of Natal and Transvaal; and
> c) with specialised farming in the vicinity of cities and large towns such as the Cape Flats and areas bordering the Rand and Durban.

Less than a decade later, the Marais/Du Plessis report (1968, paras.3.36.4 and 5), on evidence from the Orange Free State, determined economic unit viability for cattle farms in the eastern part of the Molopo region at 2,057 ha and in the far western part of Molopo at 3,428 ha or more. In Gordonia, where units under 4,285 ha were considered 'undeniably too small', some 22.4 percent of farms fell into this category. In all, the Commission estimated that some 30-40 percent of white-owned farm units in South Africa were too small to be economically viable. That these smaller units come under the greatest economic (and political) pressure is indicated indirectly by the rate of transfer of rural immovable property. In the period April 1982 to March 1983, some 9,414 farms, covering 3.5 million ha, were sold. Of these, 56.2 percent were less than 100 ha in size. 72.8 percent were smaller than 300 ha, and only 8.7 percent 1,000 ha or larger. (Central Statistics 1981).

Clearly, restructuring has entailed a relative increase in the land area devoted to commercial agricultural production. The source of this land has been African-owned land outside the reserves and African-owned or state-owned land within them. It has also entailed an absolute decline in the number of farm units, accompanied by an increase in the average physical size per unit. In short, there has been a simultaneous tendency towards land concentration and farm unit consolidation.

The concentration of capital

The period since World War Two has seen the ownership of production units accumulating in the hands of a declining number of people and/or organisations which, in turn, has produced a merging of capital both within agriculture and with capital from other sectors. These processes have occurred with and through the state as well.

At the most elementary level, the extent of capital concentration can be assessed in terms of the number of individuals or companies owning farming enterprises. The actual number of farmers, however, is not known and it cannot be assumed from the statistics on farm units that the number of farm owners is equal to the number of units since, for census purposes, a return is made for each unit, and each respondent is considered 'a holder' irrespective of whether he (or it) actually owns the enterprise.

When taken together with the fact that more than one enterprise can be owned by an individual or company, the number of farm owners is likely to be fewer than the number of units. With this in mind, and assuming that the rate of decline in the number of farm owners is identical to that in farm unit numbers, the number of owners has contracted by some 40 percent between 1950 and 1984, to a figure little over 70,000.

Ownership and concentration is not only about absolute numbers. It reflects too the size of enterprises measured not only in terms of acreage but, more importantly, in terms of volume of production and the market share commanded by individual enterprises. In South Africa most commercial farms are owned by whites as private individuals, or private companies, and production is dominated by a very small group of capitalists. In 1970, 50 percent of farmers produced 95 percent of the total agricultural output and 20 percent of farming units were responsible for 75 percent of agricultural production outside the reserves (Stadler, 1976).

If account is taken of agricultural production in the reserves, the degree of concentration is even greater since there are many producers making small, if not miniscule, inputs into production totals. The sisal industry illustrates the point. The number of sisal estates owned by whites declined from 20 in the 1950s to 3 by 1979 (Marais Report, 1968). They worked 7,000 ha or 35 percent of land under sisal. The remaining 13,000 ha in the bantustans was held by the South African Development Trust, worked by scores, if not hundreds, of producers.[7]

This trend of capital concentration seems to have continued in the 1980s. In 1981/82 the average net income of 20 percent of farming enterprises was R146,200, compared to an average of R9,100 per unit for the remaining 80 percent, the result, on the one hand, of developments in production relations and in the political economy which are driving smaller enterprises 'to the wall', and on the other of state policy which deliberately promotes enterprise and capital 'consolidation'.

Increased capital accumulation has brought with it an expansion both in the volume of agricultural production and of wealth being concentrated in the process. For the period 1950-75, the average real value of production grew by 148 percent per farming unit, which meant that, due to the unequal distribution of wealth amongst producers, the rich grew proportionately richer than this average suggests (Schroder 1979).

Economies of scale
The extent to which the process of capital concentration helps capital generate capital and wealth generate wealth can be seen in the effect of the operation of economies of scale. Economies of scale enhance profit levels substantially,

notwithstanding the fact that there is a plateau after which they do not necessarily generate greater profit, or the rate of profit generation slows. For example, a study of dairy enterprises in Natal has shown that a farmer producing 100,000 litres of milk per annum needs to produce 5,500 litres per cow before making a profit, whereas a farmer producing 1.1 million litres of milk p.a. will have a break-even level of production per cow of only 1,600 litres, i.e., his cows have to produce only 29 percent of the milk required by the smaller producer to begin to make a profit (Schroeder 1979).

Economies of scale operate in most sections of South African agricultural production, including grapes, sugar, wool, maize and meat, and calculations have been made about the level at which such economies begin to operate for various farming types. In 1979, it was estimated that for intensive farming enterprises, such as the Vaalhartz Irrigation Scheme area, economies of scale were operating optimally on 30-50 ha units, whereas for extensive mixed farming economies of scale operated on units of 800-1,000 ha. In the extensive sheep-farming Karoo, efficiency (profit) was at its highest on units of between 3,500 and 5,500 ha (*Financial Mail* 6.7.79).

How economies of scale are achieved relates in part to capital possibilities, but, as will be shown later, it is also inseparably linked to the rationalisation and reorganisation of the workforce.

Concentration of distribution

I have so far looked at capital accumulation in agriculture only from the perspective of production. However, the whole sphere of distribution needs to be evaluated when considering the extent of concentration. This is especially so in South Africa where distribution is highly centralised and controlled by the combined action of the state and agricultural producers organised in an extensive network of co-operatives. In 1981/82, 72 percent of agricultural production (in gross value terms) was handled by specific state marketing schemes through 21 Control Boards. A further ten percent was regulated by giant co-operatives like the KWV for wine growers or the South African Sugar Association (SASA) for sugar. These enforce the compulsory sale of produce to respective co-operative societies as a provision of the Co-operatives Act of 1939. In fact, only 18 percent of production is distributed outside legislative controls. Most of this is fresh fruit and vegetables for the domestic market and here large producers or distributors, without state aid, dominate the process.

Not only do the control boards and co-operatives regulate primary distribution, but inevitably they influence production itself. This is done through, for example, setting production quotas, establishing floor prices for produce, controlling international and national outlets etc. They are designed to protect white farmers from natural hazards, from competition from manufacture, and from consumer pressures. However, they inevitably also work in favour of the large producers and distributors who dominate the market. So, for example, a 1984 report by Professor E Kassier of Stellenbosch University on the degree of concentration in the meat industry found both production and distribution dominated by 'the big three'— the Co-operative *Vleissentraal*, and two companies, Imperial Cold Storage and Karoo-

Kanhym (*Financial Mail*, 8.3.85). However, not only were they found to be the dominating interest on both sides of the auction floor, which meant directly or indirectly controlling meat producers as well as the manufacture, wholesale and retail meat trade; they were also 'conspicuously well represented' on the so-called independent organisations appointed to regulate the marketing of meat and its by-products. As Table 1.2 below shows, Vleissentraal holds an absolute dominant position.

Table 1.2
Representation of Vleissentraal on key bodies
controlling production and sale of meat

Body	Total Membership	No. of Members from Vleissentraal
Meat Board	15	7
Meat Board Executive	7	3
Cattle Committee (SAAU)	8	6
Meat Committee (SAAU)	4	3
Sheep Committee (SAAU)	11	3

In addition, one third of the members of the National Abattoir Corporation were from Vleissentraal. ICS and Karoo-Kanhym also had representations on the Meat Board and two-thirds of the Offal, Skin and Hide Committee (SAAU) came from 'the big three'. What this illustrates is that a small group of companies and individuals not only dominate production, they also control distribution.

The centralisation of capital
Finally, in this brief overview we need to consider the question of the fusing of capitals — or centralisation. In South African commercial agricultural production the process of centralisation is quite advanced. This is suggested by the extent of capital concentration and the degree of industrialisation of production in the sector. It is also suggested by the strong connection between commercial agriculture and manufacture, where an estimated 48 percent of domestic agricultural production was absorbed by secondary industry in 1974, for example. At the same time, farmers constituted a substantial market for manufactured goods and services (*Financial Gazette*, 11.10.74). As we have already seen, three large organisations dominate the meat industry, to the extent that in 1980 they controlled 75 percent of it. Yet, closer investigation reveals that these organisations are themselves subsidiaries of larger companies. Vleissentraal and Kanhym-Karoo are controlled by General Mining whilst Imperial Cold Storage is owned by CG Smith Ltd, South Africa's fourth largest conglomerate which has diversified interests apart from meat. These include sugar, milling, fishing, as well as fresh milk and industrial milk products. CG Smith is in turn owned by Barlow Rand which until the early 1980s was one of the 'eight private conglomerates ... identified as the controlling forces within South African capitalism'. Since then one of those eight — SA Mutual

— has taken effective control of Barlow Rand. SA Mutual is now the third largest conglomerate in South Africa controlling, in 1985, 18.06 percent of the total assets of non-state corporations (Davies, O'Meara, Dlamini 1988: Vol I pp 12-15).

What is apparent is that not only is there a fusing of capital within the agricultural sector but that the production of diverse agricultural products is controlled by a handful of agricultural producers, which are, in turn, controlled by non-agricultural producers through corporate and company interests. There has thus been an inter-sectoral fusing of capital, producing intensified degrees of ownership concentration. Commercial agricultural production has been transformed by capital concentration and centralisation. The full dimension of this process has yet to be thoroughly investigated but for the sector as a whole, and for the interrelation of the sector with mining, industrial and finance capital, it is clear that a small group of organisations represented by a handful of men, own and control a substantial part of agricultural production directly, and indirectly determine most if not all production within the sector. The shift towards greater capital intensity in agricultural production — so-called mechanisation — has both reflected and reinforced this trend.

Mechanisation and technological innovation

One reason why the restructuring process in commercial agricultural production is often scientifically expressed, and invariably conceived of, as mechanisation is that machines are a highly visible and materially concrete expression of this process. They stand as the physical embodiment of the shift in relations between capital and labour on the land. But this apparently 'self-evident' reality conceals or obscures the fact that 'mechanisation' is only one of several processes which have combined to bring about the restructuring of commercial agriculture in South Africa. The contribution of mechanisation to this transformation process should not, however, be underestimated.

To understand properly the concept of 'mechanisation', two factors have to be taken into account. The first concerns whether the definition is able to incorporate all aspects of the process and the second concerns the meaning of mechanisation — however defined — for production relations, i.e., its impact on and implications for commercial agriculture. In this chapter, only the second aspect is examined from the perspective of its implications for capital and the process of production excluding labour, since the impact of the combined effect of all the processes of restructuring for workers is dealt with in subsequent chapters.

Defining 'mechanisation'
Perhaps the most concrete expression of 'mechanisation' in agriculture is the presence or use of tractors as the introduction of tractive power, at least up until the 1950s, was the main, although not exclusive,[8] technological innovation in commercial agriculture. Furthermore, and more importantly, the introduction of mechanical traction (tractors), particularly for arable production, not only transformed many processes involved in planting, growing and harvesting crops, but also made possible the introduction of other mechanical innovations. Tractors therefore stand at the centre of the mechanisation process since they embody the

essence of mechanical power in agriculture and it is the use of mechanical power — as opposed to animal- or human-power — which forms the base of the mechanisation process.

A definition therefore of mechanisation as 'tractorisation' would be too narrow and confining, given the expansion of mechanical technology. Rather, mechanisation should be understood as the application of mechanical power in general, encompassing tractive power, including tractors as well as machine-based technology such as milking machines, sprinkler irrigation, micro- and macro-jet spray technology etc.

But there is another aspect to the problem. Mechanisation does not account for other non-mechanical, especially biological and chemical, technological innovations. Although they are at an earlier stage of development than machine technology, they have become increasingly important over the past three decades and their importance is likely to increase with time. To incorporate them into a notion of 'mechanisation' is to commit a double error which not only robs the concept of any substance but which also ignores the particular significance of these forms of technological innovation. None the less these processes and their impact have to be, and will be, explored under the heading 'other technological innovations'. However, for brevity's sake, when these aspects are not being dealt with separately from mechanisation, the combined reference will be to mechanisation etc.

The extent of mechanisation and other technological innovations.[9]
1. *Mechanisation*
Although it has not reached the levels of Western Europe or the USA in extent or intensity, the process of mechanisation in South African commercial agriculture has advanced considerably during the past half century, particularly since the 1960s.

To give some indication of its extent, the growth in volume of machinery as well as the increase in capacity and facility will be looked at. This, however, is only a partial indicator of the process, and four provisos must be kept in mind: (a) an adequate measure of mechanisation must take into consideration the relation of capital-machinery-land to stock-labour; (b) there is no single, universal measure that can quantitatively and qualitatively indicate the extent of mechanisation in agricultural production as a whole. The most commonly used universal indicator —tractors — reveals more about the extent of mechanisation in crop production than in pastoral farming; (c) within some branches of food production, like crops, the extent of mechanisation is uneven. Wheat and maize are the only two cash crops which are virtually fully mechanised. This fact is not incidental to production and employment in the branch as a whole, since no less than 45 percent of the total cultivated area in South Africa is under maize. Wheat, the largest of the small grain crops, covered 17 percent of cultivated land in 1981/2 and accounted for 93 percent of the 2.44 million metric tons of winter cereals (wheat, barley, oats and rye) produced in that year. The remaining field crops are only partially mechanised. This means that sometimes mechanisation is at a generally low level all round, for example, in potato production. Sometimes it means that only some aspects of the production process are mechanised whilst others are completely unmechanised. In sugar, for example, whilst about 99 percent of cane cutting is done by hand, the mechanisation of stacking, loading and transloading cane is well advanced, estimated at about 89 percent (Budlender, 1984). But more commonly, each of the stages of production for any particular crop is at various levels of mechanisation; (d) mechanisation has occurred in stages which can be demarcated for the sector as a whole, for particular branches as well as for particular products. A detailed study of maize farming in six magisterial districts of the western Transvaal over the period 1968-81 illustrates the point:

> ... in 1968, between 25 and 30 percent of the area planted with maize was being harvested by combine. ... in 1981 this had risen to about 95 percent. The greatest part of the change-over took place during 1973 and 1977 . ... The adoption of bulk handling and storage techniques was more advanced in 1968. More than half the crop — 54 percent — was already being delivered in bulk and by 1977 virtually the entire crop was reaching silos in this way.
>
> By comparison, chemical weed control was not nearly as widespread in 1968. Only 15 percent of the area planted with all crops was being sprayed ... by 1981 weed killers were being used on roughly 95 percent of the total crop surface area (De Klerk, 1983:26).

These stages are not simply a factor of mechanical (or technological) capacity or development. Rather, they are the outcome of combined political and economic pressures and constraints which can be partially resolved by mechanisation, but which in turn bring about new contradictions. Nor are they inevitable or irreversible. However, 'one innovation implies another and once on the course of mechanisation it is often difficult to halt it' (Budlender, 1984), especially when mechanisation is taken in conjunction with other processes under way in restructuring.

In the period 1975-82, some 123,528 tractors were sold in South Africa. By 1984 tractor manufacturers assessed the 'white farmer tractor market' to be nearly saturated, with sales generally only possible on a replacement basis. However, tractors had undergone significant developments in their capacity since the 1950s, including four-wheel drive, extended transmission range and a basic increase in tractive power. Taking power capacity as an example, whilst the average farmer bought medium power-class tractors (52-60 kw) during the 1970s, increasingly more were buying higher power machines. In 1983, about 27 percent of tractors sold were above 60kw capacity while just under ten percent had capacities of 105kw or more (Basson, 1984). Whilst not all farmers use their machines to full capacity, this development was indicative of changing tillage practices, haulage requirements and a more 'efficient and economical' working of larger lands, all part of the process of land concentration and an effect of economy of scale.

Similar examples of the extent of mechanisation in arable production can be found in animal husbandry, in horticulture and intensively irrigated production. Each is characterised by varying degrees of mechanisation within the branch, as well as within the product. Furthermore, the measure of mechanisation varies according to the farming type. Thus, in dairy farming, for example, an important measure of the extent of mechanisation is the degree to which milking is done by machine and retained in mechanical refrigeration units. In 1984, 95 percent of the 27,000 commercial milk producers in South Africa milked by machine and all used mechanical refrigeration (RSA Year Book, 1984).

It is thus clear that in any assessment of the impact and implications of mechanisation and other technological innovations, the extent to which the process is advanced in one product and in one branch carries with it considerable significance, not least of all for labour.

2. Chemical compounds in agriculture

A major technological development in agricultural production has been the development, and increasingly widespread use, of chemical compounds, both as fertilisers and to control pests, weeds, parasites etc. The extent of their use in South Africa and their relation to other technological developments — especially mechanisation — is generally underinvestigated and not readily available. This is particularly the case with pesticides, herbicides and parasite-control chemicals. More information, however, is available on chemical fertilisers where their use in commercial agriculture has increased steadily over the past 50 years. In 1937, 365,000 tons were used in arable farming; in 1974 the amount had risen to about 3 million tons, and by 1980/81 to 3.4 million tons.

If the evidence from maize can be generalised, it seems that this increase in usage can be attributed to the fact that more farmers were using fertilisers and that fertilisers were being applied more intensively by those already using them. Between 1966 and 1982, the amount of fertiliser used per hectare of maize rose from 20 to 100 kg/ha, or by some 500 percent. A record high usage was recorded in 1981 when average figures topped 110 kg/ha or more, whereafter mounting costs and an evaluation of yield returns, coupled with three years of drought, forced farmers to reconsider the application of fertiliser. Between 1977 and 1981 more than one fifth of expenditure on goods and services in the sector was spent on fertilisers.[10]

As with machine technology, the extent to which chemical compounds are used and the purposes to which they are put varies between branches of the sector as well as between products within branches. Summer grain farmers (maize, sorghum, etc.) constitute the largest single group of fertiliser consumers, whilst sugar farming has the highest use of chemical compounds for all cash crop production in South Africa. In fact, one-fifth of all expenditure on goods and service is on fertiliser. Since sugar-cane is very hardy, pesticides are hardly used but, in other crops, the spread of chemical compounds has meant an increasing use to counteract different sorts of problems. For example, until as recently as the 1980s farmers in viticulture used chemicals only for pest control whilst weeds were controlled by plough and shovel. Now chemicals are used widely for both pests and weeds, with implications for both the levels and conditions of employment.

In animal husbandry, although the amount spent on parasite and other chemical compound controls represents less than three percent of the total value of livestock production (1984), it is nevertheless a substantial figure of about R80 million per year. Unfortunately, there is little data on the nature, volume or extent of usage of these compounds, but the treatment of ecto- and endo-parasites through dips and deworming is widespread, if not universal. What is known of the compounds is that they are based on raw materials 'developed overseas by large research organisations' (Basson, 1984), and manufactured there as well. Sanctions busting may account for the general lack of information on the subject matter.

3. Biotechnology and related research

The most recent development in agriculture-related technology, and the least explored either in the extent or implications of its usage, is that of bio-technology and related research. Research into stock, seeds and plants is not new. But the combined and mounting impact of developments in these fields, both in extent and implications, is only now beginning to be widely felt. In South Africa there are eleven specialist research institutes, seven regional organisations and the Division of Agricultural Engineering of the Department of Agriculture, all conducting research into many aspects of agricultural production. The range includes the development of hybrid seeds which are both high-yield and adapted to specific local soil and climatic conditions (potato seeds, for example) and those which are able to resist disease and pests (tobacco plants, for example). Illustrating the extent of the application of research developments, the integrated biological programme to control citrus pests developed by the Citrus and Subtropical Fruit Research Institute currently involves one-third of the nine million citrus trees in South Africa. The implications of such an experiment are not simply confined to a reduction in the cost of pesticides, but carry with them enormous import for levels of employment.

These research institutions and organisations work closely with producers, manufacturers and the state. As such, they are guided by the demands and requirements of these interests, which in turn are dominated by the quest to increase profits through increased output, improved production and reduced costs.

Impact and implications of mechanisation and technological innovation.

As a significant component in the process of agrarian restructuring, mechanisation and other technological innovations have had a profound impact on both capital and labour within the sector, as well as on the relation of commercial agriculture to the political economy as a whole. Since later chapters will deal with the effect on labour, I will here look briefly at how some aspects of the technological transformations have affected capital and production relations in general. It does need to be noted, however, that whilst these developments can not be attributed solely to mechanisation etc., these processes have often been central to them.

1. An increase in the volume of production

In all branches of agriculture there has been an absolute increase in the volume of production. The compound growth rate in physical volume in the 20-year period 1958/9 — 1977/8 was 4.6 percent p.a. for horticultural products, 4.3 percent p.a. for field crops and 2.6 percent p.a. for livestock (Nattrass 1981:103).

Table 1.3 gives some idea of the actual volume of production of meat etc., and the changes that have occurred over time. In all, over a ten-year period, meat production grew by 83 percent. This, in part, was made possible through horizontal expansion, but more so through the reorganisation of production, given the limits of water, 'overgrazing, uneconomic unit sizes and expensive land prices' (Meat Board, 1984:16) and through technological innovation.

Table 1.3
Volume of livestock production in 1973 and 1982
(excluding non-commercial production)

Product	1973	1982	% + / −
Beef	428 652	481 969	+ 12.4
Mutton	82 305	133 895	+ 62.6
Pork	74 100	81 487	+ 10.0
Chicken	197 000	425 000	+ 115.7
Total	**787 057**	**1 112 351**	**+ 41.3**

Source: Meat Board, 1983 and 1984

Feedlots increasingly are contributing to the supply of beef and mutton. In 1983 the standing capacity of beef feedlots was 314,000 head and annual throughput was about 785,000 or some 39 percent of the total number of cattle slaughtered. In the case of sheep, not only are they being herded in smaller pens, but 'feedlots are being established in increasing numbers ... (and) the intensive finishing of sheep is also increasing to supplement more extensive production systems' (Meat Board, 1984:16). However, the most spectacular increase, as the table shows, has been in poultry production. Where in 1973 chicken represented about 25 percent of the total volume of meat produced, by 1982 it almost equalled the volume of beef, representing 38 percent of the total.[11] Furthermore, unlike the increases in beef and mutton, growth in the volume of chicken has been almost solely related to intensive production methods, with technology playing an indispensable part in this rationalisation and reorganisation. This has made the production process highly capital-dependent and led to the emergence of a chicken (and egg) producer oligopoly dominating production in these fields.

Eggs
Egg production volumes increased from 3,426,194 eggs in 1972/73 to 6,779,656 in 1981/2 and some 7.1 million in 1983/4. This represented a 98 percent increase over a decade and a further four percent in the following two years. Egg production represents factory-farming at its zenith. Not only has volume been raised by an absolute growth in laying units, but also by the relative increase in the productive capacity of chickens so that 'the present average production of 275 eggs per hen per year is a new all-time record high' (Egg Control Board, 1984:1) and is amongst the highest in the world. It has been achieved by technological developments which allow producers to maintain such a high housing density that 'the entire demand for eggs for the SA market could be produced on three to four big farms' (Egg Control Board, 1984:3). This has led to a highly oligopolistic control of production, which only recently is beginning to come under any significant threat from an anticipated diversification of production away from maize.

Field crop production.
In field crop production there has been an overall increase in volume, despite climatic

fluctuations which particularly affect yields in dryland production. For maize (the largest field crop), there has been a tendency for yields per hectare to rise, even while the area planted has remained fairly constant. This tendency is confirmed in De Klerk's study of maize farms in the western Transvaal where he found that:

> despite some sharp fluctuations in the middle seventies the trend of output per hectare was firmly upward. On average, the expected yield grew by a little short of 6.5 percent per annum, resulting in a total rise of about 120 percent between 1968 and 1981 (De Klerk, 1984:6).

In wheat, the most fully mechanised field crop and where 85 percent of the crop is planted under dryland conditions, fluctuations in volume occur from year to year. So, whereas 1,385 million tons of wheat were purchased by the Wheat Control Board in the 1980/81 season, purchases increased to 2,228 million tons in 1981/82 and 2,285 million tons in 1982/83, up by 61 and 65 percent respectively over 1980/1 figures. These yield increases have been achieved partly through adapted and high-yielding cultivars and more intensive fertilisation. The effect of these technological developments has been that even in conditions of abnormally dry weather — as in the OFS in the 1983 planting season — yields can still be relatively high; for example, in that year 30 percent of the total volume of wheat produced still came from the Orange Free State.[12]

Potatoes

After maize, wheat and sugar, potatoes are the fourth largest field crop cultivated in South Africa. Unlike the first two, but similarly to sugar-cane production, mechanisation and technological innovation is much more evenly applied. Both use labour-intensive harvesting methods, for example. However, potato production differs from sugar in terms of the area planted and the yield per hectare tends to fluctuate widely. Nevertheless, taking the two years 1973/4 and 1982/3, volume increased from 659,320 to 809,969 tons. Dividing the decade into two five-year blocs, volume of production increased by an average 35 percent between the two periods. This increase was accompanied by a geographic shift in the second five-year period as production moved from the eastern Transvaal (previously the most important production area and where production decreased by 25 percent) to the OFS, where average annual production has increased by 50 percent. Given the unevenness of restructuring in potato production, and its heavy reliance on labour-intensive methods, this shift carries with it implications for the geography of the most intensive repression in the sector (Potato Board, 1984:3,6).

Similarly, an increase in production in the 1970s is evident for fruit and vegetables. For example, the production of deciduous fruit for fresh consumption grew by 65 percent between 1973 and 1982, to a total of 554,088 tons, while that for the five main vegetables grew by 48 percent to 1,010,000 tons.

The general increase in the volume of agricultural production has been achieved through the combined effects of horizontal and vertical expansion. In arable cultivation, this has meant that more land has been brought into production. Often this land was formerly considered too marginal to be profitable to cultivate under the given set of production relations. In other instances, the process of land concentration and the increase in farm unit size, as well as the reorganisation of production to make more rational use of land (and resources in general), has contributed to the actual increase in the area cultivated. Outside the reserves the area under cultivation rose from 7.4 to 11.6 million ha between 1946-71, or 56.7 percent. Since the early 1970s it has remained fairly constant, declining by some fourteen percent to a current 10.2 million ha in 1984. As I shall show later, the early expansion was accompanied by an initial increase in absolute employment levels, and particularly a rise in seasonal and 'non-regular' work.

The increase has also been a product of more intensive cultivation practices. In maize production, for example, the introduction and subsequent universalisation of combine harvesting not only affected harvesting techniques, but also significantly altered planting patterns (De Klerk 1984:11). Maize is now planted in three foot (0.9 metres) rather than in seven foot rows, as was the practice in the past. This has increased the maize yield per hectare and has to be taken into account when assessing the source of greater yields.

In pastoral production, the volume increase was also initially due to horizontal expansion — a growth in animal numbers. However, limitations of natural resources (particularly land and water) and pressures to raise productivity, which in livestock, particularly in beef production, is relatively low, has also led to an intensification of production. This is clearly evident in poultry and egg production, but is also indicated by the growing use of feedlots for cattle and sheep.

In the course of this process volume growth between the two branches of agricultural production has been uneven. In consequence, mechanisation and technological innovation combined with other restructuring processes have brought about a shift in the ratio of arable and pastoral farming. Whereas South Africa was once considered 'a poor crop-raising country' (Nattrass 1981:103), by 1950 pastoral and arable production were on a par. By 1970, however, arable production had outpaced pastoral farming and represented 60 percent of total gross agricultural output, a position that has been maintained with a slight increase over the next decade. In 1980/1 it constituted 63 percent of gross value.

2. A shift to greater capital intensity in production relations
Mechanisation and technological innovation have been at the centre of the shift to capital-intensive production in agriculture. This is especially so since about 1970. Until then both the rate of job growth and capital investment had grown, the latter somewhat faster. Since 1970 employment has declined both absolutely and relatively, whilst capital investment rose at an average rate of 3.5 percent p.a. for the twelve-year period 1970-82. This shift to capital-intensive production has increased the volume of production quite substantially although, when considered in relation to the growth of capital investment, it is not particularly large. Physical volume increased at an average rate of 2.9 percent p.a. between 1970 and 1982, a rate of 0.6 percent p.a. slower than capital investment. As such, the extent of capital investment was not rationally related to increased output as the prevailing dominant ideology is quick to argue. This fact is underlined by a second contradiction, namely the growing credit dependency and indebtedness of agricultural producers that the shift to capital-intensive production in agriculture has produced. Land Bank advances in the period 1948-77 increased by 366 percent. The interest load on agricultural

debt is the largest single burden on farmers in the current economic and profound agricultural crisis. Whilst farmer debt increased by 317 percent between 1970 and 1982, the interest load on agricultural debt increased by 1.122 percent and rose at an average annual rate of 33.8 percent between 1976 and 1982, to reach some R904 million in 1982.

Inevitably, company and large private capital has greater access to finance than medium and small farmers whose capacity to withstand such economic pressures is limited. This means that the shift to greater capital intensity has reinforced, if not accelerated, the process of production and capital concentration.

Other contributing factors to this trend include i) limited capital fluidity; ii) a relatively higher rate of inflation on the price index for what have become farming necessities — tractors, fertilisers, fuel etc. — compared to the consumer price index (15 percent p.a. cf 11.6 percent p.a. over the period 1970-82); iii) the tendency to overcapitalise, which means that many small and medium-sized farmers are being pushed out of production, whilst larger producers are still able to profit, albeit on a reduced scale.

3. Reorganisation and rationalisation of production

With mechanisation and the introduction of new technology there has also been a reorganisation of the production process itself. Sometimes, this has been stimulated directly by the technology. This is illustrated by the maize example where planting in three foot rows has also made weed spraying

> at or shortly after planting a natural complement to the use of a combine harvester with three-foot intakes, since the use of tractors in weed control is no longer possible and even hand-hoeing is difficult once the maize is a foot or two high (De Klerk 1984:11).

At other times, it is a process which is already under way and which is reinforced by mechanisation. In pastoral husbandry, for example, this has meant the introduction of smaller grazing camps and feedlots, the use of sheep-dogs etc.

But increasingly, rationalisation of production is itself directly related to growing capital intensity, central to which is mechanisation etc. Having borrowed money to buy equipment, fertiliser and fuel, the farmer is under pressure to put these goods to maximum and (hopefully for him) most efficient use in order to minimise costs and maximise profitability. This has generally, although far from universally, led to the identification, breakdown and calculation of so-called inputs and their costs in order to locate sources of profit and loss.

The rationalisation process is expressed beyond the particular enterprise or even branch. The very way in which the sector as a whole is divided testifies to this. Mechanisation and technological developments both generate and reinforce a process of division and subdivision tending towards mono-production, not only within branches but also within enterprises in particular farming-types.

Dairy farming provides a good and by no means exceptional example. It is itself a specialisation — the use of livestock (cows) for the production of milk. But within dairy farming there are sub-specialisations according to which producers are divided by the type of milk they produce in relation to its end usage, for example, those who produce for fresh milk consumption and those producing industrial milk. In turn, industrial milk producers are divided between those producing a butter fat component for manufacture into cheese and butter etc., and those with a low or no fat component for condensed, powdered and similar milk products. The relevance for workers of this and other examples of the tendency within agriculture towards mono- and specialised production lies particularly in its effects on pay and conditions of employment, as will be shown in chapter five, i.e., forms and methods of payment.

4. The intensification of exploitation of resources

As part of capitalist relations of production, both generally and, as these have developed in the repressive and abusive conditions of minority-ruled South Africa, one of the outcomes of mechanisation etc. is the intensified exploitation of natural, human and manufactured resources. This intensification is facilitated by the technology itself, which stimulates and allows for the concentrated working of land, labour, plant and animal life. In turn, this reinforces and exacerbates at least two already existing contradictions.[13]

One is the tendency to over-produce goods, creating so-called 'mountains' of food which are surplus to the cause of profit-making, although not to human need given that poverty and hunger is endemic to most of South Africa's population. Examples of over-production can be found in every type of farming and occur in most, if not all, cycles of production.[14] In 1974, for example, surpluses were recorded for butter (5,700 tons), eggs (114.5 million), maize (4.5 million tons) and wheat (420,000 tons). The destinations of these surpluses vary. Sometimes they are stockpiled, creating butter, cheese and meat mountains. Sometimes they are destroyed. In 1973, for example, 540 tons of bananas were ploughed back into the land in the northern Transvaal because producers faced 'financial ruin if they were to sell their crops at less than the controlled price' (*Rand Daily Mail*, 8.12.73) and welfare organisations were unable to raise state or private aid to cover the distribution costs of the bananas. There have been occasions when milk has been poured into the sea to overcome the 'problem' of what to do with the surplus. But, most frequently, the practice has been to export the surpluses at a loss, something which helps conceal the extent of the surpluses and over-production, especially in deciduous and citrus fruits and other goods produced mainly for export. At the same time, it ensures that local consumers pay doubly — first in high and continually rising prices, and second in widespread hunger and poverty. So, in 1975, 200 million eggs were broken over a nine-month period, recycled into powder and then exported at a loss of some R4 million, whilst local egg prices increased by 1c per dozen. In the two years prior to this, the loss on egg exports totalled R1.56 million and R3.1 million respectively.

Maize was exported at a loss for 23 of the 30 years in the period 1954/5-82/3, with profits of more than one million rand realised only in the four-year period 1973/4-1976/7. Until fairly recently this state of affairs has not unduly perturbed maize producers since they have been protected from directly bearing the cost of this loss by state-guaranteed minimum prices. The burden of such protection has been borne directly by consumers and it is in this capacity that farmers have also had to bear these costs. But since the late 1970s the economic crisis, both internationally and within the South African social formation, has generated a crisis in maize production. The low level of the international price, amongst other things, makes it difficult for producers to export their surpluses since the world market is already experiencing a glut. Maize producers refer to this as a 'penalty for efficiency'.

> The more efficiently maize is produced, the more maize will have to be offered on the international market, but the price relationship between export maize and inputs makes it increasingly unprofitable to produce maize for the export market (Maize Board, 1983:2).

Sugar, locally and internationally, is experiencing a similar crisis, although here the problems are exacerbated by competition from sugar substitutes.[15] Wheat producers face similar problems. In 1983/4, 145,000 tons of surplus wheat were exported at a loss of R150 per ton.

Related to the problem of over-production is the tendency to over-capitalise and thereby create over-capacity. So, for example, 'there is a bulk capacity for about 16Mt of summer grains in the summer rainfall area while the average receipts by the Board are ten million tons — 1937/8 to 1982/3' (Maize Board, 1984:9).

Clearly, over-production and over-capacity are related and generated by the growth in capital intensity in production relations. In the particular conditions that pertain to South Africa these problems are compounded by what is a fundamental contradiction of the combination of colonial and capitalist relations in one social formation. This is nothing other than the growing need for a home or domestic market to consume the goods produced by developed capitalist relations and the incapacity of a system based on cheap super-exploited labour (generated by conditions of national oppression and racial discrimination) to create this internal market. An internal market requires pay and working conditions to enable many people to purchase many products, but the provision of such pay and conditions would undermine the cheap labour base on which the set of relations rests. Within the system, the problem is insoluble and can only be exacerbated by increased production capacity.[16]

The second contradiction is the tendency to over-exploit resources. Historically, capitalist agriculture in South Africa has been abusive of both natural and human resources. With mechanisation and other technological innovations this tendency has been intensified, although it does not necessarily apply in every instance. The best example of an exception is in irrigation, where the common practice of surface flooding is not only particularly wasteful of water — a scarce resource in South Africa — but has led to silting up and waterlogging of formerly fertile soil. A more extensive use of sprinkler irrigation and the development of microjet and drip techniques could prove less destructive of natural resources. Yet, at this point in time, 70 percent of state irrigation schemes outside the reserves (covering just under 430,000 ha) is surface-irrigated, 20 percent is irrigated by sprinklers, but only one percent by microjet and drip.

In general, the pressures to intensify production at the expense of the resources upon which production depends persist. Thus, the drive to increase volume as a means to boost profit has led to continued overstocking practices in pastoral farming. This creates excessive grazing pressure, which, coupled with denudation of soil by water and wind erosion and destruction of natural plant life, leads to 'a vicious circle of progressive drying up of soil ... which in turn lowers the usefulness of the rainfall and which adversely affects the development of plant cover.'[17] Much research has been done on the decline of the environment, with each successive report reaching similar conclusions, such as that 'climatic hazards, destructive farming systems ... low educational standards, shortage of working capital and farm units that were too small,'[18] were the cause of the problem. Yet, in a study of white farmers in the Midkar region[19] to answer the question 'what type of farmer persists in overstocking his farm?', it was clear that:

> Overstocking occurred amongst farmers of all age groups and educational qualifications: farmers with no debt were overstocked as were farms that had been entirely inherited: and there was no clear relationship between overstocking and farm management and farm size.[20]

Thus, it is apparent that the cause of the problem does not lie in the social and psychological traits of individual farmers. But neither is it a 'random phenomenon', as McI.Daniel suggests. Rather, it is the consequence of the system itself which demands the pursuit of profit at any cost. This question needs to be rephrased and directed to asking what type of system encourages persistent overstocking and the destruction of the environment. In pursuit of the answer, the inevitable link will have to be drawn with a system which is so destructive of its human resources.

Over-exploitation of the land is, not surprisingly, also occurring in arable production. So, for example, excessive use of nitrogenous fertilisers in the past decade in maize and other summer grass production has had 'a disastrous effect on soil acid levels. The situation has reached crisis proportions as soil acidity retards root development; plants die of nutritional imbalances and are more exposed to drought risk as roots do not grow in acidic soils' (*Financial Mail*, 10.8.84). Such soil acidity and toxicity increases the risk as the slightest lapse in normal rainfall patterns reduces yields not only in the short-term but over the long-term due to increasing desertification.

Their significance for workers apart (to be examined in detail in later chapters), the four points above are the main implications of mechanisation and technological innovation. The increases in the volumes of production and of capital intensity in production relations have reinforced capital concentration and centralisation which, in turn, has intensified producer indebtedness as capital dependency has grown. At the same time it has generated problems of 'over-production' and 'over-capacity' exacerbating the insoluble but familiar contradiction of production relations under apartheid where food is destroyed while the black majority go hungry. Mechanisation etc., has also spurred the process of reorganisation and rationalisation of production such that the increasing division of labour between producers has led to mono-production and specialisation. Finally, the possibilities which these technological innovations open up in conditions where exploitation dominates all social relations of production have meant a greater tendency to over-exploit resources.

The process of mechanisation etc. has been stimulated and reinforced by state policy, for which restructuring, but particularly 'mechanisation' is the panacea for all ills in agriculture, including the so-called *'swart gevaar'* ('black peril').

The role of the state

The role of the state in actively promoting the restructuring of commercial agricultural production can only be understood in the context of its historical relation to the land question. In South Africa the land question — of which commercial agriculture is a significant part — is central to national domination and capitalist development because access to and control over land has been as important to the assertion of white minority rule — by concentrating land ownership in the hands of whites — as it has been to creating that class which, separated from the land, constitutes a necessary condition of modern production relations.

Since 1910, state policy on the land question has aimed at the promotion and support of whites on the land and the dispossession and systematic erosion of the position of Africans. Thus, the policy aims underlying the Land Settlement Act of 1912 (and all subsequent ameliorative legislation) were much the same as those which underlay the Native Land Act of 1913 and the prohibitive and proscriptive laws and decrees which have followed its passage. The former laid the base for state promotion of whites on the land as farmers and as landowners and was the forerunner to a range of legislative supports for 'white farming', including direct and indirect financial assistance,production and marketing services and research, support and compensation in times of disaster and adversity. These services have been provided by various departments of state concerned with land and agriculture (now condensed into one) as well as the Land and Agricultural Bank, various State Marketing Boards, and Co-operative Societies.[21]

The Land Act of 1913 and the Natives Land and Trust Act of 1936 established and developed the reserve system on a national scale. It stripped the African majority of its legal access to land outside limited and defined areas, which initially comprised little more than seven percent of the total surface area and ultimately will total some 14 percent, and has been the means by which the state has transformed the relation of the African majority to the land to one of landlessness.

However, changing political and socio-economic conditions in the social formation as a whole after 1945, including shifts in the balance of forces within the ruling class, meant that state strategies to achieve the national and class interests of the ruling white minority had to change.[22]

Whilst there has been continuous promotion and support for restructuring, three phases in state ideology and practice towards commercial agriculture can be discerned:[23]

1. From 1948 to the early 1960s state intervention 'acted to push capitalisation of agriculture on to a higher plane' (Morris, 1977) by intensifying its control over African labour. This was reflected in moves to force workers into the unfavourable conditions of commercial agriculture to overcome the labour shortages created by these very conditions and to establish the farm labour force by acting against squatting (rent tenancy) and limiting the practice of labour tenancy.[24]

2. From the early 1960s to the late 1970s the state attempted simultaneously to raise farm productivity and reduce white farmer dependence on African labour.

These actions stemmed from concern about the voluntary exodus of whites from the land, the so-called problem of 'platteland depopulation'. This 'problem' was the subject of a Commission of Inquiry in 1960 which concluded that *'if the tide does not turn and the growth of the non-white preponderance on the white platteland continues, this state of affairs will in the end hold out a serious threat to white civilisation in this country'* (emphasis original) (Du Toit, 1960:48).

The state perceived its task as two-fold. First, to keep whites in the sector through improved productivity and profitability to ensure them 'a civilised standard of living'. Second, to remove Africans from the sector by removing the need for their labour and simultaneously forcing those made superfluous by this process into the reserves.[25]

Taken together, policy thinking on the subject concluded that the answer lay in 'mechanisation'. As a result, incentives to encourage 'mechanisation' were introduced. These included the subsidising of fuel and fertiliser through rebates of fifteen and ten percent respectively of direct state grants in 1975; a special production loan scheme under the Agricultural Credit Board which made up to R8,000 (1977) p.a. available 'for the purchase of fertiliser, seed, fuel and pesticides, the payment of repairs to tractors, implements, parts and electric power ...' (SAAU, 1980:62) and allowing the deduction of investments in agricultural implements, including bulls, from taxable income in the year of purchase.

In addition, the drive to raise productivity saw the promotion of land consolidation into 'economic farm units'. This reinforced the trend towards concentration and centralisation. Paradoxically, however, it also accelerated the exodus of whites out of the sector. But, for several reasons it did not evoke significant concern at this stage. One lay in social changes in agrarian capital and a shift in the balance of state forces towards the interests of large and corporate capital. A second lay in the massive forcible depopulation of the 'white platteland' of so-called 'superfluous' Africans.[25] Between 1960 and 1982 no fewer than 1,129,000 Africans living on white-owned land as workers, families of workers and/or as tenants (cash or labour) were evicted and channelled into the reserves .[26] And finally, it was the sheer complacency of the state generated by a general economic expansion and relatively low levels of resistance to the intensive repression of the early 1960s.

State promotion of 'mechanisation' during this phase clearly based itself on an assumption of the widespread and continued replacement of workers by machines, so much so that it chastised farmers for being unsystematic in their approach. Thus, the Minister of Agriculture told farmers that 'it is no use mechanising on a piecemeal basis only to find that the same labour as before is required' (*Financial Gazette*, 11.10.74). This policy had the effect of generating unemployment, on the one hand, while over-extending farmers' capital commitments by encouraging excessive and over-capitalisation on the other. In other words, it promoted two of the primary sources of crisis underlying the current turmoil in the South African political economy, including in agriculture.

3. The third and current phase dates from the mid-1970s and is inseparable from the onset of a deep political and economic crisis in the social formation as a whole. It appears that the state is trying to do several things at once in so far as policy towards commercial agriculture is concerned. These include reducing its

commitment to subsidising agriculture so highly; sharing the cost burden of apartheid with private and corporate agricultural capital by, for example, encouraging them to invest in agricultural 'development' projects in the reserves; attempting to come to terms with the consequences of economic and land concentration, especially *vis-à-vis* their implications for 'strategic and national security' in the face of mounting popular resistance. (The 'desertion' of remote border farms — 'South Africa's first line of defence', according to SADF Chief of Defence General C. Viljoen, (*The Star*, 10.7.81) — reached a peak in 1979, whereafter the state intervened by pouring in R100 million to support a white presence in the remote 'border' regions);[27] a shift in policy regarding labour in the light of changing needs of advanced restructuring, rising capital costs of production and the social cost of high unemployment. The Chief Director of the Department of Agriculture has warned:

> The further replacement of labour through mechanisation must be done with the greatest caution. We must bear in mind that in relation to other countries mechanisation in South Africa is relatively more expensive. In contrast, labour is relatively cheaper. South Africa cannot afford large scale mechanisation while we have large scale unemployment ... large scale unemployment of uneducated workers in South Africa, and the fact that this is expected to increase further, is most disturbing (Hattingh, 1983).

A case of closing the gate after the horse has bolted, as later chapters will make clear.

The conclusion, which emerges from this preliminary look at state policies regarding agricultural restructuring is that, even despite many contradictions, the state, in actively promoting capital intensive production in commercial agriculture, has increasingly supported, reinforced, and generally come to articulate the interests of large and corporate agrarian capital. This has especially been the case in the second and third 'phases' of policy, during which these interests established and consolidated their position of dominance in the sector.

It is in this context that such developments as the farmer protests of February 1985 where small- and medium-sized farmers publicly rallied against 'price fixing cartels which were fleecing them, control boards which were not doing a proper job or marketing their products and government which was not paying enough attention to their grievances' (*Financial Mail*, 15.2.86) can be assessed. More importantly for our concern here, as will be shown, it is also the context in which to assess policy developments regarding farm workers, expressed in their most condensed form by the appointment in 1982 of the first-ever state inquiry into farm labour.

This chapter has identified some of the more important forces involved since 1945 in the process of restructuring commercial agriculture. What is apparent is that this transformation — in so far as the interests of capital and the white minority as a whole are concerned — has not resolved the many basic problems of agricultural production in South Africa and that even those problems that have been resolved have, in turn, generated new contradictions.

Notes

1. In 1980, there were some 2,090 Indian farmers who owned about 72,000 ha. Few owned more than 20 ha and few had sole title to the farms. Group ownership was common. The extent of land ownership by Coloureds is even less (SAIRR, *Annual Survey* 1980:121).
2. For full details see *The Surplus People's Project Reports*, 1983: vols.1-5.
3. SAIRR, *Annual Survey* 1972:193. Until 1972 state policy had prohibited direct private white access to land in the reserves. Nevertheless, it had been possible through the state-created development corporation — the Bantu Investment Corporation (BIC). Formed in 1951, BIC (subsequently named the Corporation for Economic Development) was registered as 'A Bantu' in order to get round the obstacle of whiteness in areas specifically designated as exclusively African. Its board was entirely white and remained so long after whites were granted direct access by the state.
4. The actual amount made available was more since the operation of this measure was also applied in Namibia.
5. *The Financial Mail* (15.8.69) exlaimed 'Hurrah!' when the measure was first mooted by the Department of Bantu Administration in 1969. They saw in it the opening of large tracts of cheap land for grazing and cultivation. The subsequent flow of investment was somewhat less ebullient and this stemmed from the general absence of infrastructure etc. in the reserves.
6. Consolidation has been a source of considerable land speculation and profit for white farmers and has also acted to raise the price of (particularly marginal) land.
7. Almost all land added to the reserves since the passage of the 1936 Natives Trust and Land Act has been purchased by or through the South African Native Trust — a para-statal created by the Act. Between 1936-69, it bought 3.2 million ha but only 11.9 percent of that amount was bought by Africans. For them to do so, they also required the permission of the State President — not usually given — who imposed a condition that the purchasers must accept 'measures for the proper use and rehabilitation of the land, agree to the land being declared a betterment area and align themselves with any steps taken under the Bantu Authorities Act'.
8. To assert that 'technological innovation was synonymous with tractorisation' (Budlender, 1984) at this stage is to overlook important technological developments in wheat production, for example. As the first arable crop to undergo substantial mechanisation, Keegan (1981) has observed that: 'the rapid extension of wheat production in the OFS in the 1930s was made possible by improved techniques of production, fertilisers and very importantly, the introduction of the self-binder which not only reaped the crop, but bound it into sheaves'. The number of reaping and binding machines in the OFS increased from 979 in 1926 to 3,199 in 1937. Only in the late 1930s and particularly in the 1940s did the tractor make its appearance on a very large scale.
9. For analytic purposes, the extent of mechanisation and other technological innovations are treated separately from their implications, although in reality these are inseparable.
10. Compiled from The South African Agricultural Union, *Annual Reports* 1980, 1981 and 1983/4. Goods and services accounted here are fuel, maintenance and repairs, fertilisers, stock and feed, expenditure on capital goods, vehicles, machines and implements.
11. From the viewpoint of producers, 'poultry meat is the main competitor of red meat' (Meat Board, 1984:17).
12. Data drawn from Wheat Board 1983, 1984. Figures exclude the reserves.
13. I have excluded from consideration here the contradiction of creating a weak home market arising from the nature of labour exploitation in conditions of national oppression.
14. Although, of course, not in every product or in every year.
15. Such as from High Fructose Corn Syrup (HFCS). In order to suppress the competition that HFCS poses to sugar, African Products (formerly the sole supplier of limited quantities of HFCS) was taken over by the Tongaat Group, since when HFCS has not been available in the country. (*Financial Mail*, 8.3.85).
16. 'Inward industrialisation' advocated by Dr Simon Brand (SADB Chairman) and other 'reformists' in 1988 is nothing less than an appeal to develop the domestic market in order to break out of this contradiction and generate economic growth.
17. Marais Commission, op.cit. cited in Mc I. Daniel 1984:1.

18. Ibid.
19. That is the false Karoo and Grassveld regions of the magisterial districts of Bedford, Cradock, Graaff-Reinet, Maraisburg, Middelburg, Pearston and Somerset in the Cape Midlands and eastern Karoo.
20. Marais Commission in McI Daniel, op.cit. 5.
21. For a more detailed account of the content of these supports see Myburgh 1976.
22. For issues raised concerning the significance of apartheid see Wolpe (1972) and the subsequent debate and research that this stimulated. Also of importance here is the development and elaboration of the reserve policy. For an excellent analysis of its significance see NUSAS (1983).
23. This line of argument supports the view that apartheid cannot be treated as an undifferentiated ideology, policy and practice. Rather, it should be conceived of as having gone through stages which reflect shifts in the balance of forces within the whole minority as well as between them and the black oppressed majority. These need to be identified for adequate analysis. This is not, however, to suggest that these stages are discrete and unrelated. On the contrary, they are not, and to identify them in such terms would also fail to enhance our understanding of apartheid and the state.
24. Morris (1977) provides an interesting analysis of farm interests in the early forties and their relation to the state, particularly their support for the National Party as the vehicle to pursue their interests through the taking of state power and thereby putting the machinery of the state at their disposal.
25. As the Surplus Peoples Project Reports (1983) point out:

> In many respects, this massive movement of agricultural workers and small peasant producers off the land is not unique to South Africa. It has been a feature of the capitalisation of agriculture world-wide. The intervention of the state to force this movement into the bantustans and away from the urban areas ... is, however, specific to South Africa ... (Vol.1, 41).

26. The Surplus Peoples Project Reports (1983) note that the removal of farm workers represented the largest single category of people (about one-third) forcibly relocated during this 22-year period (Vol.I, 41).
27. *The Star*, 10.7.81. If the figures are accurate, about 500 white families benefited from this subsidy, i.e., approximately R200,000 per family. Although this action was said to have 'stemmed the exodus', this fact is belied by subsequent legislation and 'aid', including a stringent law which made state loans subject to the fulfilment of a set of regulations, amongst which was that each farm had to be occupied by a white; that farm units had to be actively farmed and that roads and fences had to be kept in order.

2. Restructuring and Employment: A Macro-Survey

The impact for labour of the restructuring of commercial agricultural production cannot simply be 'read off' the technology, ideology or any other aspect of the process. These do, of course, contain within them considerable implicit as well as explicit significance, at least in theoretical terms. However, it is their application in historically given social relations, specifically within agriculture but generally within the social formation as a whole, which has determined and will determine the form, direction, pace and overall implications of this process in practice. To understand this, a concrete examination of the specific conditions is required.

One of the key indicators of the extent and significance of agricultural restructuring for workers is its effect on employment within the sector. This will be examined at the national level as well as according to regional variations, the branch of farming activity, and the variations between enterprises within a particular branch of production.

The problems of productivity and of under- and unemployment will also be examined briefly in the context of general levels of unemployment.

First, a few general cautionary remarks need to be made about the data base. The primary sources of statistical information for an analysis of employment levels and trends in commercial agriculture — especially with regard to national and regional data — are the National Population Censuses (NPC) compiled every ten years and the Agricultural Censuses, which are compiled intermittently. Both are flawed, not simply by the inadequacy and ambiguity of definitions, the irregularity of data collection, the collection of census information by means of compulsory returns and 'with the aid of the South African Police'[1] but more profoundly by the assumptions of white minority power and the reserve system of its creation. These lead to enormous omissions, distortions and confusion, such that so-called 'national' statistics exclude nine million South Africans who, as a result of Pretoria's 'homelands' independence' drive, have since 1976 statistically disappeared.

Whilst the National Population Census is generally considered more reliable than the Agricultural Censuses, this is only relatively so. In 1985, for example, it was announced that the statistics collected in the 1980 NPC were no longer valid (*The Star* 8.2.85). These problems with the statistical data contained in the censuses are compounded further by separating commercial agricultural production on the 'white platteland' from that in the reserves and by not distinguishing between petty peasant production and employment on commercial agricultural enterprises within the bantustans. This means that statistics for employment in commercial agricultural production exclude thousands of women, children and men employed on enterprises within the reserves. In 1982, the Corporation for Economic Development (CED) — a parastatal formerly known as the Bantu Investment Corporation (BIC) — ran 77 projects in the so-called 'non-independent' reserves and employed at least 14,500 workers.[2] In that same year, the SA Development Trust leased out 807 farms encompassing just over 500,000 hectares in these reserves, but the numbers employed on these enterprises is not stated, nor is it clear in which set of statistics they would be included.[3]

Agricultural censuses distort other aspects of the data they gather. They are particularly unreliable with regard to statistics on 'part-time' and 'casual' employment and therefore, *inter alia*, on the sexual composition of the workforce, given that women predominate in these forms of employment. Up until 1965 information was not collected on 'casual' labour at all. Thereafter it was, but the fact that the censuses are undertaken in August means there is considerable under-reporting of the workforce, at least for some important farming types which use relatively large numbers of seasonal workers. For example, in the Western Cape fruit-growing area August 'is completely unrepresentative' of seasonal employment levels (Antrobus 1984).

In short, the census statistics exclude a significant fraction of workers in commercial agriculture and misrepresent and distort other aspects of the information they collect. These problems are further exacerbated when attempts are made to draw comparisons over time. Clearly, far from being 'hard facts', national statistics have to be treated with caution and can only be said to provide general trend indicators.

However, in the absence of an alternative data base analysts are forced to use these statistics. Some (Simkins, 1984) have been explicitly more cautious than others (Nattrass, 1981) in their use of the censuses, but all have had to draw on non-statistical information as well as implicit and explicit theoretical assumptions, which have led at times to some 'rather heroic assumptions and extrapolations' (Budlender, 1984a). This highlights another weakness of the data base, namely, the general absence of in-depth enterprise and branch studies which would provide an alternative source of information against which the general statistics could be evaluated. Only relatively recently has such work begun on anything more than an incidental scale, and it remains preliminary.

National trends

Several aspects to the question of the impact of restructuring of commercial agricultural production on employment levels on a national scale need to be considered. First, there is the effect that restructuring has had on the absolute numbers of people employed in the sector. This is not a simple matter. The inadequacy of the data base, especially with regard to so-called 'part-time' and 'casual' employment, leads to much guess-work and frustrates a sophisticated analysis of what is a complex process. What the figures suggest is that absolute employment rose in each decade up to the late 1960s/early 1970s, then declined absolutely. One set of figures which includes in its calculations everyone who did some work on farms outside the reserves gives total employment in the sector as 1.22 million (1960); 1.35 million (1970) and 0.97 million (1980) (Du Pisanie in Bromberger 1984). These are likely to be underestimates given that figures given by agricultural censi are consistently higher and they are considered to be under-estimates. Even so

it is generally agreed that in employment terms the first phase of restructuring
— up until about 1970 — saw an increase in the number of people employed in
the sector as production, particularly arable cultivation, was extended. Simpkins
(1984) is an exception. Basing his analysis on 'regular' and 'domestic' employment
— what he misleadingly refers to as 'core farm employment' — he argues that
from the mid-1950s onwards employment in these categories began to level off.
In other words, the increase in the number of workers in commercial agricultural
production was attributable to a relative increase in the number of people employed
in seasonal or 'part-time' jobs, and that for full-time on-farm workers employment
was static or had already begun to decline.[4] After 1970, the second of what has
been termed a two-phase reduction in farm employment set in, with an absolute
decrease in all forms of farm employment.[5]

Second, there is the question of the relation of employment in agriculture to
employment in other sectors of the economy and its relation to the economically
active population in general.

Historically, in sectoral terms, commercial agriculture has been the single largest
source of work in South Africa. Partly as a result of the growth in manufacture
and in the state sector, and particularly as a result of agricultural restructuring and
the reduction of job opportunities that this entailed, this is no longer so. According
to official statistical calculations, in June 1983 commercial agriculture ranked third
in employment terms (with approximately 1.2 million 'employees') behind 'government' (1.2 million) and manufacture (almost 1.4 million) (SAIRR Survey 1983:144).

When considered in relation to the economically active population, the impact
of restructuring in capitalist agriculture is even greater than either the decline in
absolute employment levels or the relative sectoral decline suggests. Agriculture
has represented a steadily declining sector for employment as the economically active
population grew from 4.59 million in 1951 to 9.49 million in 1980. In 1951, 32.9
percent of the economically active population was engaged in commercial
agricultural production compared with less than 13 percent by 1980. This overall
figure masks the fact that in employment terms the brunt of restructuring has been
borne by the African majority. For various historical reasons the involvement of
whites and Indians in agricultural employment has declined into relative unimpor-
tance. The percentage of the white labour force employed in commercial agriculture
dropped from 14.8 percent in 1951 to 6.5 percent in 1970, and that of Indians from
13.7 percent (1951) to 4.0 percent (1970). For the Coloured population, the
agricultural sector was and has remained relatively more important for employment. In 1951, 24.1 percent of the labour force was employed in agriculture, dropping to 16.3 percent in 1970, and to 15.4 percent in 1980 (Riekert 1979. para 2.22).

For the African majority, commercial agriculture still represented a significant
employer in 1970 with 27 percent of the African economically active population
engaged in this sector. By 1980, this had dropped to 15 percent and, although
higher than any other sections of the population, marked a steep decline. (Nattrass
in SAIRR Survey 1983:126).

The impact of restructuring on African employment and the generation of a rural
surplus has been shown by Simkins. In his analysis of 'full-time' ('regular' and
'domestic') employment referred to earlier, he shows that, in so far as the on-farm

population was concerned, there was a rapid drop in employment as a percentage of labour supply after 1955. This reflected a 'levelling off of employment in absolute terms at a stage when labour supply continues to grow' (Simkins op cit:6-8). Between 1936 and 1956, the proportion was consistently 90 percent or higher, whereas from 1955 it fell, ranging around 80 percent through most of the 1960s and declining to about 73 percent in 1970.

It is only in the context of rising unemployment in commercial agriculture that the full import of the following two points can be grasped.

One, that between 1960 and 1971, about 500,000 African 'full-time' farm workers left the sector for employment in the towns and in industry (Nattrass 1981:107) with little opposition from white farmers. Two, white farmers increasingly began to co-operate and participate in the state drive to remove the growing number of Africans surplus to agrarian needs off the so-called 'white platteland' and into the reserves.

Sexual division of labour

The consequences of the decline in employment levels in agriculture has been unevenly spread with regard to the sexual division of labour. Here, even more than elsewhere, it is difficult to quantify adequately the changes due to the inadequacy of the data base concerning female economic activity, particularly that of African women who also happen to constitute the majority of women agricultural workers. It is here again that African women have had to bear the heaviest burden of declining employment, especially in the second phase of this process. The radical cutback in seasonal, 'part-time' and 'casual' jobs has seen a sharp drop in the primary forms of work open to them in the political economy as a whole. This is because of the particular interrelation of national and gender oppression, which has hinged upon the maximal restriction and containment of African women within the reserves. In consequence, the only two areas in which African women could work in any substantial numbers have been domestic service and commercial agriculture. The impact of diminished employment opportunities in commercial agriculture has thus been particularly severe as the loss of the primary source of household income hugely undermines the endless struggle against poverty. We will return to this theme in chapters three and four.[6]

Whichever way employment levels are assessed, the impact of restructuring has been to reduce the number of people employed in commercial agriculture. In terms of the numbers employed, for 'full-time' farm workers a decrease in employment began before the overall absolute decline in employment levels after 1970. When looked at in relation to the economically active population, the actual rate of decline is even more intense. Here again the impact of the decline in employment has not been evenly spread, with the greatest burden of rising unemployment in agriculture falling on African workers, and particularly African women workers.

The picture is, however, more complex than national trends reveal as the actual course of the employment decline has been influenced by regional, branch and intra-branch variations. These stem not only from physical and geographical peculiarities, but also in response to political and social forces.

Regional variations

South Africa is a vast country embracing some 1.2 million hectares and stretching across the southern tip of a continent. In this huge area there is considerable variety in terrain, soil types and climatic conditions which gives rise to a range of agricultural possibilities. Additionally, politically determined policy practices vary, and these in turn give rise to regional differences in the levels and conditions of employment in the sector.

The main problem here is to define the regions. However, the more refined the definition, the more the data will reveal the subtleties of the restructuring process.

Provincial divisions

Based on Agricultural Census statistics for the years 1961, 1965, 1969 and 1973, the percentage drop in 'regular' farm employment was 15.3, 18.6 and 20.7 respectively. However, in Natal a decrease of only 0.2 percent was recorded over the 12-year period (Hendrie et al. 1976:5, Table 5). This suggests that the decline in 'full-time' employment in Natal began later than in other provinces, which is possibly the case. However, Natal was not as exceptional as these statistics imply. What they reflect, as shown in the next chapter, is the specific characteristics of farming and land relations in Natal, in particular the widespread use of migrant labour and the extensive practice of labour tenancy. The workers covered by both these labour forms would not have been recorded in the census category 'regular employee'. From the late 1950s to the mid-1970s, the major victims of farm evictions were labour tenants and 'squatters'. During this period several hundred thousand people were forced to leave the 'white' farms on which they were living. In Natal, however, the abolition of labour tenancy began in earnest only in the late 1960s and this therefore may largely have contributed to the delay in the decline of agricultural employment in that province relative to the others.[7]

Agricultural regions

The Department of Agriculture divides South Africa (excluding the bantustans) into seven agricultural regions on the basis of broad farming conditions within the country and with regard to administrative (provincial) boundaries (Antrobus 1984:28). These regions are:

1. *Winter Rainfall Area:* fruit- and crop-growing areas of the Western Cape and north-western and southern Cape coastal belt.
2. *Karoo Region:* extensive sheep-grazing areas of the Great Karoo and Cape Midlands.
3. *Eastern Cape:* includes the grassveld and sheep-grazing area of the North Eastern Cape, central Eastern Cape, Border and coastal cropping areas between Humansdorp and East London.
4. *Orange Free State (OFS)/Northern Cape:* extensive cattle-grazing areas of the Northern Cape and sheep-grazing and diversified crop areas of the OFS.
5. *Highveld:* the northern and eastern rainfed cropping areas of the OFS and Southern Transvaal.
6. *Transvaal:* the Northern, Eastern and Western Transvaal.

7. *Natal:* includes Natal and East Griqualand.

This is a more useful division since it takes into account predominant farming activities and can thus reveal the significance of the type of farming practiced as a regional factor influencing employment.

Table 2.1
Regional distribution of 'regular' farm workers
according to colour as a percentage of the year 1976

Region	White	Coloured	Indian	African	Region%
1. W. Cape	4.5	79.1	—	16.4	12.8
2. Karoo	2.2	67.6	—	30.2	3.4
3. E. Cape	2.5	9.5	—	87.9	6.4
4. OFS/N.Cape	1.1	16.5	—	82.4	9.5
5. Highveld	0.9	0.6	—	98.5	17.1
6. Transvaal	2.0	0.3	—	97.7	30.1
7. Natal	1.8	0.2	2.4	95.6	20.8
Total	**2.0**	**14.8**	**0.5**	**82.7**	**100.0**

Source:Antrobus, 1984:30.

Table 2.1 shows that the distribution of employment is more uneven than provincial divisions suggest. In 1976, 30 percent of the 'regular' farm workforce was concentrated in the Northern, Eastern and Western Transvaal, while the Highveld region was also an important area of 'regular' work for farm workers. In the Cape, whilst it is provincially the second largest in absolute employment terms within the sector, farm workers were concentrated in the Winter Rainfall Area, representing approximately 40 percent of the provincial total (12.8 percent of the national figure).

Regions defined by employment

Another approach is to use employment as a percentage of labour supply to define regions of agriculture. Simkins (1984) carried out a cross-sectional study on the basis of the 1960 Agricultural Census for the magisterial districts north and east of the so-called Coloured labour preference zone, Western Cape.[8] What his analysis revealed was that the rate of on-farm 'regular' and 'domestic' employment was not evenly spread across the districts. In a couple 'on the edge of the Ciskei, in Northern Natal and a swathe from the Southern to the Northern Transvaal with a westward expansion' (Ibid., p9) employment fell below 60 percent of the resident population. In most of the Orange Free State and Southern Natal, on the other hand, employment percentages were above 80. But in the vicinity of most of the major reserves around the Ciskei, Northern Natal, parts of the north-eastern Orange Free State and in much of Southern, Central and Western Transvaal, the rate of 'regular' farm employment was between 61 and 80 percent of the population in these districts.

Apart from indicating that there was considerable *de facto* African occupation of farms outside the bantustans, what this shows is that already in 1960 a relatively large surplus rural population existed, particularly in the districts close to the bantustans. Why this should be the case requires further investigation and cannot be gone into here, but certainly this explanation of proximity itself is insufficient. Part of the answer must surely lie in the already existing pressure on land within the reserves, even before the large-scale relocations of the next two decades. It perhaps also lies in the restriction of access to towns through influx control and possibly, at least for some regions, the movement out of the reserves to the towns through the commercial agricultural sector. These factors, especially the latter, require further research.

Regional divisions and racial and national oppression

Finally, there are the varying conditions of national and racial oppression which have acquired regional characteristics and which have also influenced the effect restructuring has had on employment levels.

In the Western Cape, the operation of the 'Coloured labour preference policy' has meant that part of the burden of a growing agricultural surplus population has been transferred from Coloured farm workers to Africans. In the first ten to fifteen years of this policy, its impact was not so clear-cut. It is possible that, within the general decrease of full-time farm employment, the rate of decline was slightly lower for Coloured farm workers than for Africans. The average annual growth rate of African and Coloured agricultural employment in the Eastern, Central and Western Cape between 1965 and 1972 was −2 percent and −1 percent respectively.[9] However, in the period 1972-75, whilst African farm employment continued to decrease, Coloured employment began to rise, with respective growth rates of −3.2 percent for Africans and +1.1 percent per annum for Coloureds. As has already been shown, in terms of the Coloured economically active population, this increase should be seen in the light of a decline in the percentage of working people engaged in commercial agriculture. In other words, the operation of this 'policy led to a more rapid decline in African agricultural employment than would otherwise have happened' (Surplus Peoples Report 1983: Vol.3).

So the impact of restructuring in the Cape agrarian working class most seriously affected African employment levels. However, as will be shown when pay and conditions are examined, the advantage to Coloured farm workers through the operation of this policy, which is also reflected in pay levels, is only a relative one. It is not particularly great when compared with other sectors of the political economy, nor is it sufficient to protect them from the general conditions of exploitation and oppression on the farms, as the extensive poverty in Western Cape districts amply testifies.

The bantustans have also been viewed as a politico-economic region. Although physically separated, they are all characterised by similar geo-political and socio-economic features. The ideology of 'development' espoused by the state places inordinate importance on agriculture as the route to economic regeneration within the bantustans, with dual (but not equal) emphasis on subsistence and commercial production. It is an emphasis well beyond the real significance of either the commercial projects or the reality of subsistence production, as Table 2.2 illustrates.

Table 2.2
Gross domestic product, the contribution of agriculture and the contribution of commercial production to agriculture to each of the bantustans — 1980

Bantustan	Total GDP (R 000)	Agriculture (%)	Com. Agric. as % of Agriculture
Bophuthatswana	584 300	6	9
Ciskei	131 919	8	18
Gazankulu	62 329	25	13
KaNgwane	46 053	18	16
Lebowa	221 685	29 7	
KwaZulu	425 674	28	18
QwaQwa	29 606	6	6
Transkei	547 339	27	9
Venda	60 791	19	12
Total	**2 109 696**		

or 3.4% of RSA's GDP

Source: SAIRR, *Survey of Race Relations*, 1983:363.

This notwithstanding, there are two interrelated consequences of restructuring for employment in commercial agricultural production within the bantustans.

First, the drive to generate commercialisation of production within the reserves is inseparable from developments within the sector as a whole. It began in earnest in the early 1970s and was coincident with the absolute decline in employment within the sector and the prevailing ideology of maximal labour substitution. As a consequence, commercial farming within the reserves has tended towards capital-intensive production methods, especially on irrigation schemes which are the main arable projects. The involvement of white private and corporate capital has reinforced this tendency since it is inclined to reproduce the same relations existent on 'white farms'. This, in turn, has meant that projects have generated relatively few jobs, even on plantation schemes based on labour-intensive crops such as cotton, tea and sugar.

Second, the impact of commercial agricultural ventures is even further diminished when looked at in the context of:
a) the surplus population generated by restructuring on the land and removed to the bantustans;
b) the already high level of unemployment arising from structural contradictions in the social formation and the concentration of the vast majority of this pool of unemployed in the reserves;
c) the rising rate of unemployment generated by the current economic crisis;

d) the drought and its effect on already severe levels of job reduction in commercial agriculture.

Thus, the creation of 10,500 jobs by the CED in 1981/2 in agriculture in the reserves (but not including the so-called independent bantustans of Transkei and Venda) has to be assessed against a background of mass unemployment in this region where, for example, there were an estimated 70,000 unemployed people in the Ciskei rural areas alone in that year.[10]

In summary, therefore, the significance of regional differences on agricultural employment lies in the specific combination of natural and social characteristics peculiar to an area. Administrative divisions are not in themselves significant unless they demarcate differing policy practices. In such cases, physical and geographic factors become subordinate to politics, as the Coloured labour preference policy and the creation of the reserves clearly indicate. These latter express the consequences of a political geography which is drawn, first and foremost, on the basis of African national oppression.

Perhaps as important in determining regional differences and shaping the direction which employment trends have taken has been the type of farming practised and the variations between the predominant forms of agriculture.

Differences between arable and pastoral production

Farming practices fall into two broad categories — arable or pastoral — according to whether they centre on cultivation or livestock. Both branches have undergone substantial restructuring over the past several decades, although the relative significance for employment has varied in important ways.

First, pastoral farming has historically been less labour intensive than arable production. In a statistical analysis of Agricultural Census figures on 'regular' employment and the impact of 'mechanisation' (tractorisation), Budlender (1984a:18) found that 'pastoral areas mechanised relatively more quickly during the 1955 to 1976 period.' Although she cautions that care should be taken in interpreting these results, it seems that the impact of restructuring has been greater on the smaller workforce, suggesting that the rate of transformation was somewhat faster in pastoral than in arable areas. This is so for at least 'full-time' farm workers. The significance of this, however, needs to be looked at more closely and its actual implications can be illustrated by way of example. Sheep farmers have increasingly introduced sheep-dogs and are grazing sheep in smaller pens with the effect that two out of three 'full-time' workers have been replaced per 35,000 ha used for sheep-rearing. In other words, measured per 1,000 ha, the workforce has declined by 66.6 percent. In maize production, however, where nine out of 18 'full-time' workers have been replaced by mechanisation per 1,000 ha, the rate of decline is somewhat slower, with only 50 percent of workers losing their jobs. But in absolute terms, four-and-a-half times the number of people were made redundant through restructuring in maize than occurred in the process of restructuring in sheep farming. So, although the rate of decline may have been sharper in pastoral areas, the effect on absolute employment levels is greater in the arable areas.[11]

Second, the growth in employment in the first phase of restructuring, which especially involved an increase in seasonal and 'part-time' employment, was almost entirely confined to arable production. This has also meant that in the second phase of the decline in employment — post 1970 — workers in arable production were more severely affected than those in pastoral farming.

It would be incorrect to infer from the above that restructuring occurred relatively earlier in animal husbandry than in crop cultivation and horticulture. Instead, it seems that the nature of the production process determined the course of restructuring and that, in turn, these differences influenced the rates and levels of employment within each branch.

Differences within arable and pastoral production

There is also considerable variation within the branches according to types of farming specialisation. Here the focus will be on arable production mainly because arable farming is the largest source of employment in the sector, and in part because the variations within the branch pertain also to pastoral production, although differing in detail.

In South Africa, the only two crops which are all but completely mechanised are wheat and maize. De Klerk's study (1984:7) on the effects of mechanisation on employment on maize farms in the Western Transvaal showed that this process led to a dramatic and absolute decline in employment, with a differential rate of decline between seasonal and 'full-time' workers, although the extent depended on how it was measured. Between 1968-81, the number of 'full-time' workers used to harvest and deliver the maize crop fell by 20 percent per farm unit, whilst the number of seasonal workers doing the same tasks dropped by 50 percent. For workers employed seasonally to weed, the decline was slightly less steep, falling by 25-30 percent per farm unit. However, when measured in terms of workers per 1,000 ha, the absolute decline in the number of jobs was even sharper, although the differential between 'full-time' and seasonal workers was less marked. By this measure, 'full-time' farm employment for these tasks fell by 50 percent and seasonal workers by 70 and 60 percent (depending on the tasks) over the period. In all, approximately 40,000 jobs were lost from 1970 in the course of restructuring maize production (Budlender 1984:16). As will be shown in chapter four, such a huge decrease in employment has had a radical effect on pay. Seasonal employment represents a fraction of income to total wages where households have a worker in 'full-time' work, but where there is no such employment, the contribution of the seasonal worker is significant, if not vital, for thousands of black households in the reserves.

For other arable products, the shift to capital-intensive production has not been as complete or as even, not because technological alternatives do not exist or are not being developed, but because of their relative expense compared to labour. Sugar production in Natal and the Eastern Transvaal is an example. Although the industry has done research into the mechanisation of cane production, it is not for immediate use but rather an insurance against the day when workers will not 'want to dirty their hands.' However, according to major farmers, 'labour problems will have to be very severe before it becomes worthwhile' (Ibid).

This is not to suggest that there has not been a decline in employment levels in sugar production. Nelson (Ibid) in her study of sugar farming in Natal for the period 1972-82 showed that in the first five years there was a definite trend towards labour-saving methods. However, in the second five years this trend slowed or even reversed. Labour substitution occurred mainly in weeding and soil preparation through the extensive use of chemicals which reduced the need for labour to a considerable degree, and in stacking and loading of cane where 89 percent of farmers surveyed had mechanised. Nonetheless the most labour-intensive area in the industry — the harvest — was still in 1982 almost universally (99 percent) done by hand.

The slowdown in labour substitution in sugar was related to the rising rate of unemployment in the second half of the 1970s and early 1980s, and also to problems and uncertainties with some of the technology. Yet, it is interesting to note that where technological developments brought about a change in the composition of the workforce — that is, replacing men with women and children in stacking and loading procedures in the fields — the reversion to former practices has been the slowest. It is a change which has allowed sugar farmers to reassess their labour supply pool, and begin to exploit the relatively cheaper labour of the large number of women and children concentrated in the reserves.

Nevertheless, even for those arable products which are still labour-intensive — particularly vegetable, potato and plantation cropping (wattle, cotton, tea, coffee, viticulture etc.) production and employment has been affected by restructuring. The concentration of farming units, the extension (or contraction) of the area under a particular crop, the reorganisation of one or more of the processes involved in producing the crop and so on, have all had an effect on employment. For some crops it may have resulted in a relative increase of seasonal workers, given that harvesting remains the one process for many crops which has been least affected by restructuring and still tends to be highly labour-intensive. But, in all types of arable farming employment in general has declined, especially in terms of the growth in the volume of production.

Those trends contain within them at least two important implications. One, the degree to which employment levels will be affected in any particular region is determined by the particular farming mix which characterises it. In the study of the Albany District between 1957 and 1977, for example, Antrobus showed that the decline in, and simultaneous reorganisation of, hectarage under pineapples produced a decline in employment, especially for seasonal work. At the same time, chicory and vegetable production — both relatively labour-intensive at least in the harvesting process — expanded over the period. This meant that, although employment in the district declined, changes in cropping partially offset the decline in jobs which was generated by the reorganisation of pineapple production.

Two, the process of restructuring is far from complete. This means that, even though employment in the sector has already declined substantially, it can and is likely to be reduced still further. Whilst the rate of decline will probably not be as rapid as that in the period after 1970, it will vary between the different farming types. It is likely that job losses will be mainly in those types of production where restructuring is only partial, although not necessarily so. In irrigation farming, where labour costs are amongst the largest costs of production, rationalisation and restructuring centres on reducing the numbers employed. However, sugar production is likely to remain labour-intensive, at least in the harvesting process. Changes in the levels of employment in sugar are unlikely to be caused by increasing mechanisation but by shrinking markets and declining production. This applies equally to those sections of production where restructuring is well-advanced. For example, it is envisaged that the area to be planted with maize (Maize Board 1983:11) will be reduced by 1.9 million ha to overcome the contradictions generated by over-production and a weak home market. The likely job loss will be some 48,000. If, as expected, this land is given over to cattle raising, less than half the loss will be replaced.[12]

In conditions of high and rising unemployment, the ability of farmers to 'pack away' their machines and revert to more labour-intensive methods is limited, since restructuring has involved substantial reorganisation and is not simply about expensive machines in one or another aspect of production. The more the process is reliant on capital-intensive production relations, the harder it is to revert back to labour intensity. So, even in the case of Natal sugar farmers, who went back to more labour-intensive methods when labour supply increased in the late 1970s, it was the less capitalised who switched more easily and readily.

Variations between enterprises
Commercial agriculture is characterised by a lack of uniformity in production relations betwen enterprises, even with regard to the same or similar types of farming. This continues under restructured conditions, although trends towards greater uniformity can be discerned.[13] Generally, as production and wealth have been concentrated in the hands of a smaller group of farmers, the gap between large and small enterprises has widened. This has affected employment levels in several ways. First, large farms tend to be more capital-intensive than smaller ones and therefore employ fewer workers relative to the scale of the enterprise. The loss in jobs that this entails has, however, been mediated by the restructuring process itself. So, for example, many job losses occur in the course of transferring properties from one owner to another. Retrenchment is also not necessarily direct. Behind the oft-repeated claim by farmers that they are not laying off workers is the reality that they are not replacing those who leave or are no longer able to work.

Second, although the ratio of workers to land has decreased, the majority of farm workers are employed on large enterprises. In 1983, 6.3 percent of all commercial farming enterprises outside the bantustans employed 64 percent of the labour force (*Financial Mail* 5.8.83). At the enterprise level this concentration is not so apparent, partly because the number of workers and households per farm unit is affected by the combined interrelation of size, farming type and degree of restructuring. So, in the Albany District, for example, the average number of 'full-time' farm workers per farm was 10.5 for the district as a whole. But, whereas on the dryland cropping and mixed crop and livestock farms of Lower Albany, the number ranged between 7 and 13.7, on the mixed livestock and irrigated cropland of Upper Albany the range was much narrower, i.e., between 9.8 and 10.4 'permanent' workers per unit (Antrobus 1984:977). In the sheep farming district of Hanover, the extent of concentration of workers is more marked. On 17 of the district's 55 farms, farms below 9,000 morgen (one morgen = 0.857 ha) employed an average of 3.8 workers per unit, with a range of 2 to 7.

On farms between 10,000 and 13,000 morgen, the average number of workers employed was 6.5 with a range of 5 to 7.5. On the remaining farms, which ranged from 17,500 to 40,000 morgen in size, the average number of workers per farm was 12.6, with a range of 10-15 between units (Meyer 1984). This concentration of workers has, however, to be offset against the fact that these units cover vast areas, making access between workers and workers' households rare and irregular.

Third, at least amongst the large-scale producers there is a tendency towards greater uniformity in the levels and conditions of employment. Thus, in a statistical comparison of two unspecified and 'arbitrarily chosen representative districts for several crops,' Budlender (1984a:29) found that for the period 1967-75 maize and wheat showed the greatest internal uniformity, although plots on key variables for the various crops also correlated fairly closely to each other.

Fourth, smaller producers with little capital and heavier debt burdens rely more heavily on labour-intensive methods. Since their obligations to their workers in wages and conditions are subject to less stringent terms, if not a general absence of sanction, they tend to abuse this relation in order to overcome their cash flow problems. Thus, when money is short, cash wages are delayed, substituted in 'kind' or just not paid at all. Indeed, this group of farmers has been under the greatest state pressure to reduce their workforce and, therefore, the number of Africans living on their farms. This has ensnared them in a trap of mounting indebtedness. With mounting capital intensity, they have had to shoulder a large and growing share of the cost burden of production, a cost which formerly they could transfer almost wholly on to workers in the sector. The distinction between so-called 'progressive' and 'backward' farmers has conventionally been drawn around the degree of labour intensity in production relations. Those farmers considered 'progressive' are those using capital-intensive methods and who have reduced their workers to minimal levels. Conversely, 'backward' farmers rely heavily on large labour inputs. This distinction is, however, both subjective from the point of view of capital, and misleading from the point of view of labour since not only has the shift in the capital/labour ratio led to fewer jobs, less labour-using production does not necessarily mean better terms and conditions of employment. Nor does it mean that exploitation of the workforce declines, as the term 'progressive' farming might suggest. Subsequent chapters will show that exploitation has not only continued but intensified.

Productivity

This decline in relative and absolute employment levels in the course of the restructuring of commercial agricultural production also raises the problem of labour productivity. Historically, the conditions of exploitation of black farm workers have led to very low levels of output per worker. Restructuring and particularly technological developments, rather than changes in social conditions and relations, have produced a relative improvement in worker productivity. For example, between 1970 and 1982 labour productivity measured by an increase in the volume of agricultural production per worker rose from an index of 100 in 1970 to 197 in 1982 (Hattingh 1983). This increase was, however, uneven because it was primarily associated with technological changes, and therefore output per worker largely increased in proportion to the degree of mechanisation etc. (Budlender 1984a:29). This meant that productivity per worker varied between the branches and different farming types within the branches. Nevertheless, it generally increased. Taking the example of sugar production, still relatively labour-intensive, the impact of restructuring on output was stark. In 1951/2 an average of 14.9 workers were needed to produce 1,000 tons of cane and each worker produced an average of 67 tons. In 1961/2, just over ten workers were employed per 1,000 tons of cane produced, with the average tonnage per worker increasing to 97. A decade later the respective figures were 6.5 workers per 1,000 tons and 153 tons per worker. By 1977, 16,000 workers were producing what 22,000 had produced three years earlier, and it took an estimated six workers to produce 1,000 tons of cane (*Financial Mail*, 17.6.77).

However, this visible increase in productivity per worker, it must be stressed, is only relative and should not be allowed to obscure the inefficiencies and contradictions which restructuring in conditions of national oppression and super-cheap labour power have produced. As a consequence of this relation, the capacity of existing capital investment in many enterprises is both under-utilised and inefficiently used, with more workers being employed than the possession of such equipment would suggest. This means that a further reduction of employment can be anticipated without impairing levels of production. The likely outcome of the combined recession and the drought (which gripped the country between 1981 and 1984) was that large numbers of laid-off workers found their jobs vanished forever.

Furthermore, low wages and bad conditions, low levels of education, training and poor management all work to reduce efficiency and productivity and therefore reduce profit levels. So, for example, poorly-trained workers increase machine running costs such that these costs in South Africa are said to be amongst the highest in the world. In fact, in order for the reduced levels of employment not to affect productivity, a concomitant improvement in skill is required. It is these and related contradictions that pressure the state and monopoly capital to call for improved conditions and better training so that performance can be improved and wastage reduced (Horner and Van Wyk 1984:52).

The decline in employment and the increase in output per worker, which restructuring has brought about, has meant that exploitation of the workforce has continued in changed conditions, although it cannot be inferred from this that exploitation has increased. To make such an evaluation requires an analysis of pay (and conditions), and this is done in chapters five and six below.

Un- and under-employment

Inseparably related to the decline in employment levels are the facts of un- and under-employment. These are crucial to the analysis of the impact of restructuring on employment in commercial agriculture, although they are often glossed over by the statistics and ignored in discussions on the merits or demerits of 'mechanisation'. Any decline in sectoral employment carries with it the probability that unemployment will rise. This is not simply a factor of developments within the sector, but intimately connected to production trends in the political economy as a whole. Restructuring has extended under-employment in the sector and added to the growing pool of unemployed. Furthermore, the way these developments have occurred are inseparable from changes in the labour forms in the sector. On the one hand, the massive physical eviction of so-called surplus people which restructuring and the general conditions of African national oppression have generated has hidden the full extent to which restructuring has produced a general rise in unemployment.

On the other hand, the massive expulsion of workers notwithstanding, unemployment and under-employment is widespread amongst remaining on-farm agricultural workers. The paradox is that the presence of worker families on the farms is conditional upon their rendering labour service to the farmer, but, at the same time, they have no guarantee of being employed. In a survey of farms in the Calitzdorp district in 1983/4 conducted during the fruit season (when employment was at its peak), 32.9 percent of economically active people resident on the farms were unemployed, 66 percent of them women. Even when workers living on the farms are needed for labour purposes, they often experience periods of enforced unemployment, due often to their terms of tenancy. Thus, on an eastern Transvaal farm, workers were faced with five months of unemployment because, although the farmer did not then need their labour, he refused them the necessary permission to look for jobs in the nearby town over this period. He said he 'needed the women for hoeing and picking during the harvest' (Seloane 1984:18). In short, their position does not differ substantially from casual and seasonal workers drawn from the reserves. They too face long and uncertain periods of un- and under-employment.

Finally, under- and unemployment have a direct bearing on pay and work conditions in the sector. Their extent not only depresses and keeps wage levels low, but also directly affects household income, i.e., the number of people who are dependent on the wage.

This chapter has examined the effect of restructuring on the levels and intensity of employment both nationally and according to variations that arise from differences between regions, farming types and enterprises. Clearly, the variations notwithstanding, there has been both a relative and an absolute decline in employment levels. On the one hand, this decline has meant that employment in commercial agriculture has become concentrated on larger enterprises and in more capital-intensive production, the degree of concentration, however, varying within the sector and unevenly. Furthermore, it neither matches the degree of concentration of capital within the sector, nor the degree of concentration of workers in secondary industry. Concentration of the agricultural workforce is further tempered by changes in labour forms. On the other hand, the decline has contributed to rising levels of under- and unemployment in the political economy as a whole.

In order to gain a fuller understanding of the impact of restructuring on employment levels, and particularly on agricultural employment, the following chapters will look in detail at the effect of restructuring on the division of labour in commercial agriculture.

Notes

1. See Hendrie D. in Wilson F. 1977. In 1983 J.A. Grobbelaar, Senior Economist of the Unit of Futures Research at Stellenbosch University, expressed regret that official statistics had become 'subject to political developments' (since 1976, according to him) and that this was making market researchers, economists and demographers 'rather desperate for reliable vital statistics needed for population projections.' Cited in a *Survey of Race Relations* 1983:99.

2. A *Survey of Race Relations* 1983:374. In addition, there were a further 17,500 'farmer' plotholders whose conditions differ little from those of labourers.

3. The South African Development Trust (SADT) was created with the passage of the 1936 Amendment to the Land Act and all subsequent land acquired by the state is vested in it.

4. It is the reliability of the statistical data which forces Simkins to depend on statistics for regular and domestic employment *rather than* the relation of these forms of employment to labour forms in agriculture. Thus, it is unacceptable to place a value judgement on the significance of such forms of employment based solely on their statistical reliability. This is a relation which is historically established and therefore subject to change.

5. Drawing on the analogies of the US experience in the period 1930-60, Wilson F. envisaged such a 'two-phase' trend in the decline in employment in South African agriculture. Referred to in Bromberger 1984:2.

6. It is relevant to note here the misguided notion implicit in the idea that 'regular' work is primary work and that therefore the primary work is male. This is not to suggest that 'regular' male workers are not primary breadwinners for their households, but so are 'irregular' female and child workers.

7. Some left through direct physical eviction, others as a result of indirect coercion. The *Surplus People's Project Reports* 1983:70, vol.5.

8. The Coloured labour preference policy was introduced in 1955, but only effectively began to be implemented a decade or more later. Further details are given in chapter four.

9. Theron E. (1976:85, Table one. Annexure B) registers an increase in Coloured agricultural employment over the period 1960-70 of some 14.6 percent. This discrepancy may be accounted for by the different time span of the two sets of statistics and by the inclusion of 'casual' employment figures in the latter.

10. This estimate is for November 1983 and taken from the 1983 *SAIRR Survey*, p. 378. Whilst such criticism can be levelled at all development projects, the significance here is that unemployment in the South African economy is treated as though it were a problem of the reserves and separate from relations which exist in the country as a whole. It also seeks to divert attention from the facts which have created the gross unequal distribution of wealth in the country.

11. In 1973, the number of farm workers employed 'full-time' for eight farming activities per 1,000 ha were estimated at: sugar (126); maize(18); poultry, pigs, vegetables (85); non-deciduous fruit (24); cereals (14); cattle and deciduous fruit (12); about three for sheep. Cited in Wilson F. 1977:1.

12. This is so, given that the area to be withdrawn covers more than the total area under wheat at present, is ten times the area planted with groundnuts, and six times that planted with sunflowers. Using the 1973 estimate of twelve workers per 1,000 ha of cattle, the number of possible jobs that will materialise is about 23,000. This, however, is likely to be an overestimate since over the past decade the ratio of workers to farming type has undergone further reductions.

13. This does not apply only to employment levels but to all production relations, some of which will be explored in subsequent chapters.

3.   A Captive Labour Force: Blocked Alternatives

The complex interrelationship between labour forms and social characteristics has altered as a result of the restructuring process.[1] Of the two sets of changes which can be identified, the first relates to changes in labour forms: notably a shift away from labour tenancy towards a refined but somewhat altered form of farm service which minimalises the presence of workers resident on the farms and affects the location, character and form of labour recruited to meet seasonal and non-continuous labour needs. The other set of changes concerns characteristics of the labour force: the greater use of female labour, the emergence of a skill hierarchy in the division of farm work, etc.

Whilst these changes can be separately identified, changes in labour forms affect characteristics and vice versa. A distinction is, nevertheless, necessary and useful for the purposes of analysis. Identifying labour forms as the key dynamic, it is possible to analyse the significance of changing social characteristics in the context of relations of production and not as ahistorical, discrete 'factors'.

To assess the impact of restructuring, this chapter begins with labour forms found at the onset of the process and analyses similarities and differences. The part of the latter chapter considers the impact of the first phase of restructuring on these labour forms. This will provide the basis for the analysis in chapter four of changes in the labour forms and social characteristics of the workforce employed in commercial agriculture in the second phase of restructuring which began in the mid-1960s.

Labour forms in commercial agriculture at the onset of restructuring

At the onset of restructuring in the late 1930s, the two main labour forms in commercial agriculture in South Africa were labour tenancy and farm service. Labour tenancy predominated in the Orange Free State, much of the Transvaal and in Central and Northern Natal. Farm service was dominant in the Cape and in some districts of the OFS, Southern Transvaal and Southern Natal, although outside the Cape it usually occurred alongside either labour tenancy or migrant labour as a complementary but secondary labour form. A third form — migrant labour — was particularly important in sugar and wattle production and dominated the sugar belt of the Natal coast. Supplementary to these three was prison labour, which developed in this period into a significant secondary form though its geographical spread and intensity of use were patchy.

All these forms emerged in the course of colonisation and were an inseparable part of the agricultural capitalisation process. Each expressed in a particular way the historical interrelation of national oppression and social exploitation. The differences between them were not only important in shaping the composition and characteristics of the workforce at the time, but also differentially influenced and were influenced by, restructuring.

Labour tenancy

Labour tenancy represents an intermediate stage in the transition from cash or crop tenancy to full proletarianisation. Its expansion into the most common form of labour in much of South African agriculture occurred from the second decade of this century and is inseparable from the land dispossession of the African majority on the one hand, and the capitalisation of agricultural production on the other.[2] The 1913 Native Land Act not only legislated against African ownership of land or access to it through various forms of non-labour rental — so-called 'squatting' — in 93 percent of the country.[3] It also legislated *for* labour service as the only form of African tenancy on white-owned land.[4] Thus, a farm labourer was defined by the Act as

> a native who resides on a farm and is *bona fide* but not necessarily continuously employed by the owner or lessee thereof ... such native shall not be deemed to be *bona fide* employed unless he renders 90 days' service at least in one calendar year ... (Plaatje, 1981:69)

The clamour for labour tenancy expressed the determination of white farmers to break the obvious prosperity of many African peasant communities (Bundy, 1979; Beinart, 1982). These not only competed successfully for the growing home market, but also, alongside those who retained access to land through cash payments earned in wage labour, were able to evade being pressed into service on the farms. Equally, the promotion of labour tenancy stemmed from farmer resolve to secure labour without laying out cash; it was a form of labour which met the particular interests of small and less capitalised farmers.[5]

The advantages of labour tenancy to capitalising farmers was only too plain. Not only did its terms compel tenants to work for a minimum period each year for the farmer, but it made their labour a form of payment *to the farmer* in return for access to a plot of land and permission to graze stock. In securing himself a labour supply, the farmer was under no obligation to pay for the work he commanded: and payment made (invariably in a form other than cash) was entirely at his discretion. In fact, he expected and even depended on his tenants to secure their cash needs by working elsewhere during the period they were not obliged to labour for him. In consequence the tenants' 'free' months were mostly spent earning money on the mines or in the towns.

This significant characteristic of labour tenancy has often been underestimated when analysing the development and conditions of the working class in South Africa. It has at least three important implications. First, it means that labour tenancy operated in much the same way as migrant labour to lower the costs of labour power to the mines, secondary industry and service sector. Second — unlike migrant labour — off-farm employment of labour tenants directly subsidised the capitalisation of white farmers. They not only profited from the unpaid labour rendered them on the farms, but also reaped the benefits of the waged work done by tenants elsewhere.

Third, there is the more abstract question of the relation of labour tenancy to full proletarianisation. On the one hand, it seems inadequate to confine the analysis of labour tenancy to social relations on the farms or within agriculture (Morris in Keegan, 1981:235) given that these tenants, in 'binding their bodies to serve the landowners'[6] were also selling their labour to others. Their connection to agriculture was not necessarily as 'full' proletarians, but their relationship to proletarianisation was not only through agriculture. On the other hand, within agriculture, labour tenancy expressed a whole range of intermediate stages between sharecropping and full capitalist relations. The extent to which tenants had sunk into the conditions of the agrarian proletariat depended 'on the degree of control exercised by white farmers and (the) varying proportions in which the landlord and the tenant respectively owned the means of production' (Keegan, 1981:235). Therefore, there are two inseparably linked elements which have to be looked at when assessing the shift of labour tenancy away from a peasant-based relation to a proletarian one. One concerns the extent to which 'the peasant component' of labour tenancy has been eroded, the other the degree to which labour tenants depend for their subsistence on waged labour.

The 'peasant component' of labour tenancy has never rested on access to arable land. Rarely have labour tenants had access to more than two or three morgen.[7] Rather, it was to be found in livestock. Many tenants ran large herds and, as long as the farmer depended on ox-drawn carriage and ploughing, the use of tenant oxen was an inseparable part of the terms of tenancy.[8] But the very process which labour tenancy was designed to stimulate, the capitalisation of agricultural production, contained within it the seeds of destruction of the labour form. The introduction and spread of mechanical traction, and the systematic erosion of grazing rights, coupled with restrictions on the size of tenant flocks and herds to the point where few if any grazing animals were permitted, undermined the 'peasant component' of labour tenancy. This decline in conditions — rather than a rise in needs — led to greater dependency on waged labour, which in turn acted to push labour tenants more fully into the proletariat. The shift in the balance between peasant and proletarian on the land had occurred in many parts of South Africa by the early 1930s (Bundy, 1979).

Deteriorating conditions were reinforced and intensified by legislative compulsion. Through the state, white farmers acted to try and ensure that the proletarianisation of labour tenants would end in confining them within the agrarian working class. Thus, at the same time as the law served to strip tenants of their rights, it endeavoured to compel them to remain in agriculture in conditions of servitude. The provisions of the 1913 Land Act were extended to cover the Transvaal and Natal;[9] the term of minimum service was extended from 90 to 180 days;[10] the definition of labour tenant changed to encompass a man, his wife and their dependants;[11] whipping, formerly only legally applicable to farm servants under the Masters and Servants Regulations, was extended to apply to labour tenants;[12] summary eviction of the 'unit of employment' was vested in a farmer if any single member failed to fulfil his or her obligations;[13] pass laws were extended and access to the towns blocked (Lacey,1981), etc.

It became difficult to distinguish the conditions of labour tenancy from those governing farm 'servants'. The new minimum service contract meant that for at least seven months a year the labour tenant was under obligation to work for the farmer. The period over which this obligation was to be fulfilled was not defined and was therefore determined by and for the convenience of the farmer. So it often dragged out over a whole year. The effect of this was that alternative avenues of employment open to labour tenants in their 'free' months were severely restricted. Mine contracts were no longer possible. Even if the tenancy service could be fulfilled in one seven-month block, no mines accepted four-month short contracts.[14] Short-term work in industry was also hard to come by and so increasingly the only work open to labour tenants in the towns was in domestic and other service, in government employment on road construction, refuse and night-soil collection, etc., or on other farms. All of these were low-waged, even in South African terms. Thus, the unavoidable implication of extending the service period of labour tenancy was that the earning capacity of tenants was reduced twofold; first, by the shorter period open to them to take up cash-waged employment, and secondly by the further restriction imposed on employment possibilities open to them.

The harshness of the extended period of labour obligation was compounded by the extended definition of who would be obliged to meet these labour terms. Formerly, the wife and dependants of labour tenants were not legally obliged to work for the farmer. Notwithstanding those many instances where they were forced to do so, this meant that, within limits, they could choose to work for the farmer or not. It also meant that the farmer had to pay them in some form if he required their labour. But, even more importantly, it meant that at least some members of the household could work away from the farm and bring in the cash income on which the family increasingly depended. Obviously this practice was a drain on the labour pool the farmer hoped to secure through labour tenancy. Not only were these members of labour tenant households beyond his beck and call, but they were also reluctant to do farm work when they returned. Extending the definition of labour tenants to include a contracting man's entire family was an attempt to ensnare the services of all household members, mostly without payment. It not only further depleted income and effectively enslaved more people, but also added to insecurity of tenure. For whilst an individual man might contract himself to a farmer, it was exceedingly difficult for him to compel all household members to fulfil the conditions of collective servitude.

Not surprisingly, the 'peasant component' of labour tenancy had also been eroded further, partly by the reduction in the time labour tenant families could spend attending to their livestock and working their *akker* (plot), and partly be restrictions imposed by capitalising farmers. They not only whittled away at the amount of land given over to use by tenants, but directly restricted the amount of stock labour tenants were allowed to hold. This permanently diminished their wealth as it prevented them from building up their herds (South African Communists Speak: Doc.66, 1981:14). Labour tenants found they had no better access to land and cattle than workers bound by farm service.

But if deteriorating conditions of labour tenancy had brought labour tenants closer to the brink of 'complete slavery', to paraphrase a Sotho prophesy that did the rounds at the turn of the century[15], their position differed from that of workers bound under conditions of farm service in one very important respect. Whereas African farm labourers, as 'servants', were barred from seeking anything but farm work,[16] labour tenants, by the very terms of a tenancy so disadvantageous in other respects, were legally able to look for work outside commercial agriculture. The difference between the two forms of labour increasingly had less to do with relative proletarianisation, and more to do with relative confinement within a bound agrarian working class. This helps to explain the tenacious persistence of labour tenancy and the spirited resistance to its abolition in subsequent decades.

In practice the distinctions between labour tenancy and farm service, even at this stage, were not so clear-cut. Yet they were definable, especially for the tenants, who found their position eroded to the point where 'the whole family works from January to January. The man gets no money ... and is not given sufficient land on which to plough', where even the manure in the labour tenant's cattle pen was claimed by the farmer as his property.[17] They clearly saw the cause of their descent into greater poverty. It was bitterly felt, and they were led by it to the unavoidable conclusion that 'we are oppressed by our masters'.[18] Thus, by the onset of restructuring labour tenancy had undergone substantial transformation and was showing signs of relatively rapid disintegration as a labour form.

Workers in farm service

The second labour form surveyed here, farm service, embodies the outcome of rural proletarianisation in South Africa. Dispossession of precapitalist and peasant communities, on the one hand, and the abolition of slavery and the ending of the neo-slavery of indenture, on the other,[19] did not free rural workers in Marx's famous double sense.[20] Whilst they were made propertyless, they were bound by quasi-feudal ties to their employers, so that the terms under which they sold their labour power were dictated by extra-economic compulsion. Under Masters and Servants Acts of the nineteenth and early twentieth centuries,[21] farm workers were deemed 'servants' who were obliged to labour for their employers — deemed 'masters' — for twelve months a year or as long as their contract was held to apply. Like many labour tenancy relations, service contracts were invariably verbal arrangements between 'masters' and 'servants' but the provisions of the Masters and Servants regulations applied even where contracts had not been formalised, since to dispute them would mean a black man challenging the authority of a white man in the white man's court.

These laws vested 'masters' with enormous personal authority over virtually every aspect of the worker's existence. Every instruction they issued was held to be 'a lawful command' and if the worker refused to carry it out, or more often, found it impossible to carry out in the manner commanded,[22] his or her action was construed as a criminal offence which carried with it penal sanction. Rarely did these 'breaches of law' find their way to court and when they did (and this was invariably at the farmer's instigation) the ruling was almost always in the 'master's' favour. Mostly, however, the matter was settled beyond the bounds of the court, on the farm, with the farmer determining the punishment. This ranged from flogging with a sjambok (hide whip), which was a normal and common feature of farm service, to the eventual eviction of the 'offender' and his/her dependants from the farm.

Between these there was a whole range of improvised punishments which naturally incorporated physical assault and were limited only by the imaginations of farmers whose world-view was steeped in paternalism and racism and sanctioned by the Old Testament's vengeful god.

When punishment exceeded even these broad parameters and resulted in the murder of a worker, the farmer was not always brought to court, and hardly ever punished for the crime of taking another person's life. At best he would be judged as having exceeded his authority and punished for offences like common assault, etc., which often meant no more than a fine.[23]

The Masters and Servants Acts shaped the tone of relations on the farms to a very large extent. They directly applied to many black farm workers and indirectly affected all Africans working in commercial agriculture who were not classed as labour tenants, 'squatters' or contract workers. They applied to Coloured farm workers who had long been transformed into a rural proletariat and constituted the base of the agricultural workforce in many parts of the Cape. They also covered Indian workers who, on release from the obligations of indenture, found themselves bound anew by a different set of laws with the same intent of compelling them to labour for the farmer in servitude.

But by the time restructuring began, farm service as a labour form was under strain. Pressures emanated from developments outside rather than within commercial agricultural production. For whilst the terms of servitude were recognised as oppressive by millions of farm workers, few alternative avenues of employment existed. The development and expansion of secondary industry, in particular, opened up a whole range of new prospects, and farm workers in growing numbers were leaving the land for the better pay and conditions in the towns. The period 1936 — 1951 (a time-span which somewhat overlaps with the onset of restructuring in the sector) was, in fact, the period of most rapid urban population growth in South African history. This was especially so for Indians and Africans. The primary source of newly urbanised people — whether African, Coloured or Indian — was the so-called 'white rural areas' (Bundy, 1979).

This exodus did not mean that the Masters and Servants Acts had ceased to apply on the farms. These laws could and did continue to regulate relations of servitude between farm workers and their employers. But they proved an ineffective means of binding workers to the sector as a whole, and other instruments had to be sought. These were found in embryonic form in the pass laws, the elaboration of which went hand in hand with the capitalisation of agriculture and the expansion of secondary industry.[24]

The pass laws superseded the Masters and Servants' regulations as the primary means of binding workers to agriculture, perpetuating farm service as a labour form in changing conditions. But they also held particular implications for the character of the labour form and all labour in the sector. Pass laws were an instrument of national oppression directed exclusively at Africans. Indian and Coloured workers, whilst subjected to almost identical conditions on the farms, could thus escape out of agriculture, whereas Africans were compelled by the pass laws to work in the sector on the terms the white farmers dictated. It is therefore not surprising that the call to elaborate the existing pass controls and make them more effective originated from, and was frequently repeated by, white farmers.(Lacey, 1981; Morris, 1977) Through this device a substantial section of the workforce could be channelled forcibly into commercial agriculture, and the repressive relations which characterised the sector could continue uninterrupted, inseparably linked with African national oppression. The terms of the Masters and Servants laws, although secondary to securing labour power, continued to govern relations on the farms.

The other main feature of farm service was that the terms of employment initially presumed, as was the case with labour tenancy, that all members of a worker's household would put their labour at the disposal of the farmer — a presumption that became law in the course of capitalisation. The implications of this were several.

First, both labour forms were consonant with efforts by capitalising farmers to keep a pool of labour on their farms which could be tapped whenever required.

Second, for workers, this condition of employment reduced their capacity to take a stand against intolerable conditions, since the action of any one individual threatened the security of an entire household — with respect not only to income, but also to a place of abode. Since the person through whom the family/household was employed was the male household head, he invariably came under considerable pressure to force reluctant members to comply with farmers' wishes.

Third, this condition of employment meant that both female and child labour were a normal and everyday feature of working life in commercial agriculture. Whilst not necessarily employed all day or every day, children and women resident on the farms were a standard part of the irregular and seasonal workforce.

Fourth, since providing their labour was a condition of service, absence of workers from the farm for any length of time was at the discretion of the farmer. For an African man to leave the enterprise, he had to obtain a trek-pass which spelled out the terms under which he was temporarily released from service on the farm. The movement of women was generally less constrained, but alternative employment possibilities for them were fewer.

And fifth, since this household labour was a condition of service for the most part, it was also unpaid. If any payment was given, it was entirely at the discretion of the farmer and invariably was paid to the household head.

For Indian and Coloured 'servants', leaving the farm without the consent of the farmer was relatively less hazardous as they were not obliged to carry passes, but they and their families also faced eviction for failing to meet farm service conditions.

Migrant labour

The immediate problem confronting any attempt to characterise migrant labour in commercial agriculture prior to restructuring in the sector is the general dearth of literature on the subject, despite the extensive research of the past decade or so on the connection between the discovery and exploitation of minerals (particularly gold) and the development of a migrant labour system.[25] In these studies, where reference is made to the labour form in commercial agriculture, it is invariably brief and general. At best, in scientific as well as in popular thinking, migrant labour is associated with sugar and/or foreign workers. But even here, with the exception of Beinart (1982), whose work focuses on the forces in Pondoland's political economy which directed migrant labour to the sugar fields, the way the labour form developed in sugar remains relatively unelaborated.

The second and related problem is that migrant labour has taken more than one form. It presumes the existence of two sets of production relations (whether actual or not). One set (colonial capitalist) is found at the point where labour power is expended and the other (peasant) at the point of social reproduction of the labourer.[26] Changes in either one of these sets of relations, or in both, or in the way they interrelate, have all affected the form migrant labour has taken. Not only have different forms developed over time, but these have existed side by side in the same historical period. The task then is to identify the particular forms of migrant labour at a given point in time, a task made doubly difficult in commercial agriculture by the absence of ground study. In the light of these two problems, the remarks here are both provisional and preliminary. At best, they are indicators of the labour form as it occurred in capitalist agriculture prior to restructuring.

The association of migrant labour with sugar in the sector is an essentially accurate connection. It needs to be qualified in several ways. First, although it was certainly a secondary labour form in the sector as a whole, migrant labour was not confined to the sugar plantations. It is difficult to assess the extent of its practice, because some of the forms that it took make the number of people involved incalculable. This particularly applies to 'volitional',[27] and unrecruited migrant workers, as well as to those who were recruited by individual farmers in an unofficial and less systematic way. It is also likely that proportionately few migrants took up work in commercial agriculture, because of poor conditions and low cash wages (the sugar estates excepted). Evidence that foreign migrants tried to circumvent farm labour is provided by the failed special scheme devised by the Department of Native Affairs and a special committee of the South African Agricultural Union (SAAU) who between them agreed that the state was

> to take control of all non-Union Africans and distribute them among farmers. From March 1, 1947 all illegal immigrants were to be diverted to the farms. The police started intensive roundups of Rhodesian and Nyasa Africans, imprisoned them in special depots and gave them the 'choice' of signing a farm labour contract for at least 180 days or being deported ... In 1947 6,032 non-Union Africans were arrested, of whom 502 (eight percent) agreed to work on the farms. In 1948 3,474 men were arrested of whom only three percent agreed to farm labour. The scheme had cost £20,000 (First, 1959).

Nevertheless, migrant workers were to be found in general agriculture, although it is likely that they were concentrated in the farming districts, such as Bethal in the Eastern Transvaal, which faced the stiffest competition for labour from the mines, or else in the border districts of the Union. In fact, it was here that the connection was made between foreign workers and migrant labour in the sector.[28]

Second, migrant labour took two main forms. Between them there was a whole range of variations which differed in various ways, but particularly in terms of the degree of extra-economic compulsion exerted on African peasants to take up 'waged' work. In 'volitional' migrancy, Africans were pushed on to the colonial-capitalist labour market by a combination of indirect pressures. These included land alienation and the land hunger and decline in productive capacity that ensued; a myriad of tax levies which required payment in cash; restrictions on movement, trade and marketing opportunities; debt inducement through rural traders; the internal contradictions and pressures within the social relations of peasant communities, etc.

But migrant labour was not confined to this form. It is possible, although difficult to substantiate, that some farmers actively recruited migrant labour when labour was scarce or labour needs high. What is known, is that farmers established formal labour recruiting organisations in the early 1930s.[29] In 1937, twelve such firms were officially recognised. In the five-year period 1933-37, they recruited no fewer than 52,208 migrant workers, of whom approximately 30 percent (14,000) were foreign. These workers were distributed between farmers in the Transvaal and Natal, with some 22,500 being sent to farms in the former province and 29,688 to the latter (Suzman and Kahn 1947).

The essence of recruited labour was that it was solicited and involved some form of direct compulsion. Whilst further research needs to be done[30] into the way these recruiting organisations operated and whether their practices differed from those operated by the mining houses, evidence from Pondoland reveals crude and brutal methods. In the absence of adult men who were willing to take up work in the cane fields — either because they were already on mine labour contracts, or because they were able to withstand the pressures to enter the migrant labour system — sugar labour recruiters simply rounded up under-aged youths and drove off into Natal with their stolen human cargo. By this means the migrant labour system on the sugar plantations was first established on the backs of forced (male) child labour. And even when the pattern of migrancy from Pondoland shifted away from the mines, and increasing numbers of adult men took up sugar contracts, the labour needs of the sugar estates continued to be met by the extensive use of involuntary child migrants (Beinart, 1982:146).

Third, it seems that organised recruitment of migrant labour was a relatively recent development in the sector, a characteristic of the decades immediately prior to restructuring. It stemmed from the combined effects of 1) the spread of commercial production within agriculture and the rising need for labour which went with it; and 2) competition for labour, not only from the mines but, with the rise of manufacture, from secondary industry and services in the towns and cities. Recruitment of migrant workers arose out of farmers' efforts to secure labour without changing the terms of employment which drove workers out of or away from the sector in the first place. Recruitment of migrants in this period was facilitated by declining conditions in the reserves and social formations beyond South Africa's boundaries. These had long been recruiting areas for mine labour, a factor contributing to their decline as dependency on 'waged' labour became an essential part of the changed and deteriorating reproduction cycle.[31]

Fourth, recruited migrant labour only became the predominant labour form in sugar during the 1920s and 1930s. The sugar and wattle plantations, and much of colonial agriculture in Natal,[32] had been established on the indentured labour[33] of workers imported from India. On the estates this labour form had been supplemented by migrant workers, many of whom were recruited from Mozambique and other colonies outside South Africa.[34] But until the importation of indentured workers from India was halted[35] and the labour form phased out in practice (Beinart, 1982:143), it remained predominant in the plantation economy.

Fifth, in the course of establishing migrant labour as the primary labour form in sugar, recruitment came to focus on Pondoland in the Transkei. It is not quite clear why this came about. From the point of view of migration from Pondoland, the shift to the cane fields entailed a significant change in the pattern of labour movement from the area, since in 1910 about 80 percent of migrants from Pondoland worked down the mines on the Rand. This needs to be explained, especially since sugar contracts paid lower wages than those offered on the mines.[36] Dependency on waged labour in the area was on the increase.[37] In the absence of a labour recruiting agreement between sugar and mine recruiters,[38] it would seem that the pattern of migrancy was determined, to a far greater extent than is usually assumed, by rural production and social activities (Beinart, 1982:145-6). In other words, the shift to sugar migrancy by Mpondo migrants was part of an effort to sustain the base of social reproduction in the face of deteriorating conditions after the mines had raised their minimum contract period to eight months. As Beinart makes clear, the decline in size of the rural production unit and the change in its composition, with the absence of one or more (and sometimes all) young male adults, altered the organisation of rural cultivation. By the 1930s, the staple crop in Pondoland had switched from sorghum to maize,[39] which was labour intensive only for concentrated periods of the year. By the end of the decade, migrancy had assumed distinct seasonal characteristics which reflected both these changed cropping patterns and changes in the social structure (Beinart, 1982:100).

Sixth and last, it appears that, prior to restructuring, recruited migrant labour in commercial agriculture was only established as a primary labour form in sugar.[40] Whereas in all other branches of farming, recruited migrant labour tended to be a secondary source of labour, if it featured at all, on the sugar estates these workers formed the base which made cane production and processing possible. This fact, of course, had consequences for the labour form. Labour migrancy was also at its most systematised in sugar. Estate owners and companies, in order to ensure supply and conditions on their terms, organised migrancy on the pattern established by the mining houses. In fact, so closely did their conditions resemble those of migrant workers on the mines that the National Population Census of 1936 did not count sugar plantation workers as living on 'European farms' but classified them as resident in industrial compounds (Smith, 1941).

The system was based on the permanent oscillation of male migrant workers between the sugar fields and the reserve. Workers were recruited on six-month contracts to serve out their term of labour in the cane fields (and mills) as 'single labour units' housed in all-male compounds. Since it was assumed that the reserve base contributed materially to the worker's social reproduction, he was also paid as a 'single labour unit' whose wage was presumed to be supplementary to (at worst, supplemented by) agricultural production in the reserve.

For the worker, his return to the reserve at the end of the contract to participate in harvest and general agricultural and other activities formed part of his struggle to survive, not only as an individual but also as a social being with familial and community ties. Land hunger and the breakdown of production and social relations exacerbated by the migrant system, however, militated against the perpetuation of oscillating migrancy: it could only be sustained by extending the network of extra-economic control. As early as 1930, the South African Cane Growers' Association called for the introduction of a single pass (Native Economic Commission, 1930 — 1932) since already Africans were leaving the reserves permanently for the towns, although in Pondoland this movement only gained real momentum after the decade of the 1930s (Beinart, 1982:150).

For employers the merit of oscillating migrancy lay in the cheapness of labour power, inseparable from which was the absolution of employers from any contribution to the cost of reproducing the worker as a social being. The system also increased their power and control over Africans, a fact not incidental to the maintenance of white minority domination in the country as a whole. Migrant labour in its 'classical' form — i.e., where agricultural activity in the reserves contributed to the subsistence of the worker's household, and therefore acted as a *raison d'être* for his movement between town and countryside — was showing signs of disintegration. It had to be sustained by an increasingly elaborate and intensified network of laws and regulations directing and prohibiting the free movement of the worker and his family.

Migrant labour compared with labour tenancy and farm service
When compared to labour tenancy and farm service, some features of oscillating migrant labour resemble aspects of each of these forms, but there were also distinct differences.

● Like labour tenancy, migrant labour presumed a peasant component — though one which, at this stage, had a stronger base. But for labour tenants this relation was intrinsically bound up with white commercial agriculture and only indirectly connected to the reserves (through land alienation and scarcity). For migrant workers, however, the bond with the reserves was paramount in the peasant/proletarian relation. A further aspect of similarity between the two forms was to be found in the pursuit of waged labour by labour tenants in their 'free' months. In both forms the peasant component of the relation was under severe strain, if not facing complete disintegration. Both labour tenancy and migrant labour were becoming more fully proletarianised relations, with 'peasant' production at best supplementing waged labour, although at this stage not necessarily to the same extent in each form.

● Like farm service, but somewhat less like labour tenancy (although as the terms deteriorated this distinction became less marked), 'waged' labour was tied up with work on the farms. Farm workers in service were bound to labour on the farms all year long, and migrant workers worked there for the duration of their contract (where it applied). But whereas, within limits, migrant workers could take up alternative forms of waged work (mine, industrial, service), farm worker 'servants' could not.

● Migrant labour differed from both labour tenancy and farm service in that the 'unit of employment' was not the household/family. Rather, he was an individual worker who, alone, was expected to render service to the employer. He also lived without his family for the whole period during which he was employed. On the sugar estates, he was housed in single-sex compounds in similar, if not worse, conditions than those found on the mines.

● This, in turn, gave rise to another difference. Migrant workers were almost always men, including youths barely out of their childhood, whereas both labour tenancy and farm service incorporated women and children directly into the labour force.

● Furthermore, the period in which the migrant worker was employed was specified — particularly for workers recruited to the cane fields. At the end of it he was expected to leave for the reserves, although he could and probably would return on a subsequent 'contract'.

● Partly because he was unaccompanied by his 'family', and partly because the cheapness of the system rested on the presumption that migrant wages supplemented agricultural production in the reserves (although normally the opposite was the case), the migrant was paid as if he was single and detached.

● Unlike the other two labour forms, cash made up a part of the wage paid, especially where migrant workers were recruited. In sugar this practice was rationalised to the extent that pay was calculated on a daily shift basis.

These differences notwithstanding, when migrants came looking for work, their terms of employment differed little from other farm workers. All were subject to the generally brutalising conditions that characterised relations on the farms. The perpetuation of each form required a growing armoury of laws and decrees, especially as alternative avenues of employment opened up in the towns and cities.

Prison labour
A fourth labour form characteristic of commercial agriculture prior to restructuring was prison labour. The penal system under colonial — capitalism had long acted as a source of forced labour, supplying workers to various sectors in two mutually reinforcing ways.[41] On the one hand, it elaborated an ever-expanding web of tax, pass, service and other laws and regulations aimed at driving the oppressed and dispossessed black majority into 'waged' labour. On the other hand, it channelled transgressors of these laws back into the labour market through a prison labour system.

White farmers have always made use of prisoners to meet their labour needs. But the emergence of a substantial prison labour force was inseparable from the process of capitalisation within the sector. It demonstrated growing state responsiveness to farmer demands for labour and the need to counter the effects of competition for labour from other sectors, especially with the rise and expansion of secondary industry. In the space of a few years a system was elaborated to supply short-term prisoners — they were all black — to the farms on terms very favourable to the farmer. The 'criminal' nature of the overwhelming majority of the 'offenders' derived from breach of tax,[42] pass[43] and related forced labour laws, including breach of service under the Masters and Servants Acts.

In 1930 the terms of leasing[44] prison labour to farmers stipulated that: 1) a minimum 'gang' of 25 prisoners had to be hired for a period of three months, with the proviso that in the event of farmers being unable to employ so many men, arrangements could be made for central accommodation of such 'gangs' whose service could then be divided among a number of farmers in the district; and 2) the price of this labour was 1s,6d per day 'per unit', with the provision that if an employer was 'willing to supply food and accommodation the cost is reduced to one shilling per unit per day'.[45]

By 1931-2 these provisions had been refined into the '6d-a-day-scheme' which applied until 1947 when it was slightly modified. Under the '6d system', 1) the maximum sentence for short-term offenders was raised from one to three months; 2) short-term prisoners automatically lost their right to a three-quarters' remission of sentence; 3) they were handed over to the farmers (lessees) for the period of the sentence whether they agreed or not; 4) the cost of the 'unit of labour' was lowered to 6d a day and this payment was made to the Prisons Department and not to the prisoner; and 5) the farmers were given responsibility for and absolute authority over the prisoners during their period of forced labour (First, 1959; Cook 1982).

These terms made prison labour the most extreme form of forced labour practised on white-owned farms in South Africa.[46] White farmers were vested with unlimited power over the black prisoners they hired, and shocking excesses resulted. In 1947 an exposé of prison labour conditions in the Bethal district of the southern Transvaal revealed the horrors of the system in operation. Bethal had long been notorious for such abuses (*Advance*, 16 April 1953) but it was not exceptional among districts and farmers who relied extensively on prison labour (*The Guardian*, 3 July 1947) since the endemic shortage of labour that they faced stemmed partly from the extremes to which they went. Farmers clothed prison workers in discarded mealie sacks. Disused, or specially built, sheds were used for housing where they were crammed together with little ventilation, no water and no toilets. They were locked in at night and from the end of the working day on Saturday until sun-up on Monday. They slept on sacking, hay or the bare floor. They were given no eating utensils and food was thrown on sacking or on the floor, or poured into their cupped hands. At work, they were at the double all the time and if they did not move fast enough they were thrashed or set upon by dogs.[47] Physical beating was frequent and often brutal enough to result in permanent injury or death, although few of these cases reached the courts.[48]

The prison labour system acted as a conduit draining black men not required in other sectors into agriculture. In all respects, the terms and conditions of this form of labour differed from others found in commercial agriculture more in degree than in content. It was merely the most extreme of a variety of forms of forced labour to be found in the sector at the onset of restructuring.[49] This fact had repercussions not only on prison workers but on all farm workers (indeed, all black workers), since the depths of depravity which the prison labour system elicited from white farmers dragged the conditions of employment for all workers in the sector down even further. And since the system was based on the same laws which trapped workers in the other labour forms in the first place, it flushed out workers who tried to escape from, or avoid, farm service. The relative difference between workers in the various labour forms — in terms of the length of servitude, who served, and on what terms — were eroded by the prison labour scheme, expecially as the laws were both extended and more effectively implemented during the first phase of restructuring.

The impact of the first phase of restructuring on the predominant labour forms

The first phase of restructuring covers the period from the late 1930s to the early 1960s. Forced labour in the sector, the rapid growth of secondary industry, and the deteriorating position under national oppression of the African majority combined to drive black workers out of the sector. At the same time, growing capitalisation and the expansion of agricultural production (still predominantly labour-intensive) raised the demand for labour on the farms. To counter the exodus without succumbing to pressures to raise wages and improve conditions, farmers and the state acted to immobilise black workers in commercial agriculture through the instrument of African national oppression. Their efforts centred on both restricting alternative avenues of employment and concentrating agriculture's reserve labour pool in the sector, with important consequences for the predominant labour forms.

Under the greatest strain was labour tenancy, as counterposing forces operated to undermine or reinforce it. These forces were not evenly matched: whilst the forces eroding the form were dominant, their effect was limited by the relative strength of the forces perpetuating this form of labour. The offensive against labour and all forms of tenancy also brought pressure to bear on workers in farm service — and on all Africans, for that matter. This in turn meant that the prison labour system played a particularly important role in the drive to restructure the composition of farm labour in South Africa

The destruction of labour tenancy
Declining terms
The decline in the terms of labour tenancy had already been set in motion in the course of capitalisation, a process which continued to wear away at the labour form. The 'peasant component' deteriorated even further as white farmers whittled away at the amount of land and the number of animals they permitted tenants. By June 1960, a mere 1.9 percent of the total area of 'white' farm land was set aside for labour tenants *and* farm 'servants' 'to grow their vegetables and graze their herds,' (*Survey*, 1963).

More importantly, restrictions on livestock saw both a decline in absolute numbers of cattle and a shift away from cattle to other forms of stock-holding. This process was also going on in the reserves, which indicated declining pastoral and agricultural conditions and growing impoverishment.[50] Furthermore, not only labour tenants held livestock. 'Cash' tenants and workers in farm service, too, kept stock. In fact, many farmers considered stock-holding and grazing by their resident farm workers as 'one of the most significant parts of wage payment in kind' (Roberts, 1959:39) and therefore, although they restricted the number (and even the types of stock) permitted, the practice of allowing farm workers to run some animals was still fairly widespread. Nevertheless, the fact that restrictions on labour tenant herds made their livestock holdings barely distinguishable from those held by workers in farm service also indicates the decline of the labour form.

Whilst this was true at a general level, there were regional differences which reflected the way the system had developed in the different provinces, the relative extent of commercialisation in the different regions, and the relative capacity of labour tenants in the different districts to determine the terms of their tenancy. Labour tenancy in the northern Transvaal and in central and northern Natal was relatively strong after the eradication of the labour form was well under way. In the latter districts, until as late as the second half of the 1960s, 'tenant herds of 50 cattle or more were not uncommon' (Surplus People's Project, 1983: Vol.4,43).

The attack on their agricultural activities was coupled with further encroachment on tenant labour time and power, as farmers tried to tie them to their farms all year round. This reinforced pressures on growing numbers of tenants to leave the farms altogether. Some sought alternative land in the already crowded reserves, but many took up residence and employment in the better, if still bad, conditions prevailing in the towns.

The response of farmers

In turn, this generated labour shortages which met with two general lines of response from white farmers. For many, it served to intensify their agitation for greater and more extensive state intervention to block alternative employment routes for Africans as long as there was a demand for their labour in the sector. The experience of farmers in the Lydenburg district of the Transvaal in 1937 had been noted far beyond the district's boundaries. On that occasion, a series of proclamations instigated by local farmers gave notice that the state intended to impose the provisions of Chapter IV of the 1936 Native Trust and Land Act over the district. This addressed itself to the terms on which the ruling white minority would permit Africans to reside on land outside the reserves. It explicitly aimed to 'control' labour tenancy and to abolish 'squatting'. Africans could only live legally on land beyond that specified as reserves if

> they were the registered owners, or the servants of owners, or registered tenants or squatters, or wives and children of Natives exempted under these headings, or clergy or teachers, or sick or elderly people for whom special exemptions could be applied (Davenport, 1974:45).

This was the first district in which these terms were to be applied, following the passage of the Act in the previous year. On learning of these intentions, 'cash' and labour tenants demonstrated their opposition in large protests in and around Lydenburg. They demanded trek passes so that they could leave the area without being arrested and many families moved out of the district in search of alternative tenancies under the old terms. Local farmers began to clamour for Chapter IV to be implemented throughout the country, so that tenants would have no way out of the trap. But they met with little active support from the state. It was not until more than a decade later, following the rise to power of the National Party in 1948, that the state took measures which matched the demands of these farmers. Even so, tenant resistance was persistent and strong. Thus, in Natal, for example, in the late 1950s attempts to enforce registration of tenant contracts led to an exodus and the prospect of labour shortages (Surplus People's Project, 1983: Vol.4,45). Action by tenants formed part of a broader resistance in the countryside to the extension of pass laws to African women and the imposition of Betterment and Bantu Authorities.[51]

Farmers continued to agitate for active state intervention and, as Morris's study shows, the formulations of apartheid strategy were inseparable from the interests of the white rural constituency which brought the National Party to power in the first place.[52] These had been clearly articulated following the experiences of Lydenburg. The report of the 1939 Native Farm Labour Committee stated that

> farmers can see relief only in action by the government and that only in the direction of compulsion on the Natives to accept farm work and the imposition of further restrictions upon the movements of those already so employed (Morris, 1977:11).

During and after the Second World War, movement off the land rapidly increased, mainly to the towns. This aggravated farm labour shortages and stimulated farmer agitation still further. In 1942, a Special Committee of the South African Agricultural Union (SAAU) called on the state

> a) to apply Chapter IV ... to all Provinces immediately;
> b) to exercise control over unemployed Natives in locations;
> c) to revise recruitment of Native labour for mines and all public works ... (so) that these bodies will obtain their labour mainly from sources outside the Union;
> d) (that) pass laws be tightened and the Urban Areas Act be properly implemented, (*Farmers' Weekly*, 4 November 1941; Morris, 1977:11).

The state continued to resist the demands of under-capitalised farmers. The position it adopted reflected the interests dominant at the time — mining, which had secured a labour supply through the reserve system and an elaborate recruiting network which extended beyond South Africa; and manufacture, which sought an uninhibited labour flow to secure workers at 'the right price'. The state's proposal that farmers pay higher wages and improve working conditions as a solution to their labour problems was derisively declined at the Transvaal Agricultural Union Congress in 1942 (*Farmers Weekly*, 30 September, 1942; Morris, 1977:12). The reactionary intransigence of farmer spokesmen was itself a pointer to the real cause of labour shortages, despite their claim two years earlier that workers were 'impossible to maintain ... no matter how well paid' they were (*Farmers' Weekly*, 23 August 1944; Morris, 1977:12).

The underlying causes reinforcing the persistence of labour tenancy in some regions were identical to those which lay at the heart of farmer agitation for greater control over the movement of farm tenants (and African labour in general). Under-capitalised farmers, often unable (and invariably unwilling) to transform tenancy relations into waged labour — which would be at least minimally acceptable to the workers — could either perpetuate labour and other forms of tenancy, or demand direct compulsion. Deteriorating conditions of tenancy and the rise of substantial alternative employment avenues in the towns were insufficent, however, to ensure that labour demands would be met by the system. Also, the expansion of agricultural production demanded more labour and the more systematic and extensive use of natural material resources. So for many although not all farmers, the perpetuation of tenancy was not an alternative to intensified compulsion. Farmers directly linked the shortages they were facing with the labour form. As the Transvaal Agricultural Union (TAU) put it in its submission to the Native Law Commission (1946-48):

> the ruling practice of allowing Native labourers ... to leave their master's farm for a portion of any year and to be employed in towns is one of the principal causes of labour wastage ... this state of affairs would naturally be altered if a division of labour forces is created. The Native must be given the choice of becoming either an industrial worker or a permanent farm labourer (Morris, 1977:15).

Farmers implicitly recognised that the labour form was breaking down, and that it was doing so in a way disadvantageous to them. In other words, labour tenants, through their access to the towns and waged employment, were increasingly able to break the hold of farmers over their labour power and, in the process, break with the countryside altogether. In order to redress this 'natural' process, farmers demanded state intervention to ensure that the way the system was broken served their interests first and foremost. This approach not only sealed the fate of labour tenancy but also held profound implications for the way in which Africans were to be compelled into the sector in the future. Thus, within a few years of the coming to power of the National Party, the formerly flaccid response of the state was transformed into a ruthless, concerted endeavour to implement a policy which deprived African workers of any choice in the matter. The state was to establish itself as a central instrument for the channelling and directing of labour power.

Some farmers attempted to perpetuate labour tenancy nevertheless. If for a minority it was the only means by which they could get workers, for the majority it was the preferred means. Like those agitating for more control and the ending of labour tenancy, they would not or could not switch to a system of waged labour. Labour tenancy not only provided them with a 'tangible tie' between the farm and its labour supply. Since heavy labour demands 'were confined to a few peak periods during the year, for which a reservoir costing nothing to maintain was a great convenience (Smith, 1941:160), it also remained an expedient and profitable system. This especially was the case while forced labour measures remained ineffective. Although the extent of these practices has still to be uncovered, the system lent itself to widespread abuse. Farmers hired farms for the express purpose of acquiring free African labour for their own use and for sale to others (Report of the NRC, 1944:para.13). The unpaid services which 'their' tenants performed were not confined to agriculture, and some landowners were known to use their 'free' labourers for work in town (Report of the NRC, 1944, para.12). In fact, 'labour farms' had developed in Natal as a companion institution to labour tenancy, whereby farmers transformed the land they owned and had formerly used for pasturage into private labour reservoirs (SPP, 1983: Vol.4,43). The terms of tenancy differed little from 'the usual', except that the six months of service were spent away from the farm on which they lived. In some ways, the system closely resembled migrant labour, although practices varied.

Sometimes household obligations would be staggered throughout the year involving different members of the family at different times. Sometimes, however, the whole family/household would be expected to work the same six months, although not necessarily at the same place. Whatever form it took, it differed from migrant labour when it came to wages. If any wages were paid, the amount was nominal. Standard pay was R2 per month to the household head only. Dependants, who were equally obliged to work, earned nothing.[53]

Under these conditions, many farmers were reluctant to switch from the system. In other words, as long as labour tenants were able to resist being compelled to work all year round on the same terms as they now did for six months, or the state was unable to ensure an equally cheap and certain labour supply, the co-operation of all farmers in imposing and enforcing controlling measures could not be ensured. This meant that the implementation of these policy objectives was restrained, if not actually limited.

Response of the state before apartheid
Prior to 1948 the state was hesitant to take direct action against labour tenancy, despite the fact that it had enacted legislation for such a purpose (the 1936 Land Act) and was under pressure from farmers to do so. Some of the reasons have already been mentioned, including the Lydenburg resistance, the incapacity to impose controlling measures to ensure full farmer co-operation, and reluctance to make the state the pivot of forced labour measures. Apart from these reasons, there was a realisation that the state could claim that the terms on which these tenants remained on white-owned land were directly labour-related. But this was not true of 'cash' tenants. The general condemnation of 'squatting' by farmers struck a similar chord in state policy and practice. This was because, on the one hand, the land rent tenants occupied was withheld from white commercial exploitation — while on the other hand, the system enabled a fairly substantial section of the African rural population to stand outside the rural labour market, if not the labour market as a whole (Morris, 1977).

Although not directly aimed at them, and still to be applied much more purposefully and systematically in the 1950s, the campaign to abolish non-labour tenancy on white farms undoubtedly affected labour tenants. This was because the distinction between labour tenancy and 'cash' tenancy ('squatting') was often a very fine one. In practice, many 'cash' tenants paid farm owners rent 'in kind' i.e., in produce, etc. But 'in kind' payment also included the labour of some members of the tenant's household. So, whilst the first aim of anti-squatting measures — to augment labour power — may well have reinforced labour tenancy, this was not necessarily the case. The deteriorating terms on which 'cash' tenants were permitted to remain on the land may well have had a countervailing effect. In other words, restrictions on livestock holdings (imposed directly through quotas or indirectly through increased grazing fees), as well as increasing demands for labour, could equally have acted to increase the movement of tenants into the reserves or off the land altogether. The evidence on this is scant. What is clear is that prior to apartheid, state resolve to take action on 'cash' tenancy was far stronger than its position on labour tenants.[54] Following the Pike Census on 'squatting' of 1944-45, the Native Affairs Department (NAD), in agreement with several Divisional Councils, appointed inspectors to use the 1936 Act to 'peg' numbers at the census level. According to a NAD report (1945-7:24), although no details were given, matters were 'proceeding smoothly in all districts except Cathcart, which has so far declined to accept the pegging agreement'. Notwithstanding the co-operation between the authorities and local landowners that this report suggests, it would be surprising if attempts to limit 'rent' tenancy did not evoke popular resistance from tenants, though no evidence has thus far been presented.

Interrelated policies — particularly the continued promotion of the reserve system and regulation of access to towns — undoubtedly had a bearing on labour (and other forms of) tenancy. Yet their practical application, as with anti-'squatting' measures, left some room for manoeuvre and it was not until the early 1950s that machinery to enforce these policy objectives began to be constructed.

Under apartheid

Apartheid represented a new stage in white minority rule in South Africa, but this was not because the policies introduced by the National Party had no precedent. The difference lay in approach, both to the direction policy was to take and the way it was to be applied. Conflict centred on

> the effect the uneven development of capitalism had on overall labour supply and the particular *balance* that the state would be required to maintain between town and countryside as national industrialisation proceeded (Morris, 1977:26).

But it also focused on the interrelated question of the terms and conditions of African national oppression and continued white minority rule. As for administering policy, the fact that state practice was to prove more extensive, systematic and thorough-going than in all previous experience stemmed, above all else, from a new perspective on the role of the state apparatus in general. Under the National Party, the state was a key instrument by which both political and economic objectives could be advanced. This meant the promotion of specific Afrikaner interests as well as general interests of the white minority, and the extension and intensification of national oppression in changing socio-political and economic conditions.

The effect of apartheid on labour and other tenancy forms on white-owned land was profound. The 'farm labour question', of which these were an important component, was a significant aspect of efforts to control and regulate African labour in general. After a brief interlude of temporary and stop-gap measures, the basis of a coherent policy began to be laid (Morris, 1977:33), though mass popular resistance delayed the implementation of many aspects for several years. Of the battery of laws and proclamations issued during the 1950s, those which most directly affected labour tenancy (and all farm labour for that matter) included the Native Laws Amendment Act (1952), the Natives (Abolition of Passes and Co-ordination of Documents) Act (1952) and the Amendment of the Native Trust and Land Act (1954).

Laws controlling the terms of absence of Africans from commercial agriculture.
The passage of the Native Laws Amendment Act made law the 'Native policy'
project spelt out in a memorandum prepared by the SAAU some eight years
earlier.[55] In addition to the division already created between the reserves and so-
called 'white' South Africa, this Act set about transforming the social and
geographical division between town and countryside into a grid for confining and
controlling the movement of Africans. The distinction between urban (prescribed)
and rural (non-prescribed) areas was made a political division on a national scale.
The movement and employment of Africans in and between them would be controlled by a system of influx and efflux regulations operated through a network
of labour bureaux. Some labour bureaux had already been established prior to 1952,
as part of efforts to 'recruit labour for the farms'.[56] But with the passage of this
Act they were established in every magisterial district. It became compulsory for
every African man of 16 years or more to register at a labour bureau if he wished
to seek work legally in any town or district (Roberts, 1959:108). 'District' labour
bureaux controlled the movement of African workers within and from the rural
areas, and 'local' labour bureaux were set up in urban areas to control the entrance
into and flow of Africans between towns. Indeed, so closely were the provisions
of this Act tied to attempts to secure farmers an adequate labour supply that, in
order for an African man in a rural district to obtain permission to look for work
in town, he had to apply to the 'district' bureau in his area for permission to register
at a 'local' bureau.[57] This permission, in turn, could only be granted after the
'district' bureau had the permission of the 'regional' bureau, one of which was
established at the office of every Chief Native Commissioner (Roberts, 1959:112).
In urban areas this Act served to greatly strengthen influx control measures.

> Henceforth, it would be an offence for any African, women included, to remain
> for longer than 72 hours in any urban area without special permission unless
> he or she fell within a limited range of exempted categories.[58]

Labour bureaux began to operate on a national scale by the end of 1952. By
30 June 1953 there were 93 'local' labour bureaux (NAD Report, 1952-3). In
1953-4 the figure had risen to a total of 450 of which 130 were urban, and by
1957 the respective figures were 512 and 234 (Morris, 1977:43). The Native Laws
Amendment Act was not solely responsible for the rise of these institutions, since

> to pass the above legislation for the division of the labour force and to set up
> labour bureaux was not ... equivalent to the state intervening to enforce it. Efflux
> control, influx control and labour bureaux could only distribute the African
> workforce between non-prescribed and prescribed areas if the state was able
> to co-ordinate and track down the movement of all adult Africans (Morris,
> 1977:42).

To this end, the 1952 Natives (Abolition of Passes and Co-ordination of Documents)
Act was passed. Far from abolishing passes, it consolidated the myriad of
documents (tax receipts, passes, service contracts, exemption certificates, etc.)
Africans were forced to carry. In addition an identity document (photograph, finger-
print and registration number) and an employment card (which an employer was,

henceforth, to sign monthly and on discharging a worker) were added. These were all rolled into one 'Reference Book' (known as the *dompas* in the pejorative) which had to be carried by all Africans (men and women) over 16, and be produced on demand.

The state offensive to ensure that all Africans took the new passes only began in earnest in 1956. It was particularly directed at African women who, until the passage of the Act, had not been obliged to carry passes.[59] However, from 1952 onwards, local municipalities began to enforce 'Section 10' of the new Urban Areas Act.[60] They issued

> their own urban residence permits to both men and women. Although not reference books and hence outside a national system of control, these permits were still a form of pass, controlling entry into individual towns (Walker, 1982:130).

Contraventions of these local regulations provided a steady and rising flow of Africans into the prison labour system, as will be shown below, without challenging the increasingly pre-eminent role of passes in the tirelessly-repeated effort to 'recanalise' labour. By 1961 nearly eight million 'Reference Books' had been issued and the Bantu Affairs (formerly 'Native') Commissioner could report that he 'considers the reference book system to be equally as important as the system of labour bureaux' (Report, 1961).

The number of labour bureaux only tells part of the story. For the most part, it seems that the majority of people who went looking for work avoided them. Although this was illegal, it held true even at a much later date, when pass and influx control regulations were operating in a far more intensive and systematic way. So, for example, in 1977 an estimated 20-25 percent of African work seekers looked for employment through labour bureaux (Survey, 1977:22).

Even so, the overwhelming majority of workers channelled through the system were caught by and came from its operations in the urban areas. This is not surprising, for three reasons. First, mounting impoverishment in the countryside was leading to a noticeable flow of Africans to the towns.[61] This served to focus state concern on preventing what they perceived as the build-up of a 'surplus of urban Native labour (of) alarming proportions' while 'an acute labour shortage is generally experienced' in commercial agriculture (NAD Report, 1952-3). Second, it was probably less difficult to regulate the presence, entrance and access of Africans into towns than it was to control their movement off the land. And third, it was cheaper than instituting prosecution proceedings. The channelling of African men who had contravened the Urban Areas Act had begun in 1947 in Johannesburg. In 1952, when labour bureaux were first established in most major urban centres, of the 28,545 African men 'placed' in agriculture by them, 21,823 came directly from urban labour bureaux (NAD Report, 1952-3).

It is thus probable that, whatever the relation of farm workers to commercial agriculture, their chances of finding 'illegal' (i.e., non-agricultural) employment or avoiding state control measures (being 'illegally' in the towns, etc.) probably differed little from those of workers who entered urban areas from other points of origin. By contrast, if farm workers looked for non-agricultural work 'legally' through the channels set up by the state, their prospects were slim, if not non-existent. Within the system it became 'virtually impossible for an African farm worker to be anything but a farm worker all his life, and the same applies to his children and their children' (Roberts, 1959:115). Only through the inefficient operation of the system could farm workers find alternative employment. Thus in 1956, for example, when the Eastern Province Coastal Agricultural Union called on the state to stamp 'not to be employed in urban areas' in the passes of farm workers, the Chief Native Commissioner for the area assured them that this was not necessary. Like the farmers, the municipalities were keen to keep 'unauthorised Natives' out of their areas. 'The problem is that farmers fail to sign the pass book and hence the Department of Native Affairs can't act properly' (*New Age*, 19 July 1956).

Which brings us to a further point — namely, that the prison labour system was intrinsic to the operation of this political and administrative channelling of labour. The details of the way it operated will be looked at below, but the fact is that the prison system formed the catch-net into which many black farm workers (and Africans in general) who circumvented other instruments of the system fell. The enhanced significance of the penal system in this phase reflected not only the growth in laws which could be transgressed, but also the relative weakness of the other apparatuses in performing their designated functions. This meant that in 1952 the prison system provided farmers with 40,533 prisoners, that is 30 percent more than the number of people channelled through labour bureaux in the same year (First, 1959).

Laws governing the presence of Africans on white-owned farms.
The two laws discussed above could be characterised as instruments designed to direct and control the terms of absence of labour tenants, farm workers and indeed all Africans from 'white' agriculture. The third significant piece of legislation — the amendment of the 1936 Native Trust and Land Act — focused attention instead on the terms of their presence in this sector. The two questions, of course, are inseparable, two sides of the same coin (*Survey*, 1976:124).

With the passage of the 1954 Amendment, Chapter IV of the 1936 Act was made applicable throughout the country from 1 September 1956. At the same time, the terms of the law were extended and refined. Under the new provisions, no African could register as a 'squatter' unless he had been continuously resident on that land since 31 August 1936 (and he was obliged to prove this). Those 'cash' tenants who were eligible had to register as 'squatters' within three months of the new law coming into operation. Thus from January 1957, the only chance of becoming a registered and therefore legal 'squatter' was by special permission from the Minister of what were known down the years as Native/Bantu/Plural/Black Affairs. Furthermore, in order that even registered non-labour tenancy be actively discouraged, a tax was imposed on farmers. They were obliged to pay 'a fee ranging from £1 for the first year to £16 for the ninth and subsequent years ... for each registered squatter'.[62] These 'voluntary incentives' to curtail 'cash' tenancy were to apply for 15 years only (changed from an original deadline of ten years). Thereafter, all remnants of the practice would be ruthlessly crushed (Roberts, 1959a:115). In this way these measures effectively intensified existing policy practice against African access to land which was not directly related to the 'sale' of their labour power.

At the same time, under apartheid, the white minority acted with equal and unprecedented determination against labour tenancy. The tactics, tempered by a significant measure of support for the system from white farmers, differed somewhat from those taken against 'squatting'.

The amended law stipulated that labour tenants had to render a minimum of 122 days' labour service a year to the owner of the land on which they resided. He, in turn, had to pay a licence fee. Furthermore, for a labour tenant to be registered the practice of labour tenancy had to have been established on that particular farm before the Act came into force (1956). Exemptions could be applied for but were actively discouraged, since to grant them would have served to spread rather than contain the labour form. To ensure the co-operation of farmers in determining and enforcing quotas, the amended law provided for the creation of Labour Tenant Control Boards, comprised of three farmers and an official of the NAD in any district. All these provisions were conceived and applied within the perspective of 'gradual and orderly' transformation of labour tenancy into full-time (meaning exclusive) farm service.

In applying the revised law, the state had two primary and related objectives in mind. The first was that all forms of labour in the sector should be transformed, whether in the short term ('squatting') or over a longer period (labour tenancy) into exclusive farm service.[63] The idea was not that all African farm workers would have to be residentially based on white-owned land, but that those who were residing there would have to work exclusively in the sector. Farm 'servants' were advocated 'as the best type of farm labour, the most economical and the most sensible'.[64] In this, the state was expressing the interests of the most capitalised sections within agriculture, many of whom were changing the base of their workforce to 'full-time' labour. Whilst this change implied the necessity of paying some form of cash wage, the size of this could and was expected to be kept down through state intervention (labour bureaux, pass laws and influx control) to prevent competition from other sectors. Both anti-tenancy measures served in practice to promote capitalisation in the sector, complementing other state inputs (particularly financial) directed to that end.

The second objective was to promote a more even distribution of labour within the sector. By doing away with 'squatting' and limiting labour tenancy, the labour of former tenants could be released for redistribution amongst farmers to alleviate labour shortages. In this way and through Labour Tenant Control Boards, the amended law was designed to complement machinery set up to 'canalise' African labour between sectors.

Policy in practice was a somewhat less smooth affair, especially for the tenants. The NAD, for its part, actively

    set about organising Labour Tenant Control Boards and investigating the extent of squatting in the countryside. By 1960 they had held 350 meetings and made 1,531 determinations. The overwhelming majority were made in the Transvaal and Natal (Morris, 1977:51).

The majority of Transvaal farmers were in favour of vigorous state action: towards the end of the decade they were clamouring for the 'total abolition of labour tenancy'. The only objections to such calls came, in the main, from the 'historically more backward northern Transvaal' (Morris, 1977:52). Barely had the law been enacted, let alone made enforceable, than Transvaal farmers were showing tenants how ruthless they intended to be. Although much more research needs to be done, it seems that in the Eastern Transvaal, for example, some farmers handed out trek-passes to cash and labour tenants alike (*New Age*, 21 April 1953), while others tried to squeeze tenants out by imposing intolerable terms. A report in *New Age* (3 March 1955) on the plight of several hundred African tenants on two farms near Bushbuckridge in the Eastern Transvaal is revealing, not only of the callousness of the farmers, but also of the conditions of tenancy and the limits these imposed on the capacity of tenants to resist. The farmer summoned his tenants to a meeting where he notified them of the new terms of their tenancy contract. These included:

● an increase in annual rent from £1 to £17*s*6*d* for single men, an extra 10*s* for widows; and an increase of from 10*s* to £2 for pensioners;

● a labour obligation. Although no indication is given of earlier obligations, under the new contract single men would have to give three days of free labour and widows four days. The report does not stipulate whether these labour obligations covered weeks, months or a year;

● increased grazing fees on all livestock and the extension of grazing fees to pigs, for which the tenant formerly was not liable. The fee for cattle rose by 1*s*6*d* a head, for equines from 1*s* to 5*s* each, and the fee from pigs was set at 2*s*6*d*. Although the tenants were 'up in arms' and resolutely opposed the new terms, if they refused to accept them the farmer had assured them they would be evicted.

In Natal the situation was far less clear-cut. The decade began with the Natal Agricultural Union (NAU) expressing unqualified support for the principle of 'full-time waged labour' (SPP, 1983: Vol.4,45), perhaps reflecting the most capitalis-ed section of its membership. By 1956, due to the combined pressures of state activities against tenancy, strong opposition from tenants themselves, and the relative financial weakness of many farmers, local opposition within its ranks had forced the NAU to retreat to an ambivalent position. They were prepared to ac-cept change, but by 'evolutionary' rather than 'revolutionary' means (SPP, Vol.4,45). By the end of the decade, Natal farmers were so polarised that the 'Union could not indicate a clearly defined line of action' on the matter (Morris, 1977:52). So, whilst the Transvaal Agricultural Union (TAU) was in line with the demand of the national body (the SAAU) that 'existing legislation be drastically inforced (sic) and where necessary changed to ensure tight control over farm labour' this was not the case with the NAU (Morris, 1977:52). Reflecting the depth of internal tension, it could see no need for new legislation and suggested that the existing law be enforced with the 'old' objectives of 'stabilisation of the labour force and a division of labour between town and country' (SPP, 1983: Vol.4,46).

This ambivalence did not, of course, prevent individual farmers from evicting tenants — or farm workers, for that matter. SPP fieldwork in the Babanango district, for example, traces the establishment of at least three location camps — Mpungamhlope, Hlungulwana and Emakhosini — to the eviction of farm dwellers in the late 1950s and early 1960s. They suggest that more research may well uncover other settlements which 'started as relocation points for evicted farm workers or tenants during (or even before) this period' (SPP, 1983: Vol.2,18). But it also meant that labour tenancy remained widespread, especially in Northern and Central Natal and the northern parts of the Transvaal, where both undercapitalised farmers and labour tenants strongly opposed its abolition, at least in the short term.

In fact, the roots of regional differences in eradicating labour tenancy in the second phase of restructuring in commercial agriculture are to be found in the relative strengths and weaknesses of the practice in this first phase.

The response of labour tenants

The aim of this multi-pronged offensive, as has been shown, was to press tenants into exclusive farm service and to channel Africans in general into farm labour. Its effect, however, was to bring labour tenants under countervailing pressures which served to both reinforce and undermine the labour form at one and the same time. This therefore meant that while some clung tenaciously to the labour form, despite deteriorating terms, others responded to efforts to break the labour form by leaving the countryside altogether.

Both actions were forms of resistance against further dispossession and being compelled into the bondage of farm labour: two sides of the same coin which reflect the particular conditions of national oppression and class exploitation in South Africa.

Many tenants lived on the same farm for generations and they considered the land theirs. By defending tenancy on any terms, they were struggling to retain access to what remained of their national heritage. Land hunger in the reserves combined with actions to block access of Africans to the towns served to reinforce labour tenancy. For no matter how bad the terms, it was a labour form which still provided some access to land and livestock. That is not to say that the combined effect of these instruments of national oppression did not operate to erode the labour form still further. Left without options, a number of tenants moved into the reserves or African-owned land outside the reserves in the vain hope of land at some unspecified date in the future. For many others, the prospect that their access to the towns would be permanently sealed off may well have acted as a stimulus for a decisive break with the countryside and labour tenancy.

Again, bad as the terms of tenancy were, they were infinitely better than those for workers labouring under year-round service. This meant that those who clung to labour tenancy were defending the relatively better terms under which they existed in the countryside. At the same time, deteriorating conditions led to its inevitable dissolution as tenants were pressed into farm service or forced to leave the sector altogether when the terms were no longer tolerable.

Workers in farm service

The effects of the combined offensive by fractions of capital and the state were not, of course, confined to tenant relations in agriculture. Serious if less direct repercussions were felt by workers forced into or bound by farm service. The presence of Africans on white-owned land was now almost exclusively conditional on their being 'the servants of the owner' (Native Trust and Land Act, Chapter IV, Provision (b)). This, in turn, served to freeze the terms of the 'master/servant' relation into one of permanent disadvantage for black farm workers. They were robbed of even the weak bargaining power they formerly had — to leave when the terms became intolerable. The beginning of a trend towards a reduced on-farm force, with the emergence of a hierarchy of labour and skill, could just be detected: they were to come to the fore only in the next phase of the restructuring process.

In this period tenants were not the only workers leaving the land. Many of those who went in search of better terms of employment in the towns were farm workers in 'service'. Since the sweep of the laws and regulations was indiscriminate (intentionally so), they too were caught up in its functioning and pushed back into commercial agriculture. Coloured workers were also affected by these measures, because they acted to depress the terms of all labour in agriculture, and because Coloured workers, too, were thrown back into farm labour through the operation of the prison labour system. While these points need to be made, it was only in the second phase of restructuring that farm service was to come under direct and more intensive pressure, which would reorganise its form and even its content.

The expansion of the prison labour system

The prison labour system had been transformed in the course of capitalisation into a relatively streamlined conduit through which labour was channelled into the sector. With restructuring, its importance grew substantially. This was particularly so in the 'first phase', since it played an indispensable part in the construction and functioning of other 'canalising' instruments. Labour bureaux, pass laws and influx control regulations were all underpinned by the prison labour system. Failing to escape, you were caught either within the law's operations or as a transgressor of its operations, and the outcome was the same. Indeed, the development of the system from the late 1940s onwards blurred even the formal distinctions.

The new prison labour scheme

In theory there were two schemes in operation, the 'interdepartmental scheme' and the '9*d*-a-day scheme'. In practice they were two parts of the broader collaboration between various departments of state and farmers to channel Africans forcibly into farm labour.

The 'interdependent scheme' was so named because it worked on the basis of co-operation between the Departments of Native Affairs, Justice and Police. It was first practised in 1947 in Fordsburg, Johannesburg and spread across the Rand and to other large centres over the next few years (NAD Report, 1952-3). In 1954 it was formalised and made standard procedure in all urban areas, following the issue of a general internal circular entitled 'Scheme for the Employment of Petty Offenders in Non-prescribed Areas' (Cook, 1982:64). Under its terms, Africans arrested for what were officially acknowledged to be minor offences were not charged if they 'volunteered' for farm labour. They were simply transferred through the departments, from the courts via the police, or straight from police custody to the district labour bureaux. If, however, they refused to be 'threatened, forced and harassed into printing their thumb-print on to farm labour contracts' (Blaine, 1954), they were charged and prosecuted.

The 9d-*a-day scheme*, whereby the Department of Prisons leased out short-term prisoners to farmers, was the almost inevitable lot of those prosecuted on 'technical offences'. This scheme differed only in insignificant ways from the 'abolished' 6d-a-day scheme which it replaced. Formally, the prisoner had to agree to work on the farms. That meant that having refused to 'volunteer' for farm labour whilst in detention and under threat of prosecution, he now, as a prisoner, was obliged to 'volunteer' his labour for the farms. The payment of 6d was raised to 9d-a-day. It was now officially to be paid to the prisoner upon release, instead of to the Department of Prisons, as had been the practice in the past. Furthermore, in 'volunteering' for farm labour, the prisoner still remained entitled to remission of sentence, although who or how that was to be implemented once he was handed over to the farmer was not indicated, and in practice it was hardly ever likely to occur (First, 1959).

The significance of the new prison labour system

What then was the significance of these new schemes? It is true that the differences between them were negligible. But in fact, it was not in their differences, nor in the paper work that these differences entailed, that their significance lay (Cook, 1982:15). Nor was it in their novelty, since the '9d-a-day' scheme differed little from the '6d-a-day scheme' practised throughout the period of capitalisation and in the early years of restructuring. Rather, the importance of this revised and extended system was to be found in the combined effect of the two schemes, operating in the context of assertive state action to drive Africans into farm labour. They were working hand in glove with white farmers, and so, not surprisingly, the courts and prisons became focal points for farmers looking for labour at its cheapest.

The new system differed from its predecessors quantitatively in this first phase of restructuring. The number of African men press-ganged into farm labour was huge and steadily rising.[65] Under the '9d-a-day scheme' alone in 1952, some 40,500 were forced to work on the farms. The figure for the next two years rose to 100,000 and by 1957/8 had doubled to just under 200,000 (First, 1959). This total excludes the tens of thousands sent through the labour bureaux, long-term workers serving sentences on farm jails — some 4,500 men in 1954 (*Survey*, 1952/3) — and the incalculable number of people who were picked up by farmers who came to the courts and paid fines in return for an undertaking by them to work on their enterprises.

It also differed qualitatively. In this the 'interdepartmental scheme' was particularly important. Through its operation, prosecution was interpreted merely as a costly technicality to be avoided if at all possible. In this unremarked fact lay a whole series of implications. At the most general level, it exposed the law and its process under white minority rule as being devoid of any justice or due process in content (rather than in form) when it came to the African majority. The arrested person was presumed guilty rather than innocent and should he go through the processes of the law his conviction was almost guaranteed. African men were arrested on suspicion of having transgressed the law. And the source of the suspicion lay in the fact that they were African, which, in effect, made being an African under apartheid tantamount to having committed a crime. In this way, national oppression and forced labour were inseparably intertwined.

Through the prison labour system, the law and administrative decree significantly extended the licence of the state to entrap and press Africans into farm labour. Not falling foul of the growing administrative and legal snares of white minority rule ceased to provide African men with even a modicum of protection. 'Whether a man's pass was in order or not, whether he was legally employed or not, whether he had money to pay the fine or not' (Cook, 1982:16) — all were irrelevant. Thousands of Africans, youths as well as men, were snatched off the streets, dragged out of their homes, robbed of their money and parted from their documents by vindictive or corrupt members of the uniformed police and plain-clothed 'ghost squads'. Denied all rights and refused permission to contact family or employers, they disappeared, without trace, for months and even years on end, to serve time on the farms.

The criminal offence was refusal to do farm labour. If a man withstood pressures to take up farm work 'voluntarily' whilst under threat of prosecution, he most certainly would be made to 'volunteer' once sentenced. But prosecution and a fixed sentence was itself no protection once on the farms. Under either of the schemes, the priority of the state was to channel 'offenders' into farm labour. The conditions under which they worked were irrelevant. In the late 1950s the press exposed just how severe conditions were for prisoners on the farms. In the face of a litany of atrocities, (including constant whipping of prisoners, chaining them in sheds at night, robbing them of their clothes and mutilating their feet to prevent them from escaping, depriving them of food and water, forcing them to dig potatoes with their bare hands, and wilful murder), the state blacklisted only one farmer and maintained that conditions were on the whole satisfactory. In contrast, the majority of South Africans were so enraged by the reports in the press that a national potato boycott was launched to protest against and bring an end to the prison labour system.

The prison labour schemes also underlined the absence of labour freedom, especially for Africans and particularly with regard to farm work. The compulsion of the law was indistinguishable from and interchangeable with the compulsion of transgressions of the law. Force continued to underpin the labour base of commercial agriculture despite the reorganisation process it was undergoing. Indeed, this process of restructuring was being built on the foundation of a repressed and forced labour base. And the prison labour system acted very directly to drag down the terms and conditions of employment in the sector for all workers. The heightened role of the prison labour system during this phase also reflected both the relative weakness of the other state-devised instruments for channelling African workers into agriculture, and the strength of the movement off the land.

As was indicated earlier, a third scheme came into operation in 1947, whereby farmers, in co-operation with the Prisons Department, built farm prisons to house long-term prisoners. These institutions were run by the Prisons Department. Although involving far fewer people than the other schemes, these prisoners were to become a constant component part of the farm labour force. Their significance was greatest at a regional level, especially in the Western Cape, in the second phase of restructuring. By 1954 16 prison outstations had been built at the expense of farmers in return for the surety of 'free' forced labour. The first farm jail, built by the farmers of the Klein Drakenstein in Paarl, cost £18,000 in 1951 (*Guardian,* 28 June 1951) and Karoo farmers paid £12,000 for theirs a year later (*People's World*, 11 September 1952). This initial outlay was to be offset by more than two decades of forced free labour. The scheme was integral to the role assigned to prisons in serving the labour needs of commercial agriculture under apartheid.

For reasons and in ways which this chapter has tried to capture, the combined efforts of the state and predominant sections of white farming capital aimed at eradicating labour tenancy — and tenancy in all its forms — within commercial agriculture. The thrust of their policy and practice was directed at immobilising African labour within the sector as far as possible to counter the effects of inter-sectoral competition. In this way it differed little from the objectives of capitalising farmers in the period prior to restructuring. However, social, economic and political developments on a national scale, which carried with them profound implications for white minority rule, required new measures, not just in form but in practice. To this end, the 'canalised' machinery and the catch-net of the prison labour system combined to form an integral and inseparable part of these efforts. The extent of their success was, nevertheless, tempered by the capacity of tenants to withstand press-ganging into exclusive farm labour, and the capacity of Africans in general to resist being forcibly directed into the sector. Their ability to do so was, in turn, reinforced by both the unevenness of capitalist development within commercial agriculture and by the inefficiency of state machinery in practice.

The effect of economic developments and political pressure exerted by the ruling white minority had seriously begun to erode labour tenancy in the countryside. This served as a prelude to the decisive eradication of the labour form in the next phase. At the end of this first period of restructuring, whilst labour tenancy had been reduced, it was still fairly widespread in most parts of the country and existed side by side with 'full-time' farm service. Both were underpinned by the prison labour system. And as for migrant labour, whilst its form and content were little changed in the first phase of restructuring, developments from the 1960s onwards were to transform it into an increasingly significant and widespread labour form in South African commercial agriculture.

Notes

1. The interrelation between these two is a matter of much discussion. Much of the literature on labour forms as a relation of production still fails to integrate the significance of social characteristics into a general analysis of labour forms.
2. The roots of labour tenancy are to be found in the process of colonisation and land dispossession, especially in the late nineteenth century. For more details see, amongst others, the various authors in Marks and Atmore, 1980; Keegan, 1981.
3. These ranged from cash to crop and kind payments which occurred in a variety of combinations. In the OFS the predominant form of tenancy was sharecropping, at least until 1914, after which time, although it persisted, it began to decline under pressure from combined farmer

and state repression. White sharecropping, largely based on labour tenancy, continued until the 1930s (Keegan, 1981). Conditions of tenancy varied widely, but as the pressure on land and the intensification of national oppression grew, Africans were increasingly forced to accept grossly unfavourable terms. Often farmers set up private locations on land they knew to be dead — a practice known as Black Persian farming — where they not only extracted rent but also provided themselves with ready access to a labour pool (Lacey, 1981:123).

4. It should not be presumed that all whites were landowners. Many were not, and these were forced into tenancy relations with landlords. But their position differed substantially from that of their African counterparts in that 'the legal right to hire land kept many whites as part of the agrarian producing class. They acted as a conduit whereby black families were able to surreptitiously gain access to land. The Africans would undertake cash crop production, perhaps on shares, and the white lessee would subsist and pay rent on the basis of the peasant's enterprise, or he acted as a front' (Keegan, 1981:145). In fact, the destruction of African tenancy, as Keegan points out, and contrary to much writing on the subject, served to propel many whites off the land as it cut away the grounds for their parasitic relation to it.

5. Whilst the ruling class generally agreed that independent access to land by Africans had to be curtailed, there were differences in approach to the question. As Lacey (1981:131) points out, mining capital wanted Africans to be resettled on reserve land so that the migrant labour system could continue uninterrupted. Farmers wanted 'squatters' evicted from the land held by absentee landlords so as to be redistributed amongst themselves. The 1913 Act was an outcome of the struggle between these interests.

6. An unavoidable conclusion drawn by K.H. Hathorn, a retired Supreme Court Judge and himself 'a spectacular racist'. Cited in Lacey, 1981:139.

7. It was this reality that, in part, prompted resistance by sharecroppers to labour tenancy in the OFS, for example. What farmers and the 1913 Land Act demanded of them was not only that they submit to labour obligations, but that they also surrender their access to land which, through cultivation and substantial herds and flocks, provided them with the substance of their livelihood (Keegan, 1981).

8. It should not be inferred from this side that all labour tenants gave oxen service. Oxen service, whilst essentially a labour tenancy relation, combined within it a capital service which disposed relatively favourably towards the tenant (ibid.:234).

9. Under the Masters and Servants Law (Transvaal and Natal) Amendment Act 26 of 1926 (Lacey, 1981). The 1913 Natives Land Act was initially only applied in the OFS. For a moving and incisive contemporary account see Sol T. Plaatje's *Native Life* (1981:81). In writing of the devastation the Act wrought about him, he stated: 'We all knew that this law was as harsh as its instigators were callous, and we knew that it would ... render many poor people homeless, but it must be confessed that we were scarcely prepared for such a rapid and widespread crash as it caused in the lives of natives in this neighbourhood'.

10. The 1926 Amendment meant that 'in theory ... the labour tenant was tied as securely to the farmer as the full-time servant, except that the labour tenant's term of compulsory service, now the same as in Natal, ran for six months of the year' (Lacey, 1981:158).

11. Under the Native Service Contract Act of 1932. In evidence to the Native Economic Commission of 1930-32 the African Residential Association of Benoni declared this provision to be 'a mode of contract which enslaves the natives, their families and their stock and was bitterly resented by all' (ibid.:141).

12. Under the 1926 Masters and Servants Amendment. Whipping had been introduced as an alternative to imprisonment, since going to jail meant that the offender was freed from labour obligations.

13. Under the 1932 Native Service Contract Act. For more details on this period and the law governing labour tenancy see Lacey, 1981. She estimates that, in all, some two million Africans were bound by this measure to serve in agriculture. In the light of this reality it is hard not to be cynical when the state and white farmers decry labour tenancy as 'feudal' and 'backward' — which it is — given that it was they who created and enforced it.

14. It was at about this time that the minimum short-term contract to the mines was raised from six to eight months.

15. The prophecy said: 'That the Imperial Government, after conquering the Boers, handed back

to them their old republics and a nice present in the shape of the Cape Colony and Natal — the two English Colonies. That the Boers are now ousting the Englishmen from the public service and when they have finished with them they will make a new law declaring it a crime for a native to live in South Africa, unless he is a servant in the employ of a Boer, and that from this it will be just one step to complete slavery'. In Plaatje, 1981:71.

16. The practice of endorsing a pass 'Farm Labour Only' predates apartheid by some 20 years.
17. Unpublished evidence, Native Economic Commission, 1930-32.
18. Ibid. The decline in conditions of labour tenancy was fiercely resisted in a variety of ways. These included 'trekking' to other farms in order to negotiate better terms; permanent migration of some, if not all, household members to the towns; and organisation. The popularity of the Industrial and Commercial Workers' Union of Africa (ICU) in the countryside in the 1920s can be explained by the deteriorating conditions facing black workers living on farms. In rural Natal and among farm labourers in the Transvaal, OFS and the Cape it became the embodiment of rural protest (Wickens and Lacey, 1981:140).
19. Slavery was practised in the Cape until it was abolished in 1834, by which time many Khoisan were labouring under conditions of indenture. The source of slaves was external to the Cape Colony and, largely, southern Africa. But the trekker colonies of the OFS and Transvaal also lived by slave raiding and trading. The source of indentured labour was not only from colonised and dispossessed Khoisan. Indenture replaced slavery in the international trade in forced labour as well, with Calcutta and Madras becoming the new world centre. Indentured workers were first imported into Natal in 1849 (Meer, 1980:4). For further discussion see, amongst others, Ross, 1983; various authors in Marks and Atmore, 1980; and Meer et al., 1980.
20. Since workers are not free in both senses, that is free from property and free to sell their labour power, it could be argued that they cannot be described as fully proletarianised. See, in another context, Byres in *Journal of Peasant Studies* Vol.2, 1977). What such an argument fails to take account of, is the historically specific course of proletarianisation in every particular instance. In other words, 'in different countries (proletarianisation) assumes different aspects and runs through its various phases in different orders of succession and at different periods' (Marx, 1973:355). All historical instances point to some form of political, social and/or economic constraint on the meaning of this 'freedom' and it is these specific conditions which must be accounted for in assessing the extent and the nature of proletarianisation. Yet, if the notion of 'freedom' is abstracted as an absolute, then in the South African context no section of the African working class could be said to be fully proletarianised because of the extra-economic force which coerces them to labour in conditions of unfreedom. Such a contention, in turn, would be patently absurd.
21. Various Masters and Servants Acts were passed in the territories between 1856 and 1904 (and there were subsequent amendments). Of them, the Cape Act of 1856 has been described as 'a law far more ruthless than its predecessors in the range of offences and the severity of the penalties prescribed for servants' (Simons and Simons, 1969:123). In fact, it served as a model for similar laws in the white supremacy colonies throughout southern, central and east Africa.
22. A case reported in an editorial of 1928, of a Spitzkop farmer called Combrink, illustrates the problem well. Combrink, 'himself riding on horseback, compelled a Native boy of 14 to run at a trot before him for 22 miles. When the boy became tired and slackened Combrink beat him with a sjambok. He repeated this at a farther point in the road until the boy became unconscious'. Cited in Wilson, 1973.
23. To my knowledge this area has yet to be systematically researched, yet repeated cases are cited in the press over the years. To give an example, there is the case of two brothers named Roos from Louis Trichardt, who in 1928 'pursued a Native boy (adult farm worker) some miles then thrashed him. Subsequently the boy died and the Rooses stuck the body in an antbear hole. They came before the court on a charge of murder. The only eye witness was a small *piccanin* (child) who was cross-examined at great length. Following which (and in which there are some inconsistencies) the prosecution reduced the charge to one of common assault and of this the brothers were convicted and sentenced to a fine'. Cited in ibid.
24. Pass laws date from the nineteenth century when they were aimed at controlling the movement of Khoisan and Nama in the Cape Colony. In their apartheid form — where they are at

their most elaborate — they apply to all African men and women of the age of 16 or over and they regulate every aspect of their existence from birth until death, including education, health, housing and residential location, movement, employment and even citizenship. They subsume a myriad of influx control regulations which govern access to the towns and cities and to work. They take the form of a pass or reference book which each African person must carry and produce on demand. This pass book is the South African badge of slavery.

25. This was sparked particularly by Francis Wilson's seminal study (1972:xi). He wrote of his decision to analyse the gold mining in detail as being 'dictated mainly by the fact that more information is readily available about it than any other sector of the South African economy. Not only has the necessary background to the behaviour of the labour market in that industry already been filled in ... but the annual reports of the Chamber of Mines and of the Government Mining Engineer provide a great deal of raw material ... Furthermore, the development of the gold mines has probably done more than any other industry to shape the structure of the whole South African labour market into the form in which it exists today.'

26. The difficulty of defining relations in the social formations in southern Africa is great. They are not isolated and insular, and therefore untouched by capitalist relations, as the dualist model would have it. But they are also not pre-capitalist, since the penetration of capital has altered social relations within them quite significantly, although without necessarily transforming them completely.

27. The term 'volitional' migrancy differs from the usage by Clarke (see note 28) who confines its application to the specific historical period (post-slavery 1834 until the establishment of mining in the 1880s) and to a particular form, that is one 'rooted in a flourishing peasant base as a supply response to relatively high wages' (1977:2).

28. Whilst some foreign workers could be identified, the term 'foreign' did not hold much meaning until the 1940s, and even for some until the mid-1950s, since the movement of workers between South Africa and other African colonies was regulated for the most part by the same laws and decrees applied to Africans from within South Africa's boundaries (Clarke, 1977; Stahl, in Bohning, 1981).

29. This is inferred from reference to the Native Farm Labour Committee report cited in Suzman and Kahn, 1947.

30. It is, in fact, being done. Judy Kimble's research into migrant labour in Lesotho sheds some light on these problems.

31. For details of this process there is a whole body of work: Bundy, 1979; Beinart, 1982; Marks and Atmore (eds), 1980; Marks and Rathbone (eds), 1982, etc.

32. In 1909 of the 15,455 indentured workers registered in agriculture, 6,149 (approximately 39 percent) were classified as being employed in 'general farming' (Meer, 1980).

33. Indenture as a labour form differed from slavery in that, at least formally, the length of the term of bondage was stipulated and limited.

34. This still needs further research. See First, 1959.44. The Indian government prohibited the recruitment of indentured workers to South Africa in 1911, following mounting protest over the bad conditions. The last consignment of human cargo arrived in Natal in that same year on board the *Umlazi*. By then 152,184 Indians had been brought to South Africa, of whom 62 percent were men, 25 percent women and 13 percent children. Almost all had arrived since the turn of the century (Meer, 1980:16).

35. Indian workers continued to indenture under two-year contracts, if in declining numbers, right up to 1934, a reflection of the economic climate in the country and the restricted options for alternative employment. In addition, a rising number worked on the farms as 'freed Indians' and were subject to the conditions of the Masters and Servants Acts (ibid.:21).

36. Beinart, 1982:146. In the early 1930s pay was £2 per 30 shifts on sugar estates, compared to £3 per 30 shifts on the mines.

37. Ibid.:95. In 1911, 25 percent of men in the age group 15-45 were absent from Pondoland, compared with 45 percent in 1936.

38. Such an agreement is possible, but the literature makes no reference to one, should it have existed.

39. As Beinart (1982) points out, this led to more extensive and deep-soil ploughing which resulted in erosion. Also, maize tended to exhaust the soil more quickly than sorghum, a process accelerated by the dropping of crop rotation and land shortage.

40. An explanation should be sought in the extent of capitalisation and concentration of ownership, the way production was organised and, particularly, the historical labour base on which sugar had been built — that is, indentured labour, a particular form of recruited forced labour.

41. So, for example, at the turn of the twentieth century, the largest single employer of leased prisoners in the Cape Colony was De Beers diamond mines in Kimberly. For more details on this, and on prison labour in general, see Cook, 1982:62. Lacey (1981:163) writes that in the space of seven years a series of forced labour laws were introduced to meet the demands of farming capital.

42. The 1925 Tax Act, particularly, produced defaulters who directly swelled the prison labour supply. All African men had to carry their tax receipts on them at all times and were summarily arrested if they could not produce them on demand. If they were unable to pay the fine, they were sent to serve a term of 'convict' labour.

43. The whole of the Transvaal and Natal were proclaimed pass-bearing areas in 1930, so that in addition to their tax receipts, African men had to carry a pass to seek work outside the reserves or off the farms. Failure to do so meant summary arrest and fining, or being channelled into the convict labour system.

44. 'There are two methods of hiring out prison labour: the lease system and the contract system. The lease system places prisoners under the control of the employer, outside the prison. In Britain, the lease system was abolished in 1802. Under the contract system, work for an outside person or organisation is done within the prison confines. The contract system is, of the two, less open to abuse ... But the lease and contract system are in use in South Africa today' (Cook, 1982:7).

45. Reuter report of official statement of the Director of Prisons, January 1930, cited in Wilson, 1970:321.

46. In 1930 the ILO defined forced labour as 'all work or service which is exacted from any person under the menace of any penalty for its non-performance and for which the worker does not offer himself voluntarily'. Cited in ibid:319.

47. Report to the Annual Conference of the ANC. *Guardian,* 15 November 1947.

48. *Advance,* 16 April 1953. The Minister of Justice found that the majority of Bethal farmers treated their labour 'properly' and the cases of extreme abuse were confined to seven farms (*Guardian*, 24 July 1947).

49. The 1930 ILO report (note 46) stated that a variety of forms of 'legal indirect compulsion', that is 'taxation, vagrancy or pass laws, the deprivation of lands, the restriction of lands, cultivation or cattle owning and other measures with the intention of forcing workers into employment are methods of instituting forced labour for private employers and should be condemned equally with direct forms of compulsion for the purpose' (319).

50. In 1939, for example, the national herd numbered 11.85 million cattle. 45 percent were African owned, but of the total number of Africans living on white-owned farms held a mere twelve percent. In 1962, the national cattle herd had risen to some 17 million animals. Although the breakdown of African ownership is not known to the author, this increase is likely to reflect a sharp decline in African cattle ownership in general, and an increase in white stock holding. *Race Relations News,* March 1944.

51. Betterment and Bantu Authorities were two related colonial-inspired policies. The former, begun in the late 1930s, was initially known as 'rehabilitation', becoming 'betterment' as the policy intensified under National Party rule during the 1950s. It stipulated the redivision and reorganisation of land, and also its usage and occupation in the reserves, according to schemes devised in Pretoria. It imposed limitations on stock as well as land size and access, arrived at by pseudo-scientific deductions which took apartheid and the appropriation of the overwhelming majority of the land by the white minority as its basic premise. It also forced population resettlement and the concentration of people in villages or settlements.

   The Bantu Authorities scheme, similarly, was devised in Pretoria. The state aimed to transform chiefly authority from one grounded in popular consent to one deriving all its substance from the ruling white minority and the force at its disposal. In effect, chiefs in due course were to become little more than paid agents of the apartheid state. Both these schemes solicited mass bloody protest throughout the countryside. For more details see Marcus, 1984.

52. Morris, 1977. Much of what follows is drawn from this work.

53. AFRA 1980, 'Labour Tenancy and Forced Evictions from Farms: Natal'.

54. These, of course, were not the first measures to be taken against the presence of the black majority on land claimed by the white colonial settlers. Between 1855 and 1887, legislation was enacted in all of what was subsequently to become the Union of South Africa to limit and control 'squatters'. Yet these measures were fiercely resisted, so that there were many more Africans on land outside the reserves in Natal, the OFS and the Transvaal at the beginning of the twentieth century than there were in the reserves (Davenport, 1974:33). The campaign against 'squatting' was inseparable from the creation by the white minority of the terms of colonialism of a special type.

55. Mike Morris (1977). This connection was explicitly acknowledged. As Morris (14) points out, the SAAU memorandum spelt out a policy which linked the farm labour shortage to the wider political problem of controlling the African population, by starting from the 'axiom that no solution is practicable except through the medium of long-term Native policy ... (therefore) it was proposed that the Native community be encouraged to advance in two main groups, agricultural and industrial, the former divided into sub-groups consisting of farmers and farm labourers. The Native farmer should be assisted to develop within Native areas under leasehold while the labourer should be accommodated on European farms not as a tenant or part-time employee ... The industrial group should be wholly cut off from the practice of agriculture ... Elimination of the, at present, usual periods of idleness would produce an enormous potential labour force, a reservoir of manpower with no corresponding increase in actual numbers.'

56. Janse, Minister of Native Affairs, cited in *Race Relations News*, March 1949.

57. Although the state planned more extensive control over the movement and residence of African women as Walker (1982:127) points out 'any analysis of why they were incorporated into the pass laws system has to take account of the specific place of African women in society as well as the changes it had undergone by the time the Nationalists came to power. One cannot look at African women as if they were on a par with African men. The available evidence suggests that, *in the eyes of the state*, (emphasis not original) the primary function of women in 1952 still lay in the reproductive, not the productive, sphere. The state was not interested in controlling their mobility as workers as it was with African men.'

58. Ibid:126. 'In order to be exempted an African had to prove that he/she had lived in the area continuously since birth, or had worked continuously for one employer for a minimum of ten years; or had lived there continuously and lawfully for a minimum of 15 years prior to the Act; or was the wife, unmarried son or daughter under 18 years of age of a man who qualified for urban residence in terms of the above.'

59. Although most men carried passes, it is not known how many did not when the Act was introduced. Research has yet to reveal how and when these were imposed and if this occurred in a different way to passes for women.

60. See note 58.

61. For more details of the impact of the war years on the political economy, see Walker, 1982: chapter five. Her account, however, fails to include either materially (notwithstanding that 'poverty and malnutrition in the rural areas goes largely undocumented', 72) or analytically the fact that a substantial part of the movement of Africans off the land originated not in the reserves, but rather in the so-called 'white' countryside. In the period 1936-50, Bundy (1979) suggests that for every person who came from the reserves five came from white-owned farms. This fact requires at least a revision of analysis of the social relations — in the earlier and the contemporary period — so that the full dimension of relations in the rural areas (both within and beyond reserves) are incorporated into political and economic interpretations.

62. And they were perceived as such. Verwoerd, as Minister of Native Affairs in 1952, introduced all three pieces of legislation together. As Morris (1977:45) points out, the reasons for the delay in enacting the Amendment to the 1936 Act lay, in part, 'in the bureaucratics of parliamentary procedures'.

63. These were tactical rather than strategic questions which arose from contradictions within the farming class, first and foremost.

64. Dr Verwoerd, Minister of Native Affairs. Cited in Morris, 1977:47.
65. Although the majority of people caught by the system were African, Coloureds also fell victim to it. Although they did not have to carry passes and were not subject to influx control regulations, they 'sometimes found themselves being herded on to farm lorries after being arrested for a pass offence. In one case a Coloured man was given a twelve-month contract instead of a six-month contract as a punishment for protesting he was a Coloured' (Cook, 1982:17).

4.   A Destabilised Labour Force: Expulsion and Reorganisation

In the first phase of restructuring the extent of reorganisation of the labour force was shaped and limited by the fact that production relations in the sector were still predominantly labour intensive. This was not the case during the next, which began in the mid-1960s and was still proceeding in the late 1970s. By the early years of this phase, capital restructuring (with state assistance) had advanced to the point where the balance of relations had shifted away from labour- to capital-intensive production. Though this shift had even more far-reaching consequences for the reorganisation of the labour force than developments in the first phase, the channelling of Africans into the sector remained of key importance. Partially this was because of the unevenness of the relations within the sector, but also it arose, in part, from the need to sustain and guarantee the cheap labour base on which production was founded. Nonetheless, the changing demand for labour and the related question of the location of agriculture's labour surpluses and supply pools saw a profoundly reshaped division of labour emerge in commercial agriculture in South Africa. The changes in labour forms that the process brought about are directly related to the initially relative, and then absolute, decline in employment which characterised this period (See Chapter 2). They are also inseparably linked to the expulsion of Africans off white-owned (and even black-owned) land outside the reserves and the relocation of agriculture's reserve army of labour in the bantustans and in the ghettos of rural towns.

How has restructuring, in this second phase, altered the social composition of the labour force in commercial agriculture? What impact did this process have on the predominant labour forms in the sector? And, of equal importance, what consequences did this hold for the social characteristics of the agricultural workforce? In answering these questions, it is possible to draw out the main forms and characteristics of the workforce labouring in commercial agriculture in the contemporary period.

Suppressing labour tenancy and expelling labour tenants

Labour and rent tenants continued to be pressed into exclusive farm service with, if anything, added vigour. Simultaneously, however, the eradication of the labour form was bound up with the emergence of a growing African population on white-owned farmland who were surplus to the labour needs of the sector and whose presence there was perceived as endangering the base of white minority rule. This was the so-called '*beswarting* (darkening) *van die platteland*'. The emergence of this pool of surplus labour derived both from the process of capitalisation ('mechanisation', etc.) and from conditions of national oppression. The latter not only blocked African movement off the land and into the towns and cities, but also generated gross overcrowding and intense land hunger by limiting African access to land to less than 13 percent of the country. This 'surplus' of people on 'white' farmland was thus anathema to ideologists of white domination as much as to farmers intent on extending, intensifying and rationalising production. In consequence, the 'abolition' of labour tenancy became inseparable from the question of 'surplus' Africans and their expulsion out of the sector and into the reserves. Implicit here is the fact, of course, that those forcibly removed out of commercial agriculture were by no means only labour (or rent) tenants. [1]

The three issues — the abolition of labour tenancy, 'surplus' populations and their eviction — were explicitly linked in changes introduced ostensibly to amend legislation on labour tenancy. In 1964 the Native Trust and Land Act of 1936 was revised, yet again, to incorporate all the recommendations made by the special inter-departmental inquiry into labour tenancy which had sat some four years earlier. [2] The amended law empowered the state to limit and abolish labour tenancy in any district by proclamation, and converted the Labour Tenant Control Boards into Labour Control Boards.

In limiting and abolishing labour tenancy, the strategy adopted was based on close co-operation and co-ordination between state and farmers. This meant that, in principle, districts would only be proclaimed against labour tenancy where the balance of farmer opinion was in favour of such action. The procedure was to 'peg' the number of labour tenants at the level existing in the district. Whether this level was determined by rulings from Pretoria, or by the local Labour (Tenant) Control Board is unclear. However, it did refer exclusively to registered tenants. Thereafter, no new contracts could be entered into and no old contracts could be renewed. In Natal, where tenant opposition was particularly fierce, farmer agitation led to a modification of the terms. Following 'pegging', the authorities allowed labour tenancy contracts to be renewed for a limited period with a view to a more gradual termination of the system. In the Orange Free State and the Transvaal, the course of the process needs to be more thoroughly researched if we are to know precisely how tenancy was broken down. [3] But this notwithstanding, it would seem that, once tenancy had been 'abolished', the pressure from farmers to press tenants into exclusive farm service, or off the land altogether, intensified considerably.

The first districts to be proclaimed were in the Transvaal in 1966. By 1969 the labour tenant system had been made illegal throughout the Orange Free State, in 25 districts in the Transvaal, in three districts in the Cape and in four in Natal (Survey, 1969). The following year, set as the deadline by when Pretoria wished to see the system abolished throughout the country, a further 36 districts were proclaimed under the Act, 17 in the Transvaal and 19 in Natal (*Rand Daily Mail,* 7 September 1970). By 1973 the state declared the system had been outlawed in all the provinces but Natal (Hansard, 1973: Vol.45, Col.1003). There, tenancy was to continue to exist legally until 1980. It had been made illegal to register new contracts from 1970 onwards, and contracts were limited to three years, with possible renewals until 30 August 1980, on which date all existing contracts were deemed to have expired (*Sunday Tribune,* 13 July 1980).

The process of proclaiming districts and its rate of progress revealed regional differences in both the extent and intensity of the practice. In the Cape, few districts were proclaimed, reflecting the general absence of formally recognised labour tenancy. Rent tenancy was widespread and no doubt concealed the practice of labour tenancy. In other words, for as many farmers who drew seasonal, or occasional workers from the ranks of 'cash' tenants, there were those who made labour service a conditional part of the terms of residence on their property (SPP, 1983: Vol.2,312). Such forms of labour tenancy, which according to Desmond's study were a common feature of 'cash' tenancy in most parts of the country (Desmond, 1971:171), were not formally recognised. In fact, they were classified as 'squatters' who were subject to unqualified eviction. But the predominant form of labour on Cape farms was exclusive farm service and, as will be shown, the 'Coloured labour preference policy' was of particular importance.

In the Orange Free State and the Transvaal the outlawing of labour tenancy proceeded rapidly. And though the practice undoubtedly continued illegally, the labour form was abolished in most districts in the short space of five years. The speed with which the policy was realised, on the one hand, indicated how far advanced the process of pressing labour tenants into farm service was in the two provinces. On the other hand, although force and the threat of force were ever present, the relative smoothness of the transition reflected the community of state and farmer interests, which in combination masked the extent of the upheaval involved and served to crush tenant resistance. Although fieldwork still needs to be done, it seems probable that the pattern of labour tenant resistance did not differ substantially from that in Natal, where, on the whole, 'it was localised, often individual and spontaneous, reacting to the crisis as it hit' (SPP,1983:Vol.5, 77). In Natal, fierce tenant opposition was strengthened by the considerably greater dependence of farmers on labour tenancy, particularly in the central and northern parts of the province. In consequence, the process of eradicating the labour form was far more protracted. Fieldwork by the SPP and AFRA [4] has made substantial inroads into documenting this struggle in all its bitterness. Their research leads them to conclude that, although the resistance served to slow the process down, the concessions won by tenants and farmers to continue with the labour form were only temporary and affected limited numbers of tenants. State pressure to register and impose quotas continued relentlessly. It was reinforced by structural changes in agriculture, particularly land and capital concentration, 'mechanisation', and the absence of farm workers' organisations to link local struggles with one another and with those being waged elsewhere. In other words:

> Many tenants refused to accept their eviction notices and had to be driven off by police and farmers, who came with dogs and guns and fire, burned down huts, impounded cattle and arrested people still living on the land. Local tenant opposition could succeed in delaying the evictions, it could even on occasions … win concessions from the state about where it would relocate the tenants. It could not, however, prevent the evictions when both the local farmer and the local authorities were agreed on the necessity or inevitability of enforcing them (SPP,1983:Vol.5,77).

This brings us to the implications of the conversion of Labour Tenant Control

Boards into Labour Control Boards. The significance of this shift has for the most part been overlooked. Yet it represented an important change in emphasis which was not only about who was to be controlled, but also about what was to be controlled. Implicit in the new emphasis was the recognition that a population surplus to the needs of commercial agriculture existed, or was being created from within. Farmers' concern that such Labour Control Boards would create labour shortages was misplaced, since the state had every intention of ensuring that the 'canalising' machinery of labour bureaux, pass laws and influx control would continue to serve the farms. Their anxiety accurately highlighted, however, the primary role envisaged for these Boards. The establishment of Labour Control Boards was the means by which 'surpluses' could be pinpointed and action taken on them. This, in turn was linked to a broader policy on African people who came to be termed 'non-productive Bantu' — namely, their forced relocation into the reserves.[5] Such removals were acknowledged to be central to the policy of creating 'Bantu homelands'.

The immediate target of Labour Control Boards was labour and 'cash' tenancy, although they did not confine their activities to them. How they actually worked has yet to be properly researched, but two general observations can be made. The first is that it is probably no coincidence that most of them appear to have been established in the late 1960s and early 1970s when evictions of tenants and redundant farm workers were particularly prevalent. By 1972, 35 such Boards had been set up in Natal, 60 in each of the Transvaal the OFS and 33 in the Cape). The second is that, where labour tenancy is concerned, the establishment of such a board in a district was closely followed by a proclamation outlawing the labour form and heightened action in implementing the decree. Their crucial role in implementing policy is implicit, for example, in an appeal by the Drakensberg Administration Board in 1980 for these Boards to be set up in all the rural areas of Natal (*Natal Witness*, 28 February 1980). It seems that, although labour tenancy had been declared illegal by Pretoria, without Labour Control Boards it was proving difficult to put policy into practice.

So, whilst the abolition of labour tenancy was still aimed at pressing tenants into exclusive farm service, equal emphasis was laid on their forced eviction off the farms and into the reserves. They resisted for the same reasons as they had done in the earlier period: they had lived on the land for generations and considered it theirs; they refused to accept the desultory conditions of 'full-time' farm employment which would only intensify their poverty; and the places to which the state intended to move them entailed further dispossession of both land and livestock, opening a gloomy future of even greater poverty and hardship. Furthermore, alternative avenues of waged work outside the sector were closed to them, in theory and increasingly in practice. The struggle against eviction was very intense, since it was so intimately bound up with a struggle for life itself.

The ways in which evictions came about were myriad, each case uniquely shaped by the interaction of farmers' needs, state pressure, and the strength and ingenuity of tenants involved. Some were offered the 'choice' of bondage to the farmer or being expelled from their homes and their land. Many were not given even this paltry option and were simply presented with eviction notices. Either way, upon refusing to move off the land they were deemed 'squatters', the catch-all into which all those 'superfluous' to the needs of white commercial agriculture were classified, scheduled for, and subjected to forced removal into the reserves.

It is not possible to quantify accurately the number of people affected by the eradication of labour tenancy, in part because many, if not the majority, of labour tenants were never registered and so cannot be distinguished in the statistics from rent tenants, a category of people living on the land whose distinction from labour tenants was itself unclear. All were deemed 'squatters'. At best, any quantification can only give an idea of the scale of the process.

There are two sources of data. Official figures on registered labour tenants, as has already been pointed out, only tell a fraction of the story. [6] Yet even they reveal that hundreds of thousands of African lives were disrupted. From a total of 200,000 registered labour tenants in 1960, the number was reduced by some 176,000 to about 24,000 in 1971, and to an official zero by 1980 (UN,1976: No 36/76,50; Mare, 1980:9). An indication of the degree to which these figures concealed the extent of the practice of labour tenancy can be gained from the official figure given when state and farmers were in conflict over the immediate eradication of the system in 1970. Labour tenancy, officials said then, involved a 'mere' 27,000 or so (registered) tenants. The Natal Agricultural Union, however, estimated that the implementation of the ban would affect as many as 750,000 labour tenants who were then living on white-owned land in central and northern Natal (*Rand Daily Mail,* 7 September 1970). It seems that, at a conservative estimate, the eradication of labour tenancy affected over one million Africans.

A second way of estimating the effect of the abolition of labour tenancy is to look at forced relocation figures. Here, too, there are difficulties. It is hard to evaluate the number of evictions specifically related to labour tenants separately from those which involved rent tenants or workers in exclusive farm service. This notwithstanding, and bearing in mind that these figures are approximations which refer to removals and not people,[7] between 1960 and 1982 there were some 1.3 million removals directly related to expulsions off white-owned farm land into the reserves.[8] Farm removals constituted the largest single category of people affected by population relocation policy in South Africa — 1.3 of 3.5 million removals in this period. It is to this massive eviction, in fact, that many huge resettlement camps inside the reserves owe their origin (Desmond, 1971:41).

The labour tenant system was formally outlawed in 1980. Indeed, by the second half of the 1970s, farmers in most parts of the country had changed the labour base of their enterprises to one grounded on some form of exclusive farm labour. What remained at the turn of the decade were some small but substantial pockets of labour tenancy, e.g., in the Weenen/Muden districts of the central Natal thornveld, in isolated northern farming districts of Natal (SSP,1983: Vol.2, 312). Under relentless siege from forced relocation, even these remnants are being whittled away.

This second phase has thus all but completely eradicated labour tenancy, which even twenty years before, and certainly at the onset of restructuring, was a widely practised form of labour in commercial agriculture. In the course of restructuring over a million (if not several million) labour tenants were simultaneously pressed down into full-time farm service, or forced off 'the white platteland'. They were removed into the reserves, or they moved illegally into the towns. It was a ruthless and brutal process /Desmond, 1971; SPP, 1983, etc.), at the heart of which lay the pursuit of both profits and continued white minority domination. White farmers and the state protested the valour of their actions in terms of 'ending feudal practices', modernisation and the promotion of 'progressive' farming. But this glib phraseology notwithstanding, both the practice of labour tenancy, and the way in which it was eliminated, carried within them the seeds of continued repressive and exploitative relations in commercial agriculture. In other words, as will be shown, exclusive farm service for African (and, in fact, all black) farm workers was hardly a synonym for progress or enlightened labour relations.

Transforming farm service and expelling surplus workers

During this second phase of restructuring a distinct shift in emphasis was articulated by the dominant sections of agricultural capital and the state alike, and practically implemented by many farmers. The reduction of the labour force resident on white-owned enterprises was actively promoted as an adjunct to 'modernisation' of production. It stemmed from quantitative and qualitative changes in the demand for labour that the move from labour- to capital-intensive production entailed. It involved the eradication of labour and rent tenancy and the propulsion of the majority of this surplus population, who were African, into the reserves.

The eviction of farm workers in 'service' was not new. It has always been a component of the unequal master-and-servant relation which vested the 'master' with inordinate powers over the workers on his farm. Orders to 'trek' were invariably expressed in personal terms: the worker was told to leave as a consequence of being 'lazy', 'cheeky', 'no good' or simply 'not needed'. But whilst there were those who left because of genuine disputes between themselves and farmers,[9] more often than not these 'reasons' were a pretext which hid more fundamental pressures arising from the economic strains on the particular enterprise, or the economy as a whole. So, for example, periodic droughts — 'normal phenomena in the greater part of South Africa'(Marais,1968: para.4.1.,5.l) — invariably saw an increase in the scale of dismissals.

However, from the mid-1960s onwards, the expulsion of so-called farm 'servants' underwent some very real changes which were masked, in part, by their continuity with past practices. This not only meant that the scale of evictions increased, but that the causes underlying them changed. It also meant that even where workers were expelled for the same reasons as in earlier times, the implications of such evictions were not the same as they had been in the past.

Farmers vs workers

The continuity with past evictions lies in the primacy of the farmer's role in dismissing worker families and ordering them to leave the enterprise. Invariably, it is a decision taken by him and carried out by him or his proxy (the farm manager). This puts the farmer, and not the state, in the forefront of action.

The longest that I've been on a farm is four years and eight months. In March I had to leave that farm. Then the farmer says that there are too many of us and he has to pay out too much money. He only wants four men. Five must leave. He gives you nothing except the money you earned. Not even food for the road. Then you must be off his property as fast as possible.[10]

In this respect, retrenchment in the farm workforce closely resembles the dismissal of workers in industry where employer decisions are taken in the context of state pressures and backing, but these are held at a relatively lower profile. The state, in the form of Bantu Affairs Department officials, police and/or soldiers is, of course, 'on call' and is used to enforce, or assist in enforcing the removal of the dismissed worker family. More often than not, however, the state's role is far more oblique. Workers on farms generally do leave when they are dismissed and ordered to do so, for whatever reason. This, in turn, highlights the extent and depth of their insecurity. The experience of Kaalbeen Ngeju graphically illustrates the point. Born and raised on Cowley Farm, near Port Alfred, he worked for its owners for close on fifty of his sixty or so years.

The white child whom he had watched growing up took over from his father and like his father he was a cruel man who 'drove the black men on his farm like they drove his cattle'. So that one day, after 45 years of labour without dignity Kaalbeen, being struck through the face by the farmer, struck back. He had to leave Cowley ... He had never in his life been on holiday, he had never been further than Port Alfred (and then only for one day a year 'for his wife's sake') but that day in the year he was uneasy. ... But then he had to leave, and if we did not mind he would prefer not to remember the day he left. He left but he did not know where to go. (SPP,1983: Vol.2, 359).

A regional variation

In the Cape 'Coloured labour preference policy' had a high priority at this time, and operated in conditions where the predominant form of labour was exclusive farm service. First expounded in 1955 by Dr WW Eiselen, then Secretary for Native Affairs, the policy called for Coloured workers to be given employment preference over African workers in a specified area of the Western Cape, until such time as Africans would be significantly if not completely excluded from the area. The policy guidelines,[11] dormant for several years, were revised, extended and began to be seriously implemented from the mid-1960s onwards. The geographical scope of their application was twice extended eastwards, and now covered employment in agriculture as well. On the one hand, Coloured workers who made up a substantial part of the agrarian workforce in many parts of the Cape were substituted for African workers. This meant that in conditions where there was a steady and absolute decline in agricultural employment (Chapter 2), especially since the decade of the 1970s, Coloured employment in the Cape actually increased (SPP, 1983:Vol.2,107). On the other hand, a spate of removals saw large numbers of Africans expelled, in-dividually or as whole communities, from the towns and districts of the Western and central Cape.

It was far from coincidental that state activity, under the auspices of this policy, coincided with intensified anti-labour and rent tenancy measures in the entire.

province. The Coloured labour preference policy was, after all 'entirely consistent with influx control and the bantustan strategy in general' (SPP,1983:Vol.2,106). — i.e., the instruments of African national oppression. As such, its operation actively contributed to the decline in the African population living and working in the Western and central Cape.

As has already been argued (Chapter 2), the operation of this policy should not, however, be read as benefiting Coloured workers unequivocally. Whilst it has placed them in a relatively advantaged position compared to African workers, it differed significantly from the 'white labour preference policy' (Davies,1979), not least because the demand for it did not emanate from and was never actively campaigned for by Coloured workers. Nor did the relative advantages Coloured workers enjoyed in getting jobs, for example, cushion them from the general regional decline of the Cape, or the specific decline in agricultural employment. In terms of pay and conditions, the relative advantages of earning wages higher than those paid to African workers did not shield them from a low standard of living and, indeed, widespread poverty.

The terms of African national oppression, and particularly the migrantisation of the workforce, served, if anything, to depress wages and to sustain generally bad conditions of employment for all farm workers. This extends beyond the work situation. For example, informal influx control measures were used against Coloureds through the regulation of access to housing. In Beaufort West, for instance, a Coloured farm worker had to supply the local Town Clerk with very good reasons for moving to town before the person's name would be put on a housing waiting list. When the Management Committee took over the allocation of housing in 1965 (as part of the operation of the Group Areas Act), although farm workers no longer had to furnish reasons why they wanted to move, they still had to put their names on a waiting list and were effectively prevented from moving by strict anti-squatting measures until their names were near or at the top. As recently as 1983 it was reportedly still very difficult to get a house. This, in turn, has acted to keep Coloured workers on the farms (Schmidt, 1984:20-1).

The operation of the Coloured labour preference policy was uneven in its intensity and application over time. Its enforcement has been the most stringent in the more westerly districts of the Cape, for example. In the Eastern Cape it seems to have been enforced hardly at all, possibly because, as the SPP researchers suggest, there is a relatively small Coloured population resident there (SPP,1983:Vol.2,108). Furthermore, whereas the policy played a more significant part in the expulsion of Africans, farm workers included, at the beginning of this second phase of restructuring, its relative importance has declined substantially. In the most recent period 'people have been forced out of the area through intensified economic pressures rather than crude GG (state) removals' (SPP,1983:107). This is consistent with experiences in other parts of the country.

For example, in Natal (SPP, 1983:Vol.4,78) the general shift to capital-intensive production in the sector has become the primary force pressurising farmers to evict workers, or forcing workers to leave because conditions are no longer tolerable.

The state's importance in channelling surplus labour

The state was not necessarily prominent in the redundancy and eviction process, but its role in channelling workers into the reserves was primary. As has already been shown, it did so by blocking African farm workers' access to the towns and other sectors of employment. It was also instrumental in determining where 'surplus' people on white-owned land would be sent.

All the farmer had to do to obtain direct backing from the state in expelling workers was to go to his local magistrate and 'lodge an application to have a person resettled elsewhere' (*Sechaba,* October 1971). Or, if he dismissed a worker and ordered him and his family to leave the land, and they still remained on his property, he had simply to lodge a complaint that they were there illegally. Either way, from then on, the fate of this 'surplus and unwanted labour' was in the hands of the state. It did not matter if they were farm workers in 'service', or living on the farms as labour or rent tenants. A series of bureaucratic procedures led to a decision as to where the person/family would be relocated. It was taken without consultation and in accordance with the white minority's ethnically-structured 'homeland' strategy. Against it there was no appeal. If workers did not move to a specified place within a specified period (often as short as 24 hours) they, and the possessions they could muster together, were thrown on trucks and transported there.

The state's efforts were not confined to measures of crude force. Alongside these were more subtle forms of inducement to entice Africans into the reserves, which seem to have led some farm workers to leave their jobs. In the Northern Cape for example, some farm workers moved into the reserves after they heard on radio Bantu that in 'their homelands there was land, housing, schools, clinics and all the facilities' (SPP,1983:Vol.3,106). Whilst the bleak, jobless and remote wastelands revealed an opposite reality, the cruelty of this deception was the greater because it played on the real needs of very impoverished people. Similar claims and appeals have also emanated from the various 'self-governing homelands'. QwaQwa, for example, now has a sustained campaign for 'South Sotho to come home'. Since this is often also the only route by which farm workers can hope to break their bondage to commercial agriculture, many have moved into them 'voluntarily'.

Changing conditions and worker consciousness

The combined effect of capital restructuring and state interventions in this phase brought a marked decline in agricultural employment. The processes involved are reflected in the consciousness of the workers. Rarely, however, have the processes not been mediated, if not completely obscured, by paternalistic relations between white farmer-masters and black worker-servants. Most studies on farm labour have concentrated on the problems as perceived by farmers and there is a yawning gap when it comes to information on farm workers and their consciousness.[12] Nevertheless, such evidence as has been brought to light in research into population relocation and poverty suggests that one of the strongest links between restructuring and unemployment is expressed in terms of changes in farm ownership. Relations between the new owner (whether kin of or stranger to the former owner) and workers often deteriorated so much that workers found it impossible to remain on the farm any longer:

'When the farmer died we moved away because the new boss was very cruel' (SPP, 1983:Vol.2,212). Or, and just as frequently, relations were not even established. Either the old farmer, or the new owner, fired them in the process of transferring the property.

> 'The new owner of the farm said they were going to locate people of their own choice. The farmer said we should leave because he was selling to the government' (SPP,1983:Vol.2,213).

Even when not all the workers were dismissed, the transfer of property meant that at least some of the workers on the newly acquired farm would lose their jobs, and frequently it entailed the expulsion of the aged or infirm — so-called 'non-productive labour units'. The experience of Mr Piet Witbooi, who worked for close on 40 years for the same farmer, has been quite commonplace. He recounts:

> 'Then the *kleinbaas* (son and new owner) came here to live about four years ago. He says to me that no he can't keep me because I can't give nicely anymore. My legs are finished. The mountains finished them. You can't go with a horse in the mountains. You have to walk to watch the sheep there, checking for insects. So that's that'.[13]

Another aspect of the restructuring process which seems to be quite strongly reflected in worker consciousness is the effect of changing techniques of production on employment, especially when machines are involved.

> 'Everywhere you went you had to go by foot and herd the sheep forward. There weren't any lorries to do the transporting. Today the lorries transport everything. There are no longer such things as shepherds and sheep drives'.[14]

The extension of the area under production is discerned in worker disquiet about the deteriorating terms of their employment, especially as payments in kind are whittled away or withdrawn altogether. So, for example, whereas a Middelburg farmer claimed workers had access to arable land 'to the extent of one soccer field' which 'the farmer plants for them free of charge' and on which 'they plant things intended for own consumption only', a worker who had lived on the farm for about 30 years challenged the accuracy of this assertion. He said that, whereas he used to have three soccer fields, these had now been declared grazing land and he had been allocated no alternative land (Seleoane,1984:15). This structural, indirect force has pressured many farm workers to leave the farms 'voluntarily'. Several people interviewed during SPP research in the Stanger district of Natal, all of whom are now tenants in overcrowded and run-down informal settlements, described

> how they used to live and work on white farms in the district but as sugar cane cultivation in the district spread, it encroached more and more on the land set aside for their use until they eventually decided to leave the farm themselves (SPP,1983:Vol.4,79).

But while sometimes the forces underlying retrenchment and the decline in employment in the sector are clear, in general the processes involved are far more obscure. This is not only because the processes themselves are not necessarily apparent in their effect on job levels. Nor is it simply because farmers have recourse to various indirect techniques of reducing the labour force they employ, for example, by not replacing workers who leave, or by spreading or reducing seasonal peaks and thereby cutting back on the number of short-term workers they employ. Equally, it is because retrenchment and evictions are invariably presented and experienced as a very individual and personalised affair, which derives from the particular relation between the farmer and the workers concerned. In a survey of 44 former farm worker households, 38 percent ascribed their leaving the farm to a quarrel or disagreement between themselves and the farmer (AFRA, 1980-94: Reel III). In this respect, the changing rationale behind the farmer actions has done little to alter earlier practices. They callously victimise workers on the slightest pretext. If they are old and unable to find a family member to replace them on the farm; if the worker has been ill, becomes infirm (whether through injury at work or not) or dies, even where one or all family members are also working on the farm; when children refuse to work on the farm; when stock dies, or implements are damaged; being 'cheeky', 'lazy', or sick 'too often' — all have proved to be sufficient grounds for farmers to lay off workers and their families.

Indeed, one of the consequences of the objective and subjective conditions of farm labour is that, although it engenders anger and bitterness and a deep sense of injustice, it also seems to have inhibited collective and organised resistance. The extent of the isolation of workers from one another is indirectly highlighted in the study of Middelburg farms. On one of them, for instance, whilst farm workers knew that some families had left when the farm they worked on changed hands, and although they seemed to know these families, they were not aware of the circumstances behind their eviction.

In all, the black population living and working on the farms — as labour or rent tenants, or as workers in exclusive farm service — has been reduced drastically in the second phase of restructuring. During this period labour tenancy has, to all intents and purposes, been eradicated. It has been replaced by a substantially reduced body of workers resident on the farms and employed in 'full-time' farm service. It would nevertheless be both inaccurate and misleading to conceive of the workforce in South African commercial agriculture as being made up solely or predominantly of such farm workers. This so-called 'stabilised core' is only an aspect of the social composition of the workforce. Their existence is inseparable from an extensively destabilised body of workers, whose existence represents the other side of the reorganisation process.

A general reshaping of the division of labour

Restructuring, particularly in this second phase, has seen a complex reorganisation of the social composition of the workforce engaged in commercial agriculture. This has involved a profound change in the predominant labour forms in the sector, aspects of which have already been shown. But it has also had very far-reaching consequences for the social characteristics of the agricultural labour force. In discussing the way in which the division of labour has been reshaped, further changes in the main labour forms and the significance of changing social characteristics will be treated together.

The overarching change in the division of labour in commercial agriculture arises from the physical division of the agricultural labour force between workers resident on the farms and those drawn for shorter or longer periods from the reserves or urban ghettoes of 'white' towns. On the one hand, the repression of rent and labour tenancy and the reduction of on-farm employment has seen the workforce who live and work on the farms throughout the year reduced to a small group of worker families (variously and misleadingly described as 'permanent' or 'regular'). Almost every farm has one or more worker families living on it and the few that do not tend to be situated very close to townships.[14] On the other hand, the exodus or expulsion of black workers and their families from white-owned farms has brought about the migrantisation of a large part of the agrarian labour force. That is to say, the paring down of on-farm labour into a so-called 'core' workforce has been paralleled by, and is inseparably linked to an expansion of the migrant labour system.

At the same time the migrant labour system itself has changed in content. Under 'classical' conditions it presumed the existence of some base which would support the partial reproduction of the migrant worker as a social being. This was one of the primary forces motivating migration. Under restructured terms, (which of course do not apply only to agriculture) however, the presumption of such a base as underlying the worker's separation from and oscillation between the farms and his or her family is groundless for the majority of workers. Rather, such migration stems from the compulsion of the interrelated operation of African national oppression and the enforced displaced urbanisation which it entails. It stems from racial discrimination against people of colour and the social exploitation of class, gender and age.

On-farm and migrant labour are the two forms of labour which predominate in commercial agriculture in South Africa under restructured conditions. They are complementary to one another, so that the way they interrelate is a key to changes in the social characteristics of the restructured labour force. These are several. They include changes in the unit of employment, recruiting practices, the division of labour between full-time work, the exploitation of female and child labour, the use of prison labour and the emergence of a skill hierarchy. All of these key aspects are interconnected. To bring out their full significance, however, they have to be treated discretely.

Changes in the unit of employment

With restructuring there has been a general trend away from family and household employment towards individualising the unit of labour. In other words, more and more workers employed in commercial agriculture are hired on an individual basis. This is an outcome of the increasingly widespread practice of hiring a growing part of the workforce as migrants. Farmers recruit individual workers from the labour pools in towns, or in the settlements in the reserves, for the required period. At the end of the work period the worker is returned to the recruitment area. Workers are treated as single labour units to be used and disposed of at the farmers' convenience. They are divorced from any social context, without regard to their social reproduction.

In so far as workers who live on the farms are concerned, the process of in-dividualising employment is less apparent. Here the main unit of employment is still the 'family'.[15] Although it is usually a male adult who is taken on as the 'regular' worker, his employment is invariably conditional upon the understand-ing — a so-called 'rule of the farm' — that members of his family, or household, will be available for and are expected to work whenever the farmer demands. Yet, on closer examination, even here there are changes which can be related to a trend towards individualising the workforce. For example, farmers are increasingly un-willing to take on men who have many dependants living with them. As one farmer put it:

> 'We no longer employ the job seeker who has a large number of dependants, both young and old. Often a man of 20 seeks employment, but because he has aged parents and four to five young children being looked after by the parents, we turn them away as it is not beneficial to the worker who will continuously struggle to support the dependants' (Aires, 1976:6).

This somewhat convenient means of overcoming poverty wages without adding a single cent to the worker family's pay packet at the same time provides a cover for a change in labour demand brought about by capital restructuring. With the decline in the number of 'regular' workers needed per enterprise, large worker families with several adult members are not a particularly attractive proposition to the farmer, since he no longer evaluates the pool of labour they provide as essential to his operation.

For similar reasons, it is possible to understand why a growing number of farmers do not demand that all adults remain on the farm as a precondition for employing the 'family'. De Klerk's study of maize farms, for example, found that many farmers 'talked of younger men — the sons of older farm workers — who left their wives and children on farms and went to work in urban areas or on the mines' (1984:16).

This practice seems to be quite common, often without the co-operation of farmers, and certainly in spite of influx control and the pass laws when this consent is not forthcoming (or is given in such a manner as to make legal employment impossi-ble).[16] It reveals, amongst other things, that non-agricultural migrant labour con-tinues to supplement the income of agricultural worker families and thereby directly subsidise white farmers.

Both these examples show a tendency towards a nuclear-type family as the social base of the workforce resident on the farms. This is itself indicative of the process of individualising labour. Further evidence of this process can be seen in two other developments. The first is the expectation, on the part of farmers, that some form of payment is due to worker family members when their labour power is drawn on. That it is often not forthcoming does not detract from the argument, since even in this event farmers have to justify its absence in one way or another. The second is the effect the process has on both female and child labour. This will be looked at in more detail further on in this chapter. Suffice it to say here that, whereas in the past the 'family' as a unit of employment tended to obscure the labour of women and children in agriculture, under restructured conditions both the extent and nature of their labour are being 'made visible'.

Changes in recruiting practices

As has been shown earlier, recruitment practices in agriculture vary. On the one hand, the state has tightened the control machinery. Labour bureaux have opened in the homelands, and this phase has seen the strengthening and centralisation of administrative structures governing Africans in urban and rural areas outside the reserves. To this end, Administration Boards were established in 1971. These numbered 22 in 1973, although because of financial pressure they were reduced to 14 in 1979. They are made up of local white political representatives and their counterparts from industry and agriculture (Bekker *et al.*, 1982). They are the outcome of a state which, in its own words, has been 'doing everything in its power with its influx control and employment bureau machinery … to make sure that agricultural labour is not allowed to flow into the urban areas'.[17]

On the other hand, there has been a general reluctance on the part of farmers to use these apparatuses because of the bureaucracy, inefficiency and control that their use entails. In fact, few farmers seem to get their workers directly through the labour bureaux system. They have also expressed opposition to the assignment of the recruiting function to other apparatuses — the Administration Boards in particular (SAAU, 1978:74). Instead, most either recruit workers through the organisations they have set up themselves, or each man 'recruits for himself'.

Labour recruiting organisations
Recruiting organisations in commercial agriculture seem to be closely related to the regional and branch particularities already referred to. They are predominant in the Western Cape and the Natal sugar belt.

In the Western Cape, the wine and fruit-growing farmers responded to labour shortages caused by the general movement of Coloured workers into the towns, the operation of the Coloured labour preference policy, the general inefficiency of state labour bureaux and a universal reluctance on the part of farmers to raise wages and improve conditions, by clubbing together and forming 'recruiting co-operatives'. In much the same way as they built prison outstations, they organised the recruitment, transportation and necessary paper work to bring African workers, as migrants, from Transkei and Ciskei to the farms (Wilson, 1972:19). In fact, the extent to which migrant labour and prison labour are complementary goes further and is well illustrated by the example of the Hex River Valley. When the US threatened to ban vine products from the Hex River Valley because the extensive use of prison labour allowed South African goods to compete unfairly in the market, farmers were forced to close the prison outstation they had built at De Doorns.[18] To counter the effect of the loss of prison labour, the operations of their relatively recently formed recruiting 'co-op' were radically stepped up so that by 1972 the 220-member Hex Rivier Boere Groep (Farmers' Association) was recruiting between 3,000 and 5,000 men a year (Wilson, 1972:21). In the process, it was transformed into the largest of six such recruiting organisations operating in the Western Cape in the early 1970s. In addition to the recruitment of migrant workers for the vine and fruit farms, it seems that dryland sheep farmers have also increasingly come to recruit sheep shearing teams on a collective rather than individual basis. In the magisterial district of George, for example,

> Lesotho sheep shearers move through the area under contract to the farmers' co-operative for six months of the year ... All other African farm labourers are permanently resident in the district (Levatan, 1984:36).

The other region where organised recruitment operates on a large scale is the sugar belt of the eastern seaboard. It is a sector of commercial agriculture which, as already shown, has long relied on migrant workers to provide its labour base. Formerly, however, recruiting was done by individual sugar-milling companies. In 1971 eleven companies combined their efforts and formed the (misleadingly entitled) Sugar Industry Labour Organisation (SILO) which was modelled on the gold mines' Native Recruiting Organisation (Wilson, 1972:18). The stimulus to collectivise their recruiting efforts, according to one company, was provided by

> political changes taking place in the Transkei, the long-term possibility of all recruited labour having to go through a government agency, the need to compete (for labour) with ... other industries and government departments and the need for well-directed propaganda to attract labour to the sugar industry (Wilson, 1972:18).

In the 1974/5 season SILO channelled more than 17,000 workers to the cane fields and sugar mills of Natal (*Financial Mail*, 17 June 1977). By 1977 SILO had become the largest recruiter of agricultural labour and was 'probably second only to the Mine Labour Recruiting Organisation in South Africa' (Wilson, 1972:18). As a labour recruiting organisation, it co-ordinates the recruiting efforts of miller-cum-planters south of the Tugela, setting minimum wages and stipulating basic conditions, and thereby extending control over and eliminating inter-company competition for workers.

Much more information is needed on how these recruiting organisations work, and the extent of their operations. It would be useful to investigate the impact of both production concentration and the decline in absolute employment on their functioning in order to evaluate, amongst other things, the degree to which farmers continue to depend on them for their labour.

Individual recruitment

Most farmers organise their own recruitment. Practices vary from enterprise to enterprise, shaped mainly by the distance the farmer has to travel to get workers. The nearer the labour pool is to the farm, the greater the likelihood that 'migrant' workers will be trucked on and off the farm on a daily basis, the farmer picking up the number of workers he needs for the day at pre-arranged points in the townships, or from settlements inside the reserves. This operation usually takes place before sunrise to ensure that none of the working day is lost in travel. Likewise, workers are usually returned only after dark. It is a system particularly favoured by farmers: they do not have to provide any form of housing or facilities for these workers, and can be flexible about the number of people they employ at any one time. When greater distances make daily transportation too costly, farmers usually truck workers between the farms and their homes on a weekly or monthly basis.

More long-term recruiting seems to be done through agents who recruit workers on the farmer's behalf. Cane growers, for example, extensively use traders in Pondoland as their recruiting agents (Wilson, 1972:18). School teachers, 'headmen' or 'chiefs' also fulfil this function for a fee which is deducted from or counted as part of the worker's wage.

Individual recruitment of workers tends to be far less formalised than that done through recruiting organisations. Whereas the latter includes some form of written contract, invariably individual recruitment rests on a verbal understanding of the terms of employment — the nature of the work, the pay, and the duration of the 'contract'. Often one, or all, of these terms are not fulfilled, but it is next to impossible for the worker to challenge the farmer on the matter. At best, the recruit can run away, or not agree to take up the work. The price of taking such a step is high, since the very fact that the worker takes the work in the first place reflects desperation and lack of options. For workers who live on the farms all year round, the cutback in employment has meant that few, if any, farmers have to recruit workers to fill a vacancy when it arises. Once word gets out that a job exists, the pressures of unemployment, poverty, landlessness and hunger send many workers to the farmer's door. In the words of a Riebeeck East (Albany district) farmer, 'I never have a vacancy for longer than half a day. They storm me if a man leaves' (Antrobus, 1984:82).

Yet this situation is not universal. Conditions on some farms are so atrocious that the farmer is unable to attract anyone to work 'voluntarily' on his establishment for any length of time. He must resort to prison labour, deception, compulsion or a combination of these to secure workers. So, for example, on a farm in the Middelburg district, owned by a man described as 'the best Afrikaans farmer in the area', a worker described recruiting procedures in the following way:

> My main duty is to scout for workers on behalf of the farmer. Most of these are orphans. They stay and work on the farm for six months and then get discharged, whereupon I must obtain others. They live in a kind of compound and no salary in cash or in kind is paid to them'.[19]

The general situation, though, is such that farmers can boast:

> There's a job scarcity throughout the country and it has made things easier for us. In the past they could literally throw their passes into our faces and demand that we discharge them. They can no longer do that' (Seleoane, 1984:41).

Sources of labour

The question arises as to whether restructuring, and especially the expulsion of a large part of the sector's labour supply from farmlands, has led to a change in the sources of labour. It is not easy to answer on the basis of empirical evidence available, especially in the absence of research into the operation of labour recruitment. Nevertheless it is possible to judge whether trends in labour recruitment for other sectors are being replicated under restructured conditions in commercial agriculture. These seem to have followed two patterns.

The first is a trend towards the *'internalisation'* of the labour force. By this is meant a shift away from a reliance on labour recruited beyond South Africa's borders to that drawn from within the country, i.e., a shift from foreign to local labour (Bohning, 1981). Now, whilst commercial agriculture has never been as dependent as the mines on foreign workers, they have constituted a significant minority of the farm labour force in the past. During the period under consideration, the official number of foreign workers employed in the sector seems to have fallen quite markedly — despite the fact that the state, although severely circumscribing the entry and employment of Africans from Botswana, Lesotho and Swaziland from the mid-1960s onwards, explicitly excluded those heading for the mines and commercial agriculture (Stahl, 1981:28). Thus, whereas in 1964 some 144,000 foreign Africans were said to be employed in commercial agriculture, by 1979 they totalled a mere 19,000, dropping by over 80 percent during the period (Stahl, 1981:28, table 7).

This decline represents a huge decrease in the number of foreign workers on the farms. It also signals a decline in their proportion of the total agricultural workforce. But since many foreign Africans have worked and still continue to work in the sector illegally, it is likely that the decrease in their number was not as sharp as these official figures suggest.[20] Whichever way, they nevertheless indicate a trend towards 'internalisation' of the agrarian labour force. In fact, this process is reflected in another, somewhat less obvious, way. The same period saw the setting up of farmers' recruiting organisations. But although these were modelled, organisationally, on those operating for the mining houses, unlike them, they do not appear to have directed their recruiting efforts beyond South Africa's boundaries. If anything, farm labour recruiting organisations have tended to concentrate their operations on the reserves within the country.

'Internalisation' is closely tied up with the second trend, namely the *localisation* of labour supplies. Restructuring has led to a tendency for farmers to look to the nearest source for their labour supply. Figuratively speaking, they seem to work through a band of concentric and ever-broadening circles. Beginning with the on-farm workforce, they look for labour from other farms in the district, in the black urban ghettoes of so-called white towns and in settlements in the reserves, the order being determined by which of these is the nearest, most accessible, and best supplied. It would seem, indeed, that the decline in the number and proportion of foreign workers employed in the sector has less to do with the fact that they are foreign, and more to do with their distance from the source of employment. This argument is borne out by practices in districts close to the borders. Here farmers continue to make extensive use of foreign workers. For example, in the Malelane-Komatipoort region of the Transvaal Lowveld, farmers were reported to have 'no problems in obtaining labourers as it is close to some homelands and Swaziland with their reservoirs of labour' (Brotherton, 1980:91). Mozambique, too, is a supplier of agricultural labour to this region: there were an estimated 7,000 Mozambicans working on the farms here in 1984.[21]

Localising labour supplies, it would seem, disproportionately disadvantages those workers who are furthest from the source of employment. This, of course, does not only affect foreign workers, but equally operates against the people relocated in remote resettlement camps. Few farmers come looking for labour in these isolated, overcrowded and distant places, and when from time to time their trucks do arrive, the competition for work is fierce, as unemployment and poverty are endemic.

A further point about the trend towards localisation of labour supplies is that it has not been specific to areas where labour tenancy was extensively practised, and from where people have been forcibly removed. In the Western Transvaal region, De Klerk found that:

> Labour tenancy ... appears never to have been widespread and there are only a few instances recorded of black families being removed from white-owned land ... Whereas in 1968 workers drawn from 'external' sources, i.e., Bophuthatswana, Transkei, etc., could count on about 100 work places per 1,000 ha of maize harvested, by 1981 the number was less than 20. Even those from 'internal' sources, i.e., who lived on white farms, whose share of employment had grown so much, benefited little in net terms: from ten jobs per 1,000 ha in 1968, the actual number increased to only 16 in 1981 (De Klerk, 1984:9).

As with 'internalisation', the 'localisation' of labour supply is not peculiar to commercial agriculture, but is to be found generally in the political economy. For all forms of employment, the more distant the worker is from the source the less chance there is of ever finding work. In this way the reserve system and the displaced urbanisation that its creation and establishment has entailed, has meant that the burden of unemployment is geographically (and socially) unevenly spread. The heaviest burden falls on those forced into, and contained within, the remote and rural population concentrations which fill the reserves.

Changes in the division between 'full-time' and 'part-time' employment

Restructuring has also seen a tendency for employment to become more casualised. This is most clearly evidenced by the shifts in the division between what is termed 'full-time' and 'part-time' work. The easiest way to show such a shift would be to look at changes in the ratio between these two categories. Given the available data base, however, this is not possible. The main obstacle is the question of definition, how 'part-time' and 'full-time' work are defined in commercial agriculture. The division between categories is drawn on the basis of a combination of different criteria, including the time period over which the worker is employed, his or her status and the tasks themselves. The diverse assumptions on which the distinctions are made are reflected in the terms used to describe them. Full-time workers are also called 'permanent' and/or 'regular' — emphasising now status, now the period of employment. Part-time workers, also called 'casual' and 'seasonal', are defined, in part, by the tasks they fulfil, in part by the time period of their employment, and in part by the way they are employed. All these terms are misleading, if not deceptive, because they stem, in the first place, from the subjective assessment of the employers. So, for example, migrant workers are not classed as 'full-time' or 'regular' workers because they are employed on contract, or they 'commute' to and from the farm the year round. Similarly, workers are deemed 'part-time' even though they may well be 'short-time' on a daily basis, for example, as dairy parlour workers ('dairymaids'), whose 'casual' employment means two shifts per day, lasting several hours each, seven days a week. Or in fact, they work full-time on a task which is paid by the piece. In the Eastern Cape, for example, 'often jointed cactus eradication gangs work for months if not all year but are not regarded as regular workers' because of the way they are paid (Antrobus, 1984:84). Since the statistical information available is based on these unclear definitions, it is plain that it is unreliable as an indicator of actual or comparative relations.

Instead these changes should be assessed qualitatively, in the context of an absolute decline in employment and a quantitatively fluctuating contingent of 'casual' workers. Essentially, changes have come about in two, often closely connected ways. The first is as a result of the redefinition of employment that derives from the migrantisation of a large part of agriculture's labour force. As migrant workers replace workers resident on the farms, the tasks formerly done by so-called 'permanent' workers are now being done by migrants, who, by definition, are made temporary and impermanent through the imposition of a stipulated and limited employment period. In other words, the casualisation of employment here stems directly from the changed status of the worker from 'servant' to 'migrant'. This has long been a feature of employment on the sugar fields, for example, where much of the 'regular' workload has been met by migrant workers, whether on contract and resident on the estate/farm, or 'commuters' drawn from the reserves of Natal, which are interspersed among the so-called 'white areas'. In fact, the migrant employment year is so divided that workers are contracted for nine to ten months (Budlender, 1984:28). By this means, not only are the 'regular' tasks met by 'seasonal' workers, but the overlapping contract periods also enable sugar farmers to meet their peak labour needs during the harvest period. Similarly, in the Western Cape, Wilson writes:

> One of the most interesting and surprising features of the migrant system that operates in the Hex River Valley is that the labour is not seasonal. It has been roughly estimated that up to 80 percent of the recruits are on full 12-month contracts (Wilson, 1972:21).

A decade later in the Stellenbosch district, about 70 percent of the labour force in viticulture were migrants from the Herschel district, who lived 'on the farms for the whole year bar a period of a few weeks when they were forced to return to the reserves (Budlender, 1984:14). Clearly then, their categorisation as 'part-time' ('seasonal') workers has little to do with the period over which they are employed and much to do with the fact that they are migrants. Moreover, it can be anticipated (if it is not already the reality)[22] that the more widespread the use of migrant labour, the more general this process will be.

This must seem even more uncertain when the second form of casualisation is taken into consideration, i.e., the reorganisation of the work process itself. Once again, this revolves around breaking down 'full-time' employment, since 'part-time' work is already an expression of a casualised labour force. Restructuring, and especially the trend to rationalise production, has led to many tasks in the production process being reorganised or redivided both on a daily basis and over a period of time. Breaking down the work process into its component parts has made changes in the composition of the labour force easier. So, for example, harvesting is not conceived as a single procedure but as a set of parts. For maize, these parts include reaping, threshing, transporting and storing; for sugar, cutting the cane, stacking, loading and if necessary transloading it for transport off the farm. This breakdown of tasks is considered central to 'modern farm management' and is one of the services offered white farmers by state extension officers and researchers (Brotherton, 1980). In consequence, it is possible not only to control the labour of 'full-time' workers more tightly, and to use their labour time more intensively, but also to allocate work tasks on a more piecemeal basis as so-called 'part-time' jobs.

This trend has, in turn, resulted in changes in the allocation of 'part-time' work. And, it would seem, it has diametrically-opposed implications for the two halves of a labour force physically divided between those resident on the farms and those drawn from the labour reserves. An absolute reduction of workers in the sector and a substantially reduced on-farm labour pool have meant an increase in 'part-time' employment for on-farm workers and a decline in such employment for those drawn from the reserves. This increase/decline has been two dimensional. One has stemmed from a trend towards allocating more so-called 'casual' jobs to workers already on the farm, thereby making fewer available for workers drawn from off-farm sources. This development is tied up with the localisation process referred to earlier. The other has been produced by an alteration in the ratio of what De Klerk calls 'job occupancy' for 'part-time' workers in favour of workers drawn from the farm's labour pool and at the expense of those who have been made migrant. So on-farm 'casual' workers are likely to do more than one task, and are more likely to be repeatedly employed in any given period than their counterparts from the labour reservoirs. For many of these migrantised workers, however, casualisation is taken to the extreme, where labour turnover occurs literally on a daily, weekly or monthly basis.[23] This is what lies behind farmer solutions to the problems of 'lumpiness' and harvest peaks, which derive from changing demands for labour in the course of the production cycle. On the one hand, casualisation has facilitated farmer efforts to reduce costs and their dependence on black labour by only taking on the workers they need, as they need them. On the other hand, it has made possible the more intense exploitation of those they do employ.

In short, casualisation has a direct impact on the way the labour process is divided over time. With it, not only do we see a trend to break 'full-time' employment down, but also a tendency to reorganise the allocation of the work that is made 'part-time'. These processes are made possible by the reorganisation of production procedures (Bekker, 1982:14), and the physical division of workers between those living on and off the farms. In turn, they are closely bound up with shifts in the way that the agricultural workforce is divided by gender and age.

Changes in the exploitation of female and child labour

'If the women and children don't work, we don't eat'
(*Rand Daily Mail,* 20 February 1980)

Restructuring has seen both quantitative and qualitative shifts in the gender and age composition of agriculture's workforce. In order to deal adequately with these changes, it is necessary to sketch out the framework in which these divisions can be explained. When looking at the question of female and child labour it is usual to describe them separately, since they are two forms of exploitation — one, gender, or the social definition of sexual differences; the other, age, also a socially defined relation. Yet they are intimately linked, because these forms of exploitation derive from the same set of social relations. They stem from a social system organised around 'the family' (however defined), which, in turn, is based on the presumption of the direct employment of male labour and the subordination and dependence of women and children. This is not to say that in practice only men work, or are the main breadwinners of 'the family', but, rather, that it is their labour power which is the standard against which other sellers of labour power are evaluated. Nor is it to suggest that all male labour is evaluated equally. In the South African context, class divisions combine with national oppression and racial discrimination to place black and white men — and therefore black and white women and children — in objectively different positions in the social system. In other words, there is no equality in female subordination, or child dependence, in a social formation divided by class exploitation and national domination.

In commercial agriculture, the labour of women and children has been and is commanded in one of two ways. One is as dependants and subordinates within 'the family' and the social relations imposed on a black family living on a white man's farm. Paradoxically, prior to this second phase of restructuring, commercial agriculture was one of the few sectors in which a large part of the African workforce was family based. Yet this stemmed from the quasi-feudal terms under which the farmer permitted a black worker to live with his family on the farm, and was conditional upon the free (unwaged) labour of the women and children whenever the farmer demanded it. The terms of black family life were therefore predicated on the servitude and bondage of the family.

The other way in which their labour is commanded casts women and children as individual 'sellers' of labour power. This relation has been particularly important for black and especially African women workers, since historically commercial agriculture has been one of the two largest sectors in which they have been able to find employment (the other is the service sector). Partly, this stems from the poor terms of employment in the sector, which have made it the least attractive to the working class as a whole. Therefore, and in order to meet its labour needs (aside from the use of direct compulsion), the sector has had to rely extensively on the most vulnerable sections of the working class — a category into which black women squarely fall. Partly, it arises from the specific conditions of African national oppression: a relatively high proportion of African women are employed in the sector because it has been one of the few avenues of 'waged' labour open to them.

Thus black women and children, through direct or indirect compulsion, have been drawn into and made a part of agriculture's workforce. This, in turn, is integrally related to their position in the labour force within the sector and the political economy as a whole.

Restructuring, and in particular the casualisation and migrantisation of the workforce, are central to understanding changes in female and child labour exploitation. In order to highlight the main features of these changes, it is necessary to look first at the position of women and children in the labour force and the changes that have come about in relation to male workers, adult workers and the labour market as a whole. Then separately, one must examine the way their labour is commanded. This division for analytic purposes should not obscure the fact that these two aspects of their exploitation are connected in practice. Furthermore, two forms of exploitation are being treated — female and child — and changes in one directly affect the position of the other. In consequence, it is necessary to treat female and child labour both separately and together when analysing the impact of restructuring.

The position of women and children in the workforce

The feminisation of agriculture's labour force
The second phase of restructuring in South African commercial agriculture has generally seen a steady replacement of male by female workers. Although this process has been far from straightforward, its roots lie in the structurally weak and disadvantaged position of black women in the political economy which have been outlined above. This position has been aggravated even further.

First, the shift in the ratio between men and women farm workers has to be seen in the context of an absolute decline in employment in the sector for all workers. This decline has most severely affected African women. This is not only because the number of jobs open to them in the sector has dropped by a dramatic 46.6 percent over the period 1970-81 (from an official figure of 543,900 to 289,280) (Bird, 1985:79), but also because the contraction of their employment in agriculture has served to further constrict the limited job opportunities open to them. In the absence of alternative avenues of employment, their position in the labour market has been made even more marginal.

Only in the Western Cape has the process of feminisation been accompanied by a real increase in female employment for a particular section of the agrarian working class — namely, Coloured women workers. Their employment on the farms in the region actually grew by some 143.7 percent over the decade 1970-80. The measure of this absolute increase has to be taken against that for Coloured farm labour in general, which rose by some 14 percent in the same period. Indeed, on some farms in the region, there was one Coloured man for every twelve women employed as 'full-time' workers (*Die Burger*, 2 February 1983). This regionally specific development is itself the outcome of a combination of forces centring around the particularities of African national oppression and female exploitation, which make Coloured women one of the cheapest sources of adult waged labour there. Within the overriding context of the Coloured labour preference area they are amongst the cheapest because:

1. African women (and children) are discounted as competitors in any meaningful

sense as the policy is most stringently applied against them;[24]

2. the poor terms on the farms and the bad conditions in the reserves make migrantised African male workers unwilling to take up jobs in the sector. At the same time, the trend to localise labour supplies weighs as a counter against those migrants who have no option but to accept the bad terms of employment offered;

3. the policy relatively advantages Coloured men in terms of employment possibilities in other sectors.

It would seem that it is this combination of conditions which has stimulated a real growth in Coloured female employment in commercial agriculture.

Second, the generally negative implications that feminisation of the workforce carries for both women and the working class as a whole are tied up with the way that men have been replaced by women farm workers. The trend towards feminisation of the workforce has come about in two ways. The first, when one set of workers replaces another in the same job, is a process of direct substitution. This type of substitution, whilst not representing an improvement in conditions, does not necessarily imply their deterioration either. Often, however, it does mean this as well. It is essentially a device used by employers to counteract any pressure from workers to improve the terms of employment.

In practice, particularly within 'full-time' work in commercial agriculture, this type of substitution has been relatively rare. Few women (or child) farm workers have in the past been considered 'regular' workers and it would seem that, with the exception of the Western Cape, there has been little change in the course of restructuring. Thus, in 1976 Antrobus found that, on the mixed farming enterprises of the Albany district in the Eastern Cape, women classed as 'regular' workers represented less than ten percent of the 'full-time' workforce (Antrobus, 1984:77). In the Western Cape, however, the particular conditions there, and the real growth in female employment, have been accompanied by a relatively substantial, direct substitution process, with women representing a quarter of the 'regular' workforce in 1980 (*Die Burger*, 2 February 1983).

Direct substitution has also taken place with respect to 'part-time' work, but here it is children who replace adult women and men in the scramble for jobs. Thus in his study of maize farms De Klerk (1984:10) found that

> women formed the backbone of almost all seasonal harvest teams and appear to have always done so. Men made up a declining and children a steadily rising proportion. Whereas in 1968 all but a few teams included men and only 30 percent included children, 13 years later only about 40 percent had adult male members as against 65 percent which incorporated children.

The second, more frequent and perhaps more significant way in which women and children have replaced male farm workers relates to the casualisation of the labour force and the fact that most 'part-time' work has been and is done by female and child labour. In other words, the breakdown and reorganisation of 'full-time' jobs into their 'part-time' components has been accompanied by a substitution of male 'regular' by female 'casual' workers. As one farmer explained: 'We are making more and more use, with very pleasant results, of the women doing the work (which was) formerly the accepted work of the men (Darrington and Darrington, 1976:5). So we see 'one woman and a milking machine' replacing three male milkers (Van der Vliet and Bromberger, 1976); or women and children replace men in the sugar fields as mechanical means are introduced to stack and load the cane (Budlender, 1984:19). This is where the explanation lies for the paradox behind farmers' claims that they are cutting back on employment and at the same time making more use of women (Van der Vliet and Bromberger, 1976). It is clear that, if anything, substitution of this type represents an intensification of exploitation.

The substitution of children for adults

Parallel to the trend towards feminisation has been a tendency to replace adults by child workers. In part, this process (as with feminisation) can be attributed to the casualisation of the labour force, since historically children have been and remain 'part-time' workers. But this does not account for the process as a whole. At the same time as the proportion of children in the farm labour force has increased, the increase has not been evenly spread amongst them. There has been a disproportionate increase in the use of child labour resident on the farms which cannot be explained by casualisation alone. The creation of an on-farm 'core' labour force has simultaneously seen a substantial part of agriculture's labour pool relocated in distant reservoirs, and a significant reduction of the part still remaining on 'white' farm land. This fact, coupled with the tendency for farmers to draw on local labour supplies first, has meant that they have tended to mine the labour reserves of the diminished on-farm group of workers more intensely. Given that the residential workforce in commercial agriculture is family-based (for the most part), this intensified pressure has inevitably been directed most sharply at the children. It is also clear that the increased use of child labour in the sector has not only intensified the exploitation of children, but, in so doing, has further marginalised African women in the labour market as they are forced into unequal competition with children for jobs.

The greater exploitation of child labour is inseparable from the way their labour and the labour of women is commanded. And these changes are tied up with the migrantisation of a large part of the workforce. Before these matters can be considered, however, the question arises whether a figure can be put on the number of children employed in the sector or the proportionate increase in their employment? The short answer is no. Whilst all the qualitative data on commercial agriculture point to its being the most extensive and systematic exploiter of black child labour in the South African political economy, the number of children this affects is unknown. The official agricultural census does not even ask if farmers employ children, let alone how many, and although farmers acknowledge (tacitly for the most part) that child labour is integral to their 'part-time' workforce, the numbers they admit to are invariably (grossly) understated.

Quantitative data on 'part-time' employment is itself far removed from the realm of 'hard fact', not least because of its failure to account for child labour. This means that any figure which might be given for child labour is an estimate of an estimate. It is a problem which is further compounded by the qualitative aspect of this form of labour. It encourages the tendency to conceal the extent of 'casual' employment since it is less socially acceptable to employ children.

'Casual' and 'child' thus combine to disguise the extent of the employment of children in a myriad of ways. Farmer estimates are likely to exclude the work put in by a child who is told 'to get his school clothes off ... and dig sweet potatoes' to replace his father whom the farmer claims is 'shamming illness';[25] the routine work children render before and after and even during school hours; the labour utilised when they are picked up by those unenumerated lorries which move between the reserves and the farms with their cargoes of 'casual' workers, etc.

Even at the micro-level a general figure for the number of children employed is hard to come by. This is not only because few studies on farm labour have tried to quantify the extent to which child labour is used, but also because the methods and criteria used have differed from one type of work to another. This means that these results are not strictly comparable. They are nonetheless revealing. A pilot study of extensive livestock farming in the Albany district found that, of the 615 'part-time' workers employed on the ten farms surveyed, 129 or 25 percent were 18 years or under (Van der Vliet and Bromberger, 1976:5). Of these youths and children, more than 98 percent were female. This finding sheds some light on Antrobus's later study which, although it did not specifically address this question, found that 90 percent of 'casual' work was done by women (Antrobus, 1984:86). Presumably a substantial minority of this total were young girls. In another example, grape farmers of the Hex River Valley estimated that no fewer than 51 percent of the seasonal workers who did not live on the farms were children of school-going age (Levy, 1976:34). This figure is far higher than the 'roughly nine percent' estimation of the University of South Africa (UNISA) study of Coloured child 'casual' employment in the Cape.[26]

Two things are evident: first, children make up a substantial minority of the 'part-time' workforce; second, that in order to quantify the extent to which their labour is exploited in the sector, it is necessary for researchers to look explicitly into all aspects of the question.

Changes in the way the labour of women and children is commanded

Changes in the position of women and children in the agricultural labour force are also intimately connected to and shaped by shifts in the way their labour is commanded. Here, once again, both the physical redivision of the labour force and its casualisation are the key processes which explain the impact and direction of these changes.

Forced labour

It remains the unwritten understanding 'that when a man was taken into regular employment members of his family could be called upon whenever necessary to perform such work as may be required' (Antrobus, 1984:89). The labour of women and children continues to be indirectly commanded through their position as members of black worker families resident on 'white' farms. Restructuring, as already indicated, has brought about some changes which have affected both the extent and intensity of this compulsory labour. With the paring down of the labour reserve resident on the farms, this type of labour has intensified for on-farm worker families.

But the impact has not been borne equally by women and child workers.

For women working and living within the 'family' on 'white' farms restructuring has intensified farmers' demands on labour time. Farmers have not only made more use of their labour on the farms, but also extended and tightened control over their employment elsewhere. Their captive position is summed up by the experiences of workers on a farm in the Middelburg district (Transvaal).

> These farms are close to the Arnot mine and power station. Since there are a huge living quarters for the whites employed there, women on the farms could easily get jobs as domestic servants. The farmer has explicitly forbidden this as he needs the women for hoeing and picking during harvest. Hence, these women forfeit a cash income at a time when they are not needed for farm work (Seleoane, 1984:18).

To defy the farmer would mean that the 'full-time' worker would lose his job and the whole family would be expelled.

Conversely, the physical relocation of much of agriculture's labour pool into the reserves and black urban ghettos in 'white areas' has meant a decline in this type of compulsory labour for women farm workers as proportionately fewer of them are living on the farms.

This in turn has had a direct bearing on the extent and intensity of the exploitation of the child labour reserves within the black residential farm worker family. The changed position of child labour in the agricultural labour force, and particularly the disproportionate increase in the use made of on-farm child labour, is directly linked to the declining pool of adult women living on the farms.

Increasingly, employment and residence on the farm for the black worker family gravitates around the size of the family and the preparedness of children to work for the farmer. Thus,

> if you have children who are of working age — the farmer decides — and he wants them to do some work on the farm, they can refuse only at the risk of having the entire family ejected (Levy, 1976).

Greater recourse to child labour is not confined to the farmer and the workers on a particular enterprise. It extends to the general black child labour pool living in a countryside claimed and commanded by the white man. And it is also tied up with the tendency of farmers to look first for workers from the nearest local source. There is, for example, a trend towards the extensive use of schools as a ready source of labour.

The pressure for schooling in the countryside stems overwhelmingly from the working people themselves. At the same time, the existence of most, if not all, black rural schools derives directly from the patronage of the farmers. So, whether farm workers' children are allowed to attend school or not, when farm or rural schools are allowed to operate, and indeed whether they are allowed to open at all, are all matters decided by the demands of the farmer. This does not only mean that school 'holidays' are timed to coincide with seasonal peaks in the production cycle, but that the school day itself is organised around the demands made on child labour during the working day. In keeping with the power relations existent in colonial commercial agriculture in South Africa, starting and finishing times are adjusted to ensure that school does not interfere with the work children are expected to do before and after lessons. Moreover, the farmer can (and does) prevent them from attending school, or plucks them out of the classroom at any given moment. Thus, whether drawing directly on the farm, or indirectly through the collectivised child labour pools that country schools provide, restructuring has intensified and expanded the exploitation of child labour in the black worker family.

This change would also suggest a two-way shift in the balance of dependence within this particular family relation, which maintains its presence as a social unit in the 'white' countryside only through the labour resources it can muster. One shift relates to the fact that, for adult family members (and this applies particularly to the male 'unit of labour' who is also the head of a household) their employment revolves around the willingness (or otherwise) of their children to be pressed into forced labour. The ambivalent position that parents are put in, as a result of this, is expressed by one worker on a farm where children are expected to start working as soon as they turn twelve. He said that the children enjoyed working. Yet, when pressed and asked what he would do if his son, for example, did not enjoy the work and did not want to do it, his reply was 'I would make sure that he enjoys it' (Seleoane, 1984:22).

The other shift centres on the breakdown of the black worker family as a social unit on the farm. In order for children to avoid being forced into work, they have to leave the farms. Sometimes they are sent away by their parents who try to protect them from a lifetime of enslavement. Often, they leave against the will of their parents who, as has been shown, depend on them for their own employment and residence on the farm. Sometimes, they are chased off the farms by the farmers themselves who, whilst not necessarily evicting the family as a whole, will only allow people 'willing to work' to remain on their land. (It might be added here that this practice has also intensified the vulnerability of the aged and infirm who face a similar fate.) Whichever way they are forced to leave, children are unable to live with their families. As often as not, even visiting them becomes impossible due to harassment by farmers and police, who physically abuse and/or arrest them on sight (Seleoane, 1984:22).

Individual 'sellers' of labour power

The larger proportion of women, and a growing percentage of children, are entering the sector's labour force as individual 'sellers' of labour power. Whilst this is not a new phenomenon, for women at least, what is new is the extension of the practice to children, as well as its scale. Particularly, it is the outcome of the destruction of labour and rent tenancy, the cutback in the number of 'full-time' worker families living on the farms and the reorganisation of production processes. Simultaneously, there has been the physical relocation of a substantial part of agriculture's labour pool from white-owned farm land to the reserves and the urban ghettos of 'white' towns. It is from these concentrations of black unemployed people — the majority of whom are women and youth — that such 'sellers' are drawn into the sector.

What is the significance of this development for the position of female and child agricultural workers?

Clearly the exploitation of women and children as individual 'sellers' of labour power, no less than earlier forms of exploitation, presumes the socially disadvantaged position in which their gender, age and colour place them in the South African political economy.

Perhaps of prime importance is the changes it indicates in their position in the 'family', which is inseparably connected to change in the relation of that 'family' to the white farmer. At the same time as relocation removes the obligation to labour for the farmer by virtue of their dependence in a residential farm worker family, the relation of the black on-farm worker family is rephrased in the broader context of the black worker 'family' and its relation to all employers, farmers included. In other words, their position is no longer only shaped by the particular relations in the sector — that 'we are no longer under the cruel farmer' — but rather by the general relations in the political economy as a whole: 'we are starving here' (SPP, 1984: Vol.2, 212).

These, we know, are not simply determined by capitalist production relations, but also by the terms of African national oppression. This, in turn, raises the whole question of the relation of the reserves and the migrant labour system to the position of African women. It would seem that their containment within (if not confinement to) the reserves is neither accidental, nor incidental to the perpetuation of national and class oppression in changing socio-political conditions. Women are, after all, the physical as well as the social reproducers of the labour force and the African majority. Control over their location is a key mechanism in the perpetuation of oscillating migration which presumes the dislocation of production and physical/social reproduction.

The migrant labour system generates the most extreme form of familial disintegration. Social relations are so fragmented as to transform each member into a potential unit of labour, deprived of the social and economic bonds which make interdependency possible. Thus millions of men and women, old and young, are forced to find the means of socially reproducing themselves on a daily basis, in any way they can. The situation in which they find themselves does not preclude collective efforts, nor does it mean that migrant workers do not remit money to their families, but it does ensure for the majority a bitter, often atomised struggle for survival. For African women flung into these conditions the choices are few. Apart from extensive controls over their movement to the towns, industrial employment is a limited and declining opening which means that domestic and farm work are the two main avenues of 'waged' work allowed them. This is the force that drives African women back to the farms under terms little different from those applying to women compelled to labour by virtue of their position in the black residential farm worker family.

In some respects their situation is even worse, since jobs are few, unemployment is rife, the prospect of food is uncertain and, to top it all, they are forced into open and unequal competition with children. 'The white man said he didn't want mature people working for him, only children who would work for nothing … the children work for nothing'.[27]

The recruitment of children

Restructuring in commercial agriculture has seen the extensive and open recruitment of child labour. Farmers prefer children because their labour is not only cheaper but also more controllable. It is a pattern which fits comfortably into their extensive exploitation of on-farm and local sources. Whilst even in the first phase of restructuring it was not uncommon for farmers to abduct black children off the streets in urban areas, now the open lorry loads of children (and women) coursing between the farms and reserves have become commonplace throughout the country. Sometimes they are picked up and taken directly to the farm; sometimes they are transported to a central depot and distributed from there to the farmers (Anti-Slavery Society, 1984:28).

These children shoulder the full burden of the migrant labour system. For some, this means travelling to and from the reserves daily. Others spend only the weekend at home and many 'come back home once a month on a Saturday and go again on Sunday'.[28] In short, the weight of national oppression and social exploitation for African women and children means 'incredible poverty, terrible congestion, unemployment and hunger' (Anti-Slavery Society, 1984:28) in the huge concentrations of the dispossessed that the reserves and the migrant labour system represent. These are the changed terms of compulsion which drive African women and children on to the farms as 'sellers' of labour power.

At the same time, black women (and to a lesser extent children) are also being drawn from the urban ghettoes of 'white' towns to labour on the farms. The forces underlying their search for work and their compulsion into farm labour are the less extreme (relatively speaking), more 'normal' conditions of capitalist social relations.

The most important of these include the individualisation of labour and the trend towards a nuclear family; the inadequacy of a single (male) wage to sustain family social reproduction; the breakdown of the 'family' and the imposition of the dual burden on black women of bringing in income while caring for dependants (children, the aged, the infirm); the restricted avenues of employment open to them, and so on. In short, this is a combination which spells poverty and hunger, the driving forces which compel people to work in socially unacceptable and extreme conditions.[29]

The change to a more individualised workforce and the transformation of women and children into 'sellers' of labour power cannot be interpreted as a shift from compulsory to voluntary labour in the sector. Rather, and particularly in view of the way child labour is procured, it underlines the softness of the distinction between compelled and voluntary labour in a social system where the majority of workers — Africans — are directed and controlled by pass laws, influx control regulations and the migrant labour system; and in a sector which relies extensively on overtly compelled black labour — either that of women and children through the worker families living on farms, or that of male prison labour.[30] That a section of the female and child labour force comes to the farms as 'sellers' of their labour power indicates no more than a change in the form of compulsion driving them into the sector. Relatively speaking, it signals the use of less overt, more indirect force, but force nonetheless.

The depths of the oppression of black women and children

The way age and colour combine, through gender, with national oppression and class exploitation makes the oppression of African women extreme even on the South African scale. The depths to which it goes are greater than the analysis has so far revealed.

That women and children are forced to compete with one another for jobs, and that women and men are often driven by necessity to 'sell' the labour of their children, does not only reflect the extent to which the sector exploits child labour. It also indicates an intensification of female oppression and the further marginalisation of women, both economically and socially. Their position is aggravated by worsening conditions in the reserves and rising unemployment. Their need for waged work has never been so great, and the chances of getting waged work have never been so remote. Thus, the contraction of jobs under restructuring is more layered and carries more consequences than employment figures suggest.

That a substantial part of the child labour force is made up of young girls reinforces the contention that the oppression and exploitation of women has intensified. Although they are children and bear the full weight of being exploited as child labour, that they are female is not incidental to their position. They also bear the full burden of womanhood. In the South African countryside this means extensive sexual exploitation. Sexual favours (given or taken) and the sale of sex for money are often the only terms on which women can get employment on the farms, or survive in the conditions of forced labour which prevail there. This condition is not confined to adults. In other words, the fact that children are female is often part of the reason why they are recruited by farmers.

> 'On the farms not only did farmers underpay and ill-treat the children, but ... they also used girls as they pleased ... Many coloured children have come from those recruited child girls'.[31]

In somewhat similar vein, many girls are expected, after working in the fields ,or kitchens all day, to provide sexual services to the male workers.

> 'When we complain to the farmer that all our daughters are turned into prostitutes, he says there is nothing we can do about it. They want the men'.[32]

No less revealing is the content of the work that women and children are expected to perform. There are two aspects at issue here. One concerns the actual nature of the work. Closely related is the pervasive and rather elaborate, if contradictory, ideology surrounding female and child labour and its use in these tasks. Both casualisation and migrantisation have served to perpetuate and extend the concentration of women and children in 'part-time' work, which predominantly takes the form of labour-intensive, heavy, physical manual labour — sometimes formerly done by men, sometimes 'traditionally' by women. Whichever way, it is by the sweat of female and child labour that most products are now harvested. They spend from sun-up to sundown in the fields on back-breaking tasks, plucking fruit, tea, tobacco and cotton; lifting chicory, groundnuts, potatoes and cabbage; picking tomatoes, pineapples and flowers, etc. They glean behind the combine harvesters which, fitted with overhead lights, move through thousands of hectares of maize and wheat day and night. They wield hoes the year round, weeding the fields. Where this method has been replaced by chemical control, they carry the canisters in knapsacks on their backs 'covering about one hectare a day'. They plant the cane and spread the fertiliser, which, in the sugar fields, for example, is 'usually applied by workers carrying 20 kg pouches and distributing the mixture with a tin as a scoop — one tin per so many paces.[33] They thin the grapes, lay and relay the irrigation pipes, build and break down the banks of flood-irrigation canals, milk the cows, churn the cream, wash down the milking equipment and the sheds, herd the livestock, etc. They also wash the clothes of farmers and their families, clean their houses, cook their food, care for their children, tend their domestic pets and their gardens — either when they have finished their farm chores or 'full-time'. The inescapable conclusion is that on 'the farms you work very hard — even today' (Barrett et al.,1985:70).

It is true that black men are driven as relentlessly on the farms. But it is necessary to underscore the physical and arduous nature of the work done by female and child labour on the farms, both because it is not reflected in their material reward, and because it is openly contested across the broad spectrum of prevailing ideology. The myth projected is a double-headed coin expressing the currency that the work they do is light. Typical of one side is the recent work of Budlender, who writes of weed eradication work in the vineyards of Stellenbosch, for example:

'Up until two years ago (early 80s) ... women were employed where light hoes were used, but for the strenuous work of 'bankies gooi' it was necessary to employ men'.[34]

The other side is encapsulated in the widely held view that 'part-time' work is light by definition, because it is not 'full-time'. The tautology is rather extended, but for all that is no less circular, implying that, in general, women and children do light work because they are employed in 'casual' jobs which are by definition 'light' and therefore are naturally suited to female and child labour.

Restructuring has strengthened the mythology. The reorganisation of the work process has proportionately increased female and child labour and redefined gender and age characteristics associated with certain tasks — women and children are doing jobs which were formerly associated with men. Then there is the widely held misconception that machines automatically make labour lighter. 'In terms of sheer physical strength all those changes which have allowed increasing employment of women have also meant that the work is less strenuous' (Budlender, 1984:13).

The logic of the ideology can lead to an absurd conclusion, namely that the employment policies and practices of white farmers in South Africa are not guided by the combination of capitalist greed, race hatred and contempt for women that might be expected from the conditions of social exploitation that prevail in the sector. Rather, they are motivated by an extraordinary altruism which is hypersensitive to all the nuances of those allegedly natural biological, physiological and racial differences on which they believe the social division of labour to be based. In other words, they employ women and children in monotonous, strenuous, low-paid work which involves long, often unsociable and irregular working hours, not because men refuse to do the work and women and children are the cheapest form of 'waged' labour, but because women and children 'are more efficient, reliable and meticulous — especially at certain jobs like wool sorting and Sunday milking', and 'more careful and gentle with the handling of fruit than are the men.' There are even 'women's jobs like hoeing and cleaning the separator — which men won't do' (Van der Vliet and Bromberger, 1976). They do all these jobs 'so natural-ly' compatible with their gender and age, only when their equally 'natural' racial characteristics do not obstruct them. Then force has to be used to overcome the 'sheer laziness' that white farmers believe characterises African womanhood. As a farmer put it:

> 'I really have to lay down the law. Otherwise they'd be quite happy to laze their time away at the huts. They could earn R1.50 a week ... there is all the bush on the farm to be chopped ... (but) they're just not interested' (Antrobus, 1984:89).

The ideology nothwithstanding, the raw and rude reality is that women and children are employed because their labour is the cheapest and most coercible labour power available to the farmer. As GJ Knobel, MP (and farmer) explained to Parliament:

> 'I want to mention an example. When they had had good rains and the maize had to be treated with DDT against stalk borers, the hybrid kaffir corn had to be hoed and the deviations had to be weeded, my son (who runs the farm with only five Bantu) came to me and told me he did not have enough labourers. Then I told him to go to the principal of the Bantu school — it was during the holidays — and ask him whether every Bantu pupil, boys and girls, above the age of eight could work for him on the land the next day. And sir, they did that work as well as any big, fat grown up Bantu woman could do it and the work costs much less that way' (Hansard: Vol.19, Col.198).

The distribution of child labour.
The question arises whether restructuring has had an impact on the distribution of child labour in the sector. Has it led to differential employment practices between large and small farming enterprises with respect to children? On the one hand, it can be anticipated, and is in fact practice, that small farmers under financial pressures and constraints tend to make extensive use of child labour in order to keep going. On the other hand, and contrary to expectations, the practice of employing children on large enterprises seems no less widespread. Thus, on one of the then Minister of Agriculture, Hendrik Schoeman's sixteen citrus farms in the Eastern Transvaal, of the 1,800 African workers employed 80 percent were 'casuals'. According to his son, Karel 'seven lorries collected 700 casual workers — both women and children — and returned them to their villages (in the Lebowa bantustan) daily' (Anti-Slavery Society, 1984:46). In fact, there are few large estates which do not employ child labour. Nasson's recent study of 20 Cape farmers, for example, found that there was

> 'only one larger estate which expressly prohibited the employment of *all* children under the age of 16. In all other cases, farmers acknowledged that farm pupils

were often involved in what they were at pains to describe as light, part-time work' (Nasson, 1984:27).

On the available evidence, however, it is not possible to assess whether they employ proportionately fewer children than smaller enterprises, which is also a possibility. What is clear is that all sections of commercial agriculture, whether organised on large or small enterprises, exploit child labour. This means, in terms of the changing labour forms and conditions, intensified exploitation.

Changes in the prison labour system.

White farmers continue to use the state extensively as a direct procurer and provider of labour through its prison system, making prison labour an integral component of the agricultural workforce. The second phase of restructuring has only brought changes in detail to the basic system elaborated in the 1940s and 1950s. Essentially, three channels operate to supply prison labour to the sector — Aid centres, parole release and the lease system. 'As a farmer, confirming the value of rights to convict labour once explained "it's like having water on your farm"(IDAF,1980).'

Aid Centres.
When press exposure and public outrage forced it to suspend the 'inter-departmental scheme', the state could identify the problem only as a technical one. Not unexpectedly, it proposed a technical solution — to establish 'Aid Centres'. This scheme was introduced in 1964, under the Bantu Laws Amendment Act, and differed from its predecessor only in that it now gave

> statutory authority to the procedures which had previously taken place outside the law. Instead of the procedure whereby the police were instructed to hand pass offenders directly to the employment officer at the district labour bureau, the new machinery provided for the police to 'admit' or 'refer' Africans directly to the centres or transfer them to centres from police cells or prison (Cook, 1982:24).

It remains a device for channelling 'technical offenders' to the farms or into the reserves without the costly formalities of prosecution.

In 1969, farmer agitation over labour shortages stimulated the state to set these centres up in earnest, and by the end of 1973, at least 18 were in full operation in various parts of the country. Their workings, like all other aspects of the prison system, is shrouded in secrecy as it is screened by law from public scrutiny.

Nevertheless, the number of Africans 'placed in employment' through Aid Centres reveals the extent of its operations. In 1975 the scheme sent 21,636 to the farms, and in 1979, 18,627 (Cook, 1982:26).

Release on parole
Until 1986 (when the pass laws were abolished) the parole system, formerly the '9d-a-day scheme', continued to be the main channel by which farmers were supplied with prison labour. Apart from raising the 9d to an equally paltry 45c-

a-day in 1980, its practice was essentially unchanged.[35] In the euphemism of the criminologist T.M. Corry 'immediately after being sentenced, prisoners are asked if they would rather serve their sentence in prison or be released on parole to work for a private person at market wages'. The majority of these 'private persons' were white farmers, who 'employed' 'virtually all the short-term offenders released on parole' (Cook, 1982: 21,23). And the majority of parolees were serving short sentences for pass and influx control transgressions. Although figures of prisoners released to farmers are not available, an idea of the number of people involved can be given by looking at the numbers of prisoners released on parole in general. In the period July 1981 — June 1982, 85,863 (38.75 percent) of the 221,449 people sentenced to imprisonment were released on parole.[36] Many if not most of these parolees ended up working on the farms.

The lease scheme

Lastly, there is the lease system, whereby prisoners not on parole are leased by employers from prisons on a daily basis. This system, based on farm jails, is the most visible manifestation of the vested interest white commercial agriculture has in promoting the exploitation of prison labour in the sector.[37] As has been indicated,

> these jails ... were put up by groups of farmers who came together and built a jail which was handed over, filled up and run by the Department of Prisons. The capital cost of building each jail was met by the individual farmers who bought shares in the building and who then held 'rights' to convict labour in proportion to their share holdings (IDAF,1980).

Farmers profited in two ways, since this labour was not only exceedingly cheap and assured — most of these prisoners are serving sentences of two years or more — but also represented an investment asset which enhanced the value of their property. Thus, for example, in the mid-1960s Western Cape farms appreciated by at least R1,000 per convict, and in the early 1970s a prison share bought for R2,000 sold for R4,000 (IDAF,1980).

This has also been the main route by which Coloured prisoners are forced on to the farms. That half of the 22 purpose-built farm jails in the early 1970s were in the Western Cape seems to be more than incidental to the operation of the Coloured labour preference policy. While Coloured workers' unwillingness to remain in the sector has led to labour shortages, they have been pushed in involuntarily through the back door as leased prison labour.

It is not only prison outstations that supply leased prisoners to the farms. Although these jails were expressly built for the purpose, farmers can (and do) make use of other prisons as sources of leased labour. In 1972/3, in addition to the 9,489 prisoners leased out daily from 'prison outstations', it can be safely assumed that farmers were well represented amongst the other 'private persons' who leased another 20,000 prisoners from other prisons every day (IDAF,1980). In this context, the trend from the mid-1970s to close these outstations cannot be seen as the end of leased prison labour on the farms. It does, however, indicate that alternative, less controversial sources of labour — contract, migrant, female and child — proved equally suitable to the farmers' needs.

In addition to these three channels, 'several thousand' prisoners are directed to state farms for 'training in farm activities' (*Race Relations News,* November 1972). These possibly are the same as the farms run by the Prisons Department (prison farms) where Africans caught in the 'Idle and Undesirable' legislation are sent to serve out forced labour sentences for 'loitering', or being without a 'work-seeker's permit', etc. Of these farms, one is known to exist in Virginia, OFS, one in Pretoria, and several in Bethal in the Transvaal.[38]

It is clear that these various channels combine to provide a constant stream of labour which is integral to commercial agricultural relations, although not all farmers use this labour form. The Theron Commission estimated that some 13 percent of farmers used prison labour (Theron, 1976: para.141:7.18). Conservative estimates put the number of prisoners working on the farms at any one time as 100,000 — close on ten percent of the total labour force employed in South African commercial agriculture.

Any discussion of prison labour must mention the extensive violence and abuse to which prisoners are subject. Yet it is not possible to separate their treatment from that meted out to farm workers who are not prisoners, because the terms under which prisoners work shape those which apply also to 'free' labour. In this way the distinction between voluntary and forced labour is further elided.

The emergence of a skill hierarchy

Restructuring has also led to the emergence of a hierarchy of skill — significant in terms of the further differentiation of the agricultural labour force, but still relatively crudely elaborated. This fact throws into sharp relief the inherent contradiction in relations when capital-intensive production is built on an oppressed, forced, low-waged and structurally destabilised labour force. While capital inputs and techniques of production (machines, bio- and chemical technology, etc.) demand a workforce that is skilled and stable in order to maximise productivity (and therefore profit), the terms of national and social oppression, which make the labour base so cheap, mitigate against its creation. This contradiction expresses itself in a complex way, but is summed up in the problem of quality and the perennial shortage of skilled labour that many farmers face.[39]

At the most simple level, the work process can be divided according to the degree of knowledge required to perform a task. The greater the level of knowledge, the higher the level of skill and the less easy it is to substitute one worker for another. But the ordering of the division of labour into a skill (and authority) hierarchy is not so technically or 'objectively' determined as such a definition might suggest. The divisions are shaped by social judgments and struggles which are not confined to the tasks under consideration. Equally, they revolve around whether the work is considered 'full-time' or 'part-time' and who is to do it — women, children, migrants, prisoners, 'regular' male workers, blacks, whites, etc. And they are determined by the alternatives open to workers who have acquired skills. In other words, a whole set of social assumptions come into play in determining the skill hierarchy of labour.

This said, identifying skill divisions in the work process is not beyond the capacity of white farmers. In fact, in the second phase of restructuring, they have shown themselves to be increasingly willing to do so. In the Albany district survey, for example, workers considered to be semi-skilled or skilled included, amongst others, 'milkers, stockmen in positions of responsibility, stationary machine operators, tractor and truck drivers, shearers and wool cleansers, inseminators, welders and mechanics' (Antrobus, 1984:79). Other identified skills included fencing, building, glazing, poultry, leather work, shoeing of horses, etc. What is apparent from this list is that, whilst some of these tasks are indeed new to the work process — spray tractors, combine and heavy duty truck drivers, chainsaw operators, etc. — many are not. What is new is that they are *identified* as specialised in some degree.

Identifying skilled work is not all there is to the question. The second and in-dispensable aspect is that they be acknowledged in a material way. And here, of course, is precisely where the tension lies in a sector which rests so firmly on the cheap labour base that characterises the South African political economy. Whilst farmers demand that specialised jobs be done with skill, they are reluctant to train, and even less willing to pay workers accordingly. So what has happened is that, although the practice of acknowledging skills — through training or recognising the need for training and through a differentiated wage structure — has become more widespread, the process remains very uneven within the sector. It is also unevenly spread in so far as different skills are concerned, and generally it re-mains substantially out of step with the requirements of capital-intensive produc-tion relations.

Despite the extensive capital investment in machine and other technology that restructuring has entailed (see Chapter One),[40] the overwhelming majority of workers who are required to perform semi- and skilled tasks have had no formal training. Thus, for example,

> a survey conducted by the Division of Agricultural Engineering of the Depart-ment of Agricultural Technical Services concluded that fewer than 10,000 of the approximately 180,000 tractor operators in the Republic received any formal training (Farm Labour Project, 1982: para.3.8.2).

This meant that less than 5.5 percent were formally trained. But as meagre as this figure is, it overstates the degree of general formal training. On the one hand, this is because the extremely limited training facilities available in the country tend to concentrate heavily on training for tractor and other farm machinery; while, on the other hand, the few farmers who are prepared to send workers for training overwhelmingly prefer courses related to these aspects. So, in addition to training courses run by certain companies which sell tractors and related machinery, there are schemes run by the South African Sugar Association for training machine operators, as well as courses organised by state Agricultural Research Stations, e.g., in forestry. Most if not all of these were first organised only in the early 1970s. At the Boskop Training Centre, the only one in existence in South Africa for African farm workers right up until the 1980s, the same bias was to be found. The main courses offered included 'tractor maintenance, tractor maintenance and driving licence, combine maintenance, maintenance of farm implements, handling of milking machines, building maintenance and artificial insemination'[41]

In other words, few training facilities exist and most of these concentrate on tractor and tractive machinery. At the same time, the courses in most demand from farmers are those which train workers to drive and maintain these machines. The extent of this concentration in certified skills is reflected in De Klerk's study, where he found that amongst 'permanent' workers, some or all 'on 35 percent of farms had tractor driving licences; on 15 percent of farms some or all had attended vehicle maintenance courses; and on 13 percent some or all had a heavy or extra heavy duty truck driving licence' (De Klerk, 1984:52).

It is clear that the low level of formal training that these figures indicate is even greater for skilled workers who are not doing these kinds of jobs. The findings of area surveys of Vryheid (Natal) and Albany (Cape) in the early 1980s, where no one interviewed had had any training (Farm Labour Project, 1982: para.3.8.2), reflect the more generalised reality that only a tiny minority of farm workers receive any formal training.

In part, the low level of training can be attributed to the general lack of facility: courses in most demand at Boskop and Kromme Rhee (until recently the only other general state-run training centre, but restricted to Coloured farm workers) are regularly oversubscribed. Another more important cause is the reluctance of farmers to provide formal training for workers. This is so despite state incentives, such as a tax deduction worth 200 percent of the cost of training courses (SAAU, 1978:79). The problem revolves around an unwillingness to pay workers for their skills. This question will be treated more extensively below: the point here is that with certificates workers have relatively greater job mobility and so farmers are under greater pressure not only to pay for their skills, but also to pay at more competitive rates. Hence, farmers are trapped in the vicious circle of their own shortsightedness. On the one hand, the general lack of training leads to very high running costs. At the same time, the low wages they pay trained workers leads to a drain of those with certified skills, who try to move to the universally better conditions offered by other sectors. Workers, on the other hand, are doubly penalised. Without certification for the skills they have acquired, they are unable to exercise the necessary leverage to improve their terms of employment. And in being forced to handle machinery and chemicals without training, they bear the brunt of the inevitably high rate of accidents and injuries.

A differentiated wage structure

Whether skills are acquired in the work process, or through formal training, the question of pay is central to their acknowledgement. Only in this second phase of restructuring has there been a more general trend towards categorising the workforce into a hierarchy of skills and authority which is reflected in a differentiated wage structure. The ordering and evaluation of the agricultural workforce in this way seems to have developed first on the company estates, and they continue to manifest the most formalised and systematic differentiation within the sector. Thus, for example, Young, in his study of two agribusiness farms in the Transvaal, found that on one a job evaluation scheme was first introduced in 1973. A five-tier skill/job/racial hierarchy was devised for 'full-time' workers and employees (one tier ran two parallel structures) under the following classifications:

Table 4.1
Job evaluation classification scheme on a Transvaal company farm (1975)

Job Group	Classification	Race	Job Title
A	unskilled	black	labourer 1 & 2
B1	semi-skilled	black	tractor driver, clerk, combine driver,
B2		black	truck driver
B3		black	induna 1 (forman)
B1,2,3	clerical	white	telephonist, typist, bookkeeper
C1,2	junior management	white	senior bookkeeper, section manager,
	skilled		unit manager
D1	senior managerial	white	divisional manager
D2			financial manager
E1	senior managerial	white	general manager

Source: Young, 1979.

On others, the hierarchy may be less elaborate but it more or less gravitates around the same types of divisions.[42]

On most individually owned farms, which may be but are not necessarily smaller, when a differential wage hierarchy exists, it is at its most ad hoc and discretionary. The way these divisions are acknowledged is summed up in the statements of Albany farmers. Thus,

'All had a basic flat wage until two years ago (1974). Now I pay up to R2 extra to some boys'.

'I try to keep wages very much the same. I do give extra for exceptional work, but I say "Don't pass it around" — that was my dad's advice in 1940!' (Antrobus, 1984:79).

Arbitrariness is not only reflected in whether skilled workers will be paid or not, but also in which skills will be acknowledged. So, for example, the same farmers who identify the considerable skills of stockmen in their employ as including the keeping of stock records for individual camps, AI (artificial insemination), and inoculations against and even diagnosing of disease, only mention 'extra pay in connection with tractor drivers. Furthermore, although there is a tendency for more and more farmers to differentiate between unskilled and skilled workers, often the difference in pay is so little that it has no material bearing on the position of the latter.

In many different ways farmers circumvent acknowledging the skills workers have and are expected to use. These vary according to the predominant labour forms in the sector and are not confined to those farmers who exercise no (or only the most basic) skill and authority differentiation.

The use of a formalised job evaluation scheme is strongly advocated as sound management practice by the SAAU in its farmer's manual. But, whilst this represents an 'improvement on the traditional ad hoc methods of job evaluation and wage setting' (Young, 1979:15), it is far from the objective and equalising measure to which its advocates lay claim. Since the evaluation of both the categories into which workers fall and the value attached to each category is made in conditions where farm workers are oppressed by colour and gender and are not organised as a social force, the demarcations revolve around the class, racial and gender presumptions of the white male farming establishment. This is quite apparent in the categorisation systems mentioned earlier. Their introduction, therefore, does not mean 'the use of one system throughout the enterprise', nor does it remove 'partiality towards certain employees', as Nel's *Guidelines to Manpower Management in Agriculture* so quaintly puts it (Nel, 1985: 35, para.5.4.1.1).

Partiality is central to the evaluation process. The problem is not really whether the farmer uses an adequate scheme of categories. Rather, it lies in the content given to the evaluation. So, although

all duties in an enterprise can therefore be graded according to the Paterson Plan (a six-band system) in terms of a single common factor with reference to a common standard ... the common factor is the level of decision-making required in the work (Nel, 1985: 34, para.5.4),

what is not mentioned is the 'common standard' set by white domination and class power. Thus, we see that management consistently downgrades the skills of black workers. Whether they are tractor, truck or combine drivers, mechanics, builders, cane or timber cutters, shearers, milking machine operators, inoculators, AI specialists or foremen, they tend to be classified as semi-skilled rather than skilled.

The underlying presumption on which these schemes are based is that, generally speaking, they only include 'permanent', 'full-time' workers in their ambit. So, just as some farmers do not formalise their categories of employment, other enterprises avoid acknowledging skills by making extensive use of both migrantised and casualised labour. Thus, Cape farmers rely on African contract migrants for livestock husbandry as their 'innate ability in coping with animals' makes them 'natural stockmen'. Conveniently for the farmers, they also do not need to be trained and paid for their allegedly 'inherited' skills (Nasson, 1984:7).

The system also operates on the presumption that skilled labour is male adult labour. Few, if any, women or children doing semi- or skilled work are acknowledged as such. Their substitution for male farm workers (which invariably accompanies the casualisation of labour in the work process) serves as yet another means by which farmers downgrade or ignore and therefore cheapen the costs of labour in general. In other words, the fact that it is a woman who uses and maintains the milking machine, or a 'standard-four child' who is hired 'to write up the beef records' (Antrobus, 1984:197) disqualifies or devalues the work, which in other circumstances would have been considered semi-skilled at least. This is particularly so in conditions of extensive illiteracy and the all but complete absence of formal training for female farm workers.[43] It is not surprising, then, that in his small survey of farms in the Western Transvaal, Seleoane found that although 'twelve men had drivers' licences and one a certificate for operating and maintaining a milking machine ... no woman had any certified skills' (Seleoane, 1984:5). Once again what is apparent is the deep and systematic oppression of black women. They are not only the least likely to be employed in skilled work but, when they are, they stand the least chance of being acknowledged for it — either in pay, or in training.

Finally, the prison labour system — and specifically the lease system which operates within it — serves as yet another mechanism built into the social relations of production by which farmers can avoid acknowledging skills. Writing of the farm jail system, Cook makes the point that it

> is a unique device for enabling farmers to exploit forced labour to the utmost. One disadvantage of parole is that ... he (the farmer) cannot teach skills to a continually changing force of labourers on six-monthly or yearly contracts. In the farm jail system, however, a farmer can keep a prisoner perhaps for many years; he can teach him skills and end up getting a skilled as well as forced labourer for considerably less than the going rate for an unskilled labour (Cook, 1982:28).

Changes in the authority structure

Inseparable from the emergence of a skill hierarchy and the differentiation of the workforce is the development of a more elaborate authority structure within farming enterprises. Some farmers still organise and control every aspect of the work process. But, as enterprises have grown in size and production intensity, the tendency has been for black workers to do most first-line supervision, often more skilled co-ordination, and even general management tasks — as 'gang leaders', 'boss boys' or '*indunas*'.

As in the general case for all farm workers, including other skilled workers, few of these men have any formal education or training. Whilst they may well have acquired skills in the work process, for the most part they have been and continue to be chosen by the farmer or farm management from the male, on-farm 'regular' workforce. And their selection is based on what management sees as their record of responsibility, reliability and, most importantly, loyalty to the establishment. The indifference towards, or equally strong suspicion of, schooling and training that is so widespread in the sector is compounded by presumptions about what the job of first-line supervision, or even more skilled co-ordination work entails (Nasson, 1984:7).

Essentially, farmers describe such work as enforcing discipline, keeping the farmer informed about ongoing work and, especially keeping him informed about the workers. Most farmers do not consider these to be qualifications acquired through formal educational structures. Rather they believe they only have to be bought. This, of course, places workers employed in the authority hierarchy in a somewhat different position from other skilled workers. Except for those who are temporarily 'put in charge' of others alongside whom they are working on a particular operation, they have their work acknowledged by some form of payment. This is often not formalised. So, for example, 'I don't call Spanner a boss boy, but I treat him as such' (Antrobus, 1984:193). Nor does it mean that payment is in cash or is regular. Mr Z, who has worked on a Middelburg farm complex for ten years, twelve hours a day, five and a half days a week,

> gets a weekly supply of R6 worth of meat and two litres of milk and knows no other worker who received these fringe benefits. His house is remarkable both in terms of the way it is built and the way in which it is furnished. The farmer actually donated twelve bags of cement and window frames towards its construction. It is not difficult to see ... that he is the eyes and ears of the farmer (Seleoane, 1984:10).

Indeed, both farmers and workers are aware of the connection between the position of the 'boss boy' or *induna*, and that of informer. Also, they are expected to play an active part in the enforcement of 'discipline' which includes, but also extends beyond, the work situation and frequently involves physical violence. Most farmers recognise that, in order for the worker to undertake such an open expression of loyalty, he has to be motivated to do so. As has been shown above, this often takes the form of discretionary 'rewards'. But it can also take the form of a threat — for example, of eviction when the worker has become too old to work and other family members are unwilling to replace him or work on his behalf. Then his continued presence on the farm (as well as that of his family) gravitates around whether he is willing to keep the boss informed.

This should not be read as meaning that all farm workers in these positions are committed to, or collaborate with, the demands and presumptions of the farming establishment. Their response is shaped by the objective conditions they find themselves in, as well as the level of their consciousness as workers and black oppressed people. Inevitably, though, they are placed in an ambiguous and even ambivalent position, in relation both to the farmer and to other workers.

This said, the demands of the production process under restructured conditions require something more than the combination of force, fear and violence to ensure proficiency and effective output in the sector. The role of black workers in first-line supervision and, perhaps more importantly, their growing incorporation into higher levels of co-ordination and management, have meant that their work has become more diverse and responsible (in the sense of decision-making), requiring more formalised training and a more systematised reward structure. Yet, from the evidence available, this trend is only manifest — and here weakly and unevenly — on the larger, professionally managed, invariably company-owned enterprises. Although literacy and numeracy are considered when they are employed, the paramount determinant seems to be their willingness to ensure (through loyalty and the enforcement of discipline) the 'welfare of the farm' (i.e., the farmer). This is reflected, for example, in the fact that only in the higher bands in a differentiated hierarchy will schooling be considered important, and then only relatively so (Nasson, 1984:7). This emphasis is also patently evident in programmes offered those few workers who receive formal training. So, for example, the 'works foreman course' at Boskop includes

> subjects such as leadership, the enforcement of discipline, human relations, work organisation, supervising and the production abilities of farm workers

... They are also taught how to manage the farm when the farmer is absent.[44]

Furthermore, although under these conditions payment is more standardised and systematised, where formalised differentiation of the workforce is practised, most black workers in responsible organisational positions in the authority structure are classified as 'semi-skilled'.[45] In other words, and like other skilled workers, notwithstanding their often cardinal significance in the organising and running of the work process, they are systematically downgraded in the work hierarchy because of the white, paternalistic and class interests of the farming establishment. Their presumptions are encapsulated in the notion of the 'boss boy', or *'induna'* used universally by 'progressive' and 'backward' farmers alike to refer to foremen and supervisory jobs performed by Africans. At their most sophisticated and advanced (!), these interests are summed up by La Borde, who is an advocate of 'high quality scientific management'. In writing of its general absence on the wattle estates where timber and bark are produced, he argues (with two other 'experts') in a special appendix entitled 'long-term motivation and contentment', that:

— workers must be compatible with one another. Tribal differences lead to disharmony and dissension;
— *indunas* should be trained to be sensitive to others and in the basic principles of Management by Objectives in the same way farm managers are trained; and
— blacks must not lose their identity as blacks through education and association with whites (La Borde, 1980: Appendix J).

In these conditions, the role of these foremen and supervisors in running the enterprise is fraught with contradictions in their relation to other workers, on the one hand, and to the white farmer or more senior management, on the other.

As regards skilled workers, then, it is clear that:

● only a small proportion of the workforce in the sector is identified as semi-skilled, skilled or in a position of authority. Antrobus gives a figure of 38 percent of the 'permanent' workforce in the Albany district (1984:79), one of ten percent for the labour force as a whole is quoted for the Letaba district (Smit and Herbst, 1983). However, both figures need to be treated with caution as they are not likely to reflect actual skill levels accurately, and they do not reflect the sector's skill requirements;

● only a small proportion of the recognised skilled labour force is trained or paid for their skills;

● Although the acknowledgement and differentiation of the workforce is most standardised and systematised on company estates, these job evaluation schemes are imbued with prejudices and presumptions which reflect the interests of white farm management as a class and as part of the ruling white minority;
● the acknowledgement of skills is not applied to all workers equally. Farmers

are inclined to acknowledge only the skills of male on-farm 'full-time' workers. This means that not only are the skills of female, child, migrant and prisoner farm workers consistently ignored, but they are also systematically disadvantaged in both training and pay;

● reluctance to train and pay for skills and responsibility impairs productivity and profitability. Although farmers have been able to pass on the lion's share of this cost to farm workers in particular, and to the black working class in general, changing economic and political conditions make this route an increasingly less sure way of making profits in the longer term. It is this pressure which is behind efforts to improve training and introduce some form of uniformity in job classification and payment;

● finally, the emergence of a skill hierarchy contains the seeds of division within the agricultural workforce, with the prospect that some workers will be incorporated into the authority hierarchy of the white farming establishment. This is likely to be a very slow and uneven process, however.

This chapter has shown that the division of labour has undergone profound reorganisation in the course of the second phase of restructuring. At the same time as labour tenancy was effectively crushed as a widespread labour practice in the sector, the physical relocation of much of agriculture's labour pool saw a simultaneous physical division of the agrarian working class. Those resident on the farms have been whittled down to a so-called 'core' of 'full-time' workers and their families. The majority of workers, however, have been removed to the reserves and, to a lesser extent, the ghettoes of so-called white towns. From there, they are drawn on as 'migrant' and 'casual' labour, according to the needs of the farmers. As such, the stabilisation of the on-farm workforce rests on the destabilisation of the majority of farm workers.

Changes in the social characteristics of the labour force engaged in the sector have been integrally tied up with changes in the predominant labour forms. Whilst 'regular' 'full-time' employment has been concentrated amongst the male, on-farm workforce, 'casual' 'part-time' jobs have tended to become the preserve of women and children from the on-farm labour pool, as well as those (including many men) who have been made migrant and are drawn from the labour reservoirs on to the farms. Prison labour continues to be widespread. From the late 1960s, the shift from labour- to capital-intensive production has also led to the emergence of a skill hierarchy, although it is very weakly and unevenly manifest.

Indeed, from this evidence it is clear that the way the division of labour has been reorganised suggests that the dichotomy between town and 'countryside', which has been elaborated in a very specific way for mining and secondary industry, has, in this second phase of restructuring, been reproduced in commercial agriculture. This then is the so-called 'stabilisation' of farm labour that the state and sections of organised agriculture have long advocated and steadily adopted on an ever-increasing scale. It is one which is based on extensive destabilisation through the migrant labour system and continues to presume direct and indirect compulsion. The labour forms which characterise commercial agriculture are essential to understanding the conditions of pay and existence under which workers labour in the sector — a question taken up in the next two chapters.

Notes

1. The policy of forced population relocation affected millions of black people throughout the country who were moved within the urban areas, and from urban areas, the 'white platteland' and black-owned land outside the reserves into the 'homelands', and within them as well. For details of this mass forced population relocation policy, which has few historical precedents in modern history, see in particular Desmond, 1971; *Sash*, publications of the Black Sash; The Surplus People's Project Reports, 1983: Vols. 1-5; AFRA, 1980-84, etc.
2. Morris, 1977:53. The report of the Nel Committee was never published.
3. The area which has been studied in the most detail is Natal. See The Surplus People's Project Reports, 1983:Vol.4.
4. AFRA (The Association for Rural Advancement) was formed in 1980 in response to the apparent and gross hardship experienced by the black majority as a result of population relocation. Its aims are twofold: 'to monitor, enquire into, record and publicise' the social and economic position of rural people in Natal; and second, to take action to alleviate hardships, discrimination and oppression suffered by them (AFRA, 1980-84: Fact Sheets, July 1980).
5. General Circular No.25 of 1967 issued to all Native Commissioners stated:

   > It is government policy that Bantu are only temporarily resident in the European areas of the Republic for as long as they offer their labour there. As soon as they become, for some reason or another, no longer fit for work or superfluous in the labour market, they are expected to return to their country of origin or the territory of the national unit where they fit in ethnically if they are not born or bred in the homeland ... Non-productive Bantu are classified as the aged, unfit, widows, women with dependent children, families who do not qualify for family accommodation under Section 10, Bantu on European farms who become superflous as a result of age or disability, Bantu squatters from mission stations and black spots, professional Bantu such as doctors, attorneys, agents, traders, industrialists, etc. who are not regarded as essential for the European labour market and as such must also be settled in the homelands. It must be stressed that no stone is to be left unturned to achieve the settlement in the homelands of non-productive Bantu at present residing in European areas ... *Settlement must enjoy the highest priority* (emphasis not in original) (cited in Harris, et al., 1982).

6. The extent of this under-enumeration is revealed by research into resettlement. In 1980, the SPP survey of Sahlumbe, one of several relocation sites set up in the late 1960s as a 'temporary relocation area for the thousands of labour tenants then being moved off farms in the Weenen area', revealed that only two percent had formally registered contracts with the farmer on whose land they lived (SPP, 1983:Vol.4, 308-10).
7. Many people have been removed more than once.
8. The Surplus People's Project Reports, 1983:Vol.1,6. These figures are below earlier estimates, where for 1960-74 figures as high as 1.4 million people were given. However, as the SPP researchers point out, the total number of people affected will never be known, but even given this, without extensive field work, measuring relocation through secondary sources is a somewhat futile exercise. The aim of these figures is simply to give a general indication of the relative scale of the removals and the proportionate size of the various categories.
9. In fact, when such disputes arise, farm workers have tended to leave of their own accord, albeit 'illegally'. More often than not they have been pursued by the farmers who try to force them to return not only because they may be dependent on their labour, but also because their actions have violated the farmer's authority over them.
10. Schmidt, 1984:43. Although the informant refers to the workers as men, it is implicit that they are with their families. He, his wife and two children (aged four years and four months respectively) were on the trek. The fact that the farmer gave them no food for the road seems

to indicate a change in practice, which in the particular conditions of the Karoo, where moving from one farm to another on donkeycart could take a day or more, means that the dismissed worker and his family are certain of going hungry for a time, since even when they reach the next farm there is no surety of being taken on. This family expected that they would be on the lookout for work for at least a week or two.

11. Eiselen envisaged that the stages in the operation of this policy would be 1) the removal of foreign Africans; 2) a freeze on the number of African families; 3) restricted influx of migrant workers; 4) reduction of African families and 5) replacement of African migrants by Coloured workers (SPP, 1983: Vol.2, 359).

12. The most recent examples of this are to be found in the research work done for the Carnegie Commission into Poverty in 1984. So, Archer and Meyer (1984:36), in an otherwise interesting study of Hanover, write: 'It was not possible to interview farm workers directly on the farm visited, nor to study living and working conditions without changing the entire nature of the investigation'.

13. Piet Witbooi, born 1911, interviewed 1983. Cited in Schmidt, 1984:42.

14. Bekker et al., Marcus interview, 1982.

15. Family is used in inverted commas in order to make conscious the fact that it is a mistake to presume the relations we are referring to mean the 'nuclear' family. The 'family' as such has been little studied in the apartheid South African context, but what is known, in so far as the content of that social relation in agriculture is concerned, is that it often includes several generations, near and distant kin, and even people unrelated by birth or marriage but who are brought up together.

16. For example, in one of the farms in Seleoane's study (1984:8), some of the farm workers were unemployed for the five months March to July each year and were therefore 'free to seek jobs where they please'. In fact, they were made all but unemployable by the farmer because although he wrote the necessary 'letter of release' he stipulated in it the condition that they return to the farm in August. This made it impossible for them to get work at the nearby Arnot mine or power station, the main sources of employment in the area.

17. Reported speech of Dr Koornhof, *Financial Mail* 18 December 1970.

18. The use of prison labour is contrary to the International Labour Convention and also violates the General Agreement on Tariffs and Trade (GATT). From IDAF, 1980.

19. Seleoane, 1984:43. The 'chief' referred to is 'a "Ndebele" petty chief who seems to have worked himself into a favourable position on the farm. He acts as a tribunal whenever there are disputes between families on this and neighbouring farms and imposes fines. Gossip has it that the fines are shared between him and the farmer'.

20. The sharpest decline seems to have been between 1964 and 1970 when the number of migrant workers fell by just under 100,000 to 45,000. This figure seems rather high and possibly reflects a tendency for few foreign workers from Botswana, Lesotho and Swaziland to apply for entry into the country as demanded by the Aliens Control Act of 1963.

21. *Sowetan*, 8 November 1984. The legal employment of Mozambican workers only opened up as a prospect in 1982. Restrictions had been imposed on workers from there when Mozambique won independence in 1975.

22. The evidence on this has yet to be collected. The available sections of De Klerk's study — one of the few which analyses problems of this kind — do not address this question.

23. This does not mean that some workers are not employed more than once, but rather that their re-employment is essentially a matter of chance.

24. This is not to suggest that African women do not come in search of work, or that farmers do not take them on, although they are in the area 'illegally'. On the deciduous fruit farms of the Elgin Valley, farmers were found to be employing women who had come from as far as the Transkei in search of work (Levy, 1976:38).

25. Antrobus, 1984:89. He claims that such incidents are 'rare', yet from the evidence he presents it would appear that such an assertion is groundless, given farmer obsessions with workers feigning illness, the alleged laziness of 'blacks' and their strong opposition to 'brain schooling', particularly if it interferes with their labour needs. On the contrary, such incidents could, if anything, be presumed to be commonplace.

26. Cited in Theron, 1976: para.141.7.7.

27. Mrs M. Ntsele, interviewed in AFRA, 1980-1984: Microfilm Reel III.
28. Ibid.
29. This is at the very general level. What needs greater investigation is the particular combination of forces which drive women to accept the notoriously harsh terms of agricultural employment and specifically their relation to changes in their position in 'the family'.
30. On the information available, prison labour is male, although women may well be sent to the farms when caught in the influx control or 'idle and undesirable' machinery. This needs to be investigated, however.
31. The question of sexual abuse is intimately connected to the question of control and health and safety at work, all of which can only be explored in subsequent work.
32. Mrs M Ntsele, interviewed in AFRA, 1980-84, Microfilm Reel III.
33. J. Nelson cited in Budlender, 1984:18.
34. Budlender, 1984:13. Notwithstanding the fact that weeding by hoe could not be described as light, she is unable to reconcile the apparently contradictory finding that in the 1940s, for example, women were extensively employed to '*bankies gooi*' (literally 'throwing banks, i.e., digging furrows). Thus she relegates it to a note as an 'unusual task' performed by women.
35. It is unlikely that the prisoner ever sees the money, as another change in the system is that the farmer is now responsible for handing the money over to the prisoner at the end of the parole period, whereas formerly he was obliged to deposit it with the Prisons Department (Cook, 1982:22).
36. This figure is based on Coloured and African parolees who are serving short sentences only. It is in fact unrealistic to exclude male parolees serving long sentences and it is also probable that a number of the 5,249 Coloured and African women serving short sentences also found themselves labouring on the farms.
37. Which seems to me rather more important than the farmer's alleged 'vested interest in serious crime' (Cook, 1982:27), not least of all because the notion of serious crime itself has to be treated with caution in the apartheid context. For example, within this so-called category of serious criminals are people convicted of stock theft (two years for a first offence, three and up to ten years for conviction on subsequent offences).
38. House of Assembly Debates: Questions and Replies, 7 March 1978, Col.778; *Echo*, 18 December 1980 and *Rand Daily Mail*, 29 May 1982.
39. Antrobus (1984:211) found, for example, that farmers considered their biggest labour problem to be that of 'quality' although they never addressed the problem of the relations that undermined the generation of quality labour but rather expressed it in racial and class stereotypes, e.g., 'no machinery is kaffir proof'.
40. A survey of the Ruens district showed that expenditure on farm machinery absorbed about 40 percent of the total production costs of wheat, for example. *Eastern Province Herald*, 22 October 1976.
41. The SAAU Annual Report, 1978:79. In the 1982/3 Annual Report the existence of eight training centres was recorded, although some of these were not functioning due to a lack of finance. The 1984 report only mentioned one more as being operational, in addition to those at Boskop and Kromme Rhee.
42. Nasson (1984:7) found that a Paarl viticulture estate categorised its 'full-time' labour force into a four-tier hierarchy — A1, 2, unskilled, general labourer and pruner; B1-4, semi-skilled, including tractor and spray-tractor drivers; C1-4 and D1-4, skilled, clerical and occupational, which included specialised and salaried grades.
43. In the wattle industry La Borde (1980) reports that certain growers have trained women as chain sawyers, but it is unclear whether this training was formal or 'on the job'.
44. *Informa,* August 1981. Workers who are accepted on this course have to be able to read and write and have completed two skill-related courses as well. This means that they have also been subject to the general lectures given all 'candidates' on things like 'family planning, nature conservation, fuel saving and farm safety' as well as lectures where 'they are told what the relationship between the employer and the employee and farming should be. A bicycle is used to demonstrate the point. The farmer is shown as the rider and he explains that he cannot ride if all the gears (all and everything on the farm) do not work together. This analogy is rather unfathomable except that it leaves us in no doubt as to who is supposed to be in

the commanding seat!

45. Exceptional here are the sugar estates in Natal and perhaps (although probably less so) the grape and fruit farms of the Western Cape where Indian and Coloured workers respectively are employed in skilled and higher level management jobs.

5. Restructuring: Wage Forms and Methods of Payment

Forced and cheap labour has played a central role in the restructuring of South African commercial agriculture. As has been shown in Chapters Three and Four, this is manifest in changes in the division of labour affecting both the forms and social characteristics of the labour force in the sector. It is also evident in all aspects of the social conditions under which farm workers labour. As it is not possible to focus on all of these here, both this and the following chapter will concentrate on the key factor of wages.

Wages paid in commercial agriculture are not only revealing of social conditions in the sector, but also open up some more general questions. The first and perhaps most important of these is the significance of wages in the dynamics of the restructuring process. The contention that is most frequently repeated is that the evidently low wage levels in commercial agriculture have meant that 'the cost of labour' has not been a 'factor in the shift of mechanisation' (Schroder, 1979:5). It is true that rising wages were not a stimulus to reorganise the production process. Yet this line of argument overlooks the considerable restraints imposed by both farmers and the state to prevent wages from rising. These are not only visible in the predominant forms and characteristics of the labour force; they are also reflected in the levels, forms and methods of wage payment.

This raises a second and related question — namely, is the only impact of restructuring on wages that they continue to be low? Or has the process also affected how low they are and the forms they take? To answer this, it is necessary to try and establish a wage value for work in the sector.[1] This is far from straightforward, not least because levels of pay are complicated by the forms wages take and the methods by which workers are paid. Both these aspects have been affected by the restructuring process and together they have had a material bearing on wage levels.

So, in order to try and evaluate the impact of restructuring in the sector on wage levels, it is necessary — at least for analytical purposes — to treat these three strands separately, although in practice they are closely interwoven. Wage forms and methods of payment are examined in this chapter. Chapter Six goes on to consider wage levels and explore some of the implications these changes have had for the living conditions of farm workers: the main focus will be on developments in the sector from the late 1960s onwards, and especially on the more recent period. Although these changes reflect general trends, they are not necessarily universal or evenly spread throughout the sector. This, of course, raises (Chapter Seven) the question of the way capitalism has developed in the specific context of national oppression.

By wage forms is meant the material form in which the worker is paid. Cash is normally the presumed content of the term 'wages' under capitalist production relations. Yet, perhaps typical of the way the terms of social exploitation and national oppression have combined in the South African countryside, this has not been the primary content of the wage form on the farms. Whilst payment in cash has been an aspect of the wage, so has payment in kind.

Cash payment, as a wage form, is on the whole unproblematic and the comments that I have will be confined to the end of the discussion of wage forms. Wages in a non-cash form are to be questioned, however, although the literature invariably only does so in terms of the difficulties they pose for evaluating wage levels.[2] Yet being paid in kind says something more about social relations in commercial agriculture than the quantitative amount it embodies. It expresses something of the complexity of conditions whereby farmers have been able to resist some of the consequences of full proletarianisation by having recourse to non-capitalist wage forms. They have been assisted in this by the extensively forced and rightless terms under which most black workers have had to labour.

Payment in kind
Historically speaking, in farming as in no other sector of the South African political economy,[3] where a wage has been paid[4] it has invariably taken the form of a non-cash payment.[5] In fact, payment in kind — particularly food, fuel, the running of livestock and/or access to a piece of land — has been the basic and most prevalent form of wages for workers in the sector.

What impact has restructuring had on wages in kind? At one level, payment in kind continues to be widespread in the sector. It remains a substantial part of farmers' evaluations of workers' wages. This is clearly evidenced in the census figures which are supplied by farmers and form the base from which the state calculates national wage levels in the sector. Thus from statistics provided by Pretoria for 1980, as Table 5.1 shows, farmers paid a cash wage greater than the amount they attributed to the payment in kind in only one region (western Cape II).

Table 5.1
The proportion of average monthly wages of on-farm 'full-time' black farm workers in various districts which farmers attribute to the wage in kind, 1980

Eastern Orange Free State	54.7%
Western Transvaal	50.5%
North-West Orange Free State	56.5%
Highveld (Transvaal)	65.8%
Western Cape I	58.5%
Western Cape II	45.9%

Source: Barrett et al. (eds), 1985:80

Wages in kind, although more usually a feature of 'full-time', on-farm male workers' income, also make up a part of the wage of workers in so-called 'part-time', 'casual' or 'seasonal' work. Here, however, the proportion of the wage taking this form varies more widely. Some are only given food rations, others are paid in the vegetables, fruit or crops which they are employed to harvest rather than in cash. Thus, the farmers' lorries which run to and from the huge populations concentrated in the reserves along the banks of the Tugela in Natal come and announce the work they are offering and the terms of employment. In 1980, daily workers were paid in produce and had to provide their own food during the working day. Weekly work was paid in cash, but that meant staying on the farms in compounds or in sheds (*Rand Daily Mail*, 20 February 1980). Children employed from the same area to harvest the potato crop a year earlier were being 'paid with potatoes that could fill the equivalent of 3 coke tins' for a day's work (*Financial Mail*, 16 February 1979). On the maize farms, reaping and gleaning 'seasonal' workers — the women, children and men who walk behind the combine harvesters collecting the maize heads left behind by the machine — are also frequently paid in kind, this time in a proportion of the crop. De Klerk (1984:12) found that in 1981, of seasonal workers employed to reap and glean, 64 percent were paid with a proportion of the crop rather than in cash.

For other workers in 'part-time' jobs, payment is often in both cash and kind. The sugar employers' labour recruiting organisation (SILO) estimated the payment in kind to be R45 per month (*Financial Mail*, 17 June 1977). These workers earned a basic cash wage of R1.40 and R2 a day for a 26-day shift which meant that the proportion of their wage attributed to payment in kind was 55 and 46.4 percent respectively. According to sugar employers, the bonus system built into the wage structure of cutters meant that they averaged a cash wage of R3.50 a day which reduced the in-kind proportion of their income, when compared to 'full-time' on-farm workers. In fact, a substantial section, if not the majority, of the workforce employed 'part-time' receive no form of payment in kind.

The shift to a cash-based wage system
Nevertheless, one of the major consequences of restructuring for wage forms has been a shift in favour of cash payments. Though payment in kind continues to feature in the calculation of farm workers' income and often makes up a substantial part of the wage, its significance as a wage form has been and is declining. This change is manifest in three important ways:

A money payment
The first and perhaps least significant is that most workers who are paid a wage receive a proportion of it in cash. In fact, for employers the form payment takes, particularly whether pay should be in cash and kind or in cash only, has become 'one of the most discussed questions'. Antrobus (1984:200) found that although the majority of farmers he surveyed (85 percent) paid in both forms in practice, 49 percent of the sample expressed a preference for a cash-only wage. The reasons for this are several, but perhaps the most important ones relate to rationalisation and specialisation. Farmers no longer see themselves obliged to pay in food, etc., especially when it means they have to purchase it or have to draw on saleable goods.

In the survey most farmers thought, however, that a cash-only system would be 'impractical' to implement. As one so candidly put it, 'I don't think my bank balance would stand it.' This is a consideration for employers only if they mean to make up the full value of an existing wage in kind by a cash payment. Where this is not the case — and frequently it is not — then the switch to cash wages does not mean greater cash outlay by farmers, but rather represents a way of further reducing the cost of labour.

Components of wages in kind

Not unexpectedly, the shift to a cash-based wage system is also manifested in changes and a decline in content of the payment in kind. Leaving aside the value attributed to these things, what in fact constitutes payment in kind is far from clear-cut. It is subject to great variation over time as the reckoning of goods and services which are calculated as 'the wage' is historically specific. And it is also more class specific in its valuation, since the assessment of the value attributed to the goods differs quite substantially between employers and workers. Prior to restructuring and even during the first phase of the process, the main content of payment in kind generally included:

- an *'akker'* or piece of unused or low-yielding land allocated to some farm workers to cultivate — 'like most farmers I gave the worst land to the Natives';[6]
- permission to hold a limited number of livestock. This gave them access to grazing land, but did not preclude farmers from claiming the cow dung in the cattle kraals of farm workers or labour tenants on their property;[7]
- food — the green mealies, mealie meal, fruit, vegetables and milk, which together make up the spare, starch-based ration payment to workers.[8]

All of these items represented little or no direct cost to the farmer,[9] and though usually meagre were the primary, if not sole wage on which farm workers and their families struggled to survive.

Housing, fuel and water, although attributed by some farmers to payment in kind, were for the most part considered the free 'perks' of living on the farms. For workers these were necessities which they had invariably to provide for themselves (building huts, gathering firewood, fetching water), and as such they were not considered part of the payment they received for their labour.

Restructuring, particularly from the mid-1960s, has meant that two of these — access to arable land and stockholding — have become an increasingly infrequent and insignificant part of the wage calculation for farm workers. The decline in these forms of wages in kind is closely tied up with the eviction off white-owned land of hundreds of thousands of Africans and the declining proportion of the overall workforce employed as 'full-time' on-farm workers. Even amongst this group of workers these forms of payment in kind have become rarer.

Arable land: Thus the practice of 'giving an *akker*' (as the payment in terms of access to arable land is frequently put) is generally declining. People who have been removed from or who have moved off white-owned land have, of course, lost any access to it. Many of them reported having 'a field' whilst working on the farms. So, for example, a survey of former labour tenants and farm workers removed to Mzimhlope found that before their eviction, of the households interviewed '90 percent had grown mealies, a little over 70 percent had grown sorghum and potatoes and over 50 percent had grown beans as well'.[10] In the Eastern Cape, of former farm worker households now living at Sada, only 13 percent had neither land nor livestock whilst they were on the farms. Of the rest, 31 percent had had a field and 97 percent had had some stock. The provisions these provided, 'the eggs, milk and meat and the green vegetables were vital additions to the rations diet which appears to have been mainly bulk carbohydrates (samp and mealie meal).[11] Having lost access to the land, these workers return to work on the farms as migrant and 'casual' labour — forms which preclude any such methods of payment in kind.

But the decline in access to land has also affected those workers who remain in 'full-time' on-farm employment. The majority have either lost rights to land altogether, or the access they are granted is limited to vegetable plots of a quarter ha or less. In the 1977 study of farms in the Albany district, for example, only 13 percent of workers with access to land had five ha or more.[12]

This gradual devaluation of payment in kind goes even further. On the one hand, where workers continued to have more than vegetable plots, this land was ploughed and sown by the farmer. So, for example, on one farm

> each family was said to have been allocated three morgen. One family had about three soccer fields of arable land; the others about one soccer field. Another family said it had had arable land in the past and that it was removed and not replaced.

Worse still, this 'service' is often only provided at a fee, which makes it even less tenable as a form of wage payment. On the other hand, workers with access to land also report a decline in the amount of land they are apportioned. In the words of one farm worker, 'the farmer is reducing our land. I had land equivalent to three soccer fields and now I have one soccer field only' (Seleoane, 1984:34). Arable land therefore constitutes a very minor and diminishing proportion of the non-cash wage and it only affects a minority of the workers employed 'full-time' and who reside on the farms.

Grazing and non-grazing stock: Stockholding by farm workers is the other main component of wages in kind which has declined with the capitalisation process and especially in the course of restructuring. Former farm workers all report that they kept some form of livestock before they were forced off the land. In the survey of Sada in the eastern Cape, for example, 97 percent had some form of livestock, although this was most often only chickens (SPP, 1983: Vol.2:212). In Natal, cattle, sheep, and goat stockholding was even more widespread. Of the former farm workers and labour tenants surveyed at Mzimhlope, for instance, '86 percent of all the households interviewed had owned some cattle beforehand, 78 percent had kept goats, 25 percent — a quarter — had kept sheep, 16 percent had kept horses and 12 percent had kept pigs whilst almost everybody had owned poultry'.[13] These workers have been dispossessed of most, if not all of their livestock.[14]

Of those farm workers who remain on the farms, few are allowed to keep stock, particularly grazing animals. So, for example, in the maize farm study (De Klerk,

1984:10), only 19 percent of the farms allowed 'full-time' on-farm workers to graze livestock (chickens and perhaps pigs excluded). Similarly, in a study of farm labour in the Karoo, 60 percent of the workers had no animals grazing on the farmers' land (Kooy, 1976:25). And, as with access to arable land, those who are allowed to hold stock can keep only a restricted and decreasing number. Thus, in the Albany district survey, which covers a predominantly livestock-farming area, the extensive limitation of stock began after the severe drought of the late 1960s and by 1977 the number of animals per adult male 'full-time' farm worker averaged a mere 1.9 large stock units (Antrobus, 1984.17).

Food Rations. It is evident, then, that for those farm workers who receive part of their wage in kind, the predominant form has been whittled down to food rations. Here the content is preponderantly a carbohydrate diet of maize meal, mealies and beans. In conditions where farm workers are no longer able to grow vegetables or run stock, this represents not only a deterioration in their already meagre and spare diet but also a greater reliance on the cash part of their wage.

The following examples illustrate the limited nature of rations provided and their inadequacy in meeting the food requirements of farm workers. They also show the variations that exist in the quantity of the basic food rations and the intervals they are paid in. The type of farming has a limited bearing on the nature and degree of the variety of foodstuffs workers get; and this above all else affects those goods paid erratically or intermittently. There are also some regional differences.

In 1973, in the trial of a Coloured farm worker found guilty of killing a steenbok (deer), it was revealed that he earned R5 a month, ate meat about once every three months and was given a weekly ration of a paraffin tin of mealie meal, some salt and 8 cents worth of tobacco. He also intermittently received a paraffin tin of onions, potatoes and cabbage (*The Times*, 25 October 1973). Four years later, a survey in Albany District found that whilst 80-90 percent of farmers regularly allocated maize meal, grain and milk, 58 percent gave no regular meat ration. Of the 42 percent who did give meat regularly, 55 percent paid half a sheep or less a month. Fruit and vegetable rations included 'unmarketable potatoes, maize, blemished tomatoes, undergrade citrus, marrows and onions, damaged pineapples, etc.' These were only paid to 'regular' male workers. And 90 percent of farmers took no account of family size. If 'full-time' women workers or youths or 'casual' workers received any ration at all, it was invariably only a fraction of the men's (Antrobus, 1984:111).

On a citrus and horticultural enterprise of 6,500 ha in the Transvaal lowveld, 'full-time' workers were allocated a daily ration of one kg of meal, 80 kg dried beans, 60 kg dehydrated vegetables and 'fruit in season'. Meat was rationed at two kg a month (Godet, 1976:9).

In the Western Transvaal and Orange Free State wheat and maize farm rations consist of little more than a bag of maize meal a month and an occasional beast.

The depths of poverty in pay and conditions in the OFS were exposed in the press when nine workers from the Parys farm of Henning Klopper (former Speaker of the House of Assembly) were involved in a series of court cases, as they had been accused of stealing cattle and mealies. They said they stole because they were hungry. Klopper, in dismissing this as untrue and the work of 'jailbirds and agitators', revealed that apart from their cash wage (which he claimed ranged from R10 to R30 a month and which the workers said was in fact R5) 'they also get a sack of mealie meal and sometimes some meat and milk' (*Rand Daily Mail*, 26-27 June 1978). This was generally acknowledged to be the going wage rate in the area.

De Klerk found that on 60 percent of the farms he surveyed, an 80 kg maize meal ration was distributed per worker and the remaining 40 percent issued the ration per family. On about 80 percent of the farms, an ox or a sheep was slaughtered every two months and 'shared by all'. On the other 20 percent of farms meat was purchased in small quantities and distributed per worker usually for their direct consumption. Roughly 65 percent of the farmers distributed milk by family and 35 percent by worker. 90 percent of the farm workers and their families were allowed to consume unlimited green mealies (maize cobs) when they were in season (De Klerk, 1984:7). These ration payments specifically referred to 'full-time' on-farm workers and their families.

At the maize harvest it would seem that reaping and gleaning teams from non-farm sources also get rations. Thus, according to an elderly woman working on an OFS factory farm in the 1983 season:

> I think you do get less money at the maize, but you get bags of maize, you eat well there — maize and potatoes and beans ... Also an animal is slaughtered every week so you get some meat there. People also say you eat well at the potato harvest. A lot of food' (Barrett et al., 1985:66).

This payment lasts for an average season of 8½ weeks per year (De Klerk, 1984:7).

The approach to systematised rationing on larger and company-run estates is no more enlightened. As a worker on a sugar estate explained, 'if we don't finish work on one day we have to go back early the next morning and if we don't finish it we are not given a meal.' Food is porridge and beans twice a day and on Thursday meat is added. However, a worker who has missed a day's work stands to lose the meat ration (*Sunday Express*, 2 March 1980). Conditions on timber plantations are little different. At Anglo-American's De Hoek saw-mill complex, for example, rations are spare and controlled, issued twice a day on workdays only.[15] Indeed, the rationale underlying the content of rations paid to workers expresses the logic of a system based on forced and super-exploited labour. A company official of a Transvaal maize and cattle farm revealed that the company supplies 'an adequate diet in terms of calories and protein for a man, his wife and between one and two children'. The average size of worker families on the farm was 6.2 people (Young, 1979) which poses the question of what the employers expected the remaining family members to eat.

Sectoral and regional differences. Are there sectoral and regional differences in food rationing practices and have these been affected by restructuring? Whilst some can be discerned and these are of interest, they have only a qualified significance since generally the food ration is very low and unbalanced.

Sheep shearers have a payment in kind 'built in' to their wage calculation — namely, a *slagding* (slaughter animal) for every 500 to 1,000 sheep shorn.[16] This effectively means that at best they eat meat once a week or so when they are working. However, their apparently high meat diet is deceptive, as is made clear by

Isak Juris, foreman of one of five sheep-shearing teams operating from Rietbron.

> We don't work every day or even every week. At times we are laid off for two weeks, for three weeks on a run, on occasions there may not be work for a month. There is only work for about eight months in a year. You see some of the farmers shear sheep once a year, others twice a year. It's the same type of sheep only the wool is longer if you shear once a year. The price of wool on the market goes up with the length of wool, but we get paid the same rate. Goats are sheared twice a year. Their wool is more expensive.
>
> We're just from baas Jan Snyman's farm in Prince Albert district. It's about 25km from here. He came to fetch us and brought us back. We've been away for 2¼ days shearing sheep and goats ... just over 500 in all. We don't know if there will be work next week ... We just sit and wait in the meantime.
>
> The farmers slaughter a sheep for us once we have sheared 500 animals. But that doesn't mean we eat lots of meat. Not all jobs require so many sheep sheared and in any case the meat, when we receive it, has to be shared among seven workers who try to bring most of it home to their families (Wentzel, 1984:85).

Furthermore, few if any shearers receive any other form of rations and they usually have to sleep in the shearing shed or out in the open (Kooy, 1976:8).

In general, working in animal husbandry represents at best a very limited advantage when it comes to the inclusion of meat and other animal products in ration payments. In the Albany district, for instance, Antrobus found that meat rationing was not an important factor on small stock farms, although half a sheep or less was the main form in which meat was allocated (1984:115).

On crop, vegetable or fruit farms the tendency to use blemished or unmarketable products as rations may have been relatively greater. Even this is tempered by the rationalisation and specialisation of production (see Chapter 1). Where goods are not produced on the farm, farmers who buy in rations are inclined to purchase the cheapest and least perishable product — grain, dehydrated vegetables, etc. Where specialisation has occurred, the whole product is usually saleable. Thus, workers on commercial dairy farms do not necessarily receive a milk ration because, as one farmer explained, 'they used to get skim milk, but none now, now that I am a fresh milk producer' (Antrobus, 1984:113). Their experiences are likely to be replicated on fruit and vegetable farms producing quotas for factory processing rather than for the fresh market.[17] Finally, in rationalising production, farmers have tried to turn unsaleable products to profit — for example, disposing of non-marketable vegetables, etc. by setting up their own pig units or selling to other farmers. Once again, the rations of workers are affected. In these and other ways restructuring has tended to whittle away at or even remove food wages in kind.

Alcohol. One regional rationing practice which is characteristic of the Cape is that of supplying workers with a quantity of wine (or spirits) on a regular basis, popularly known as the *dop* system (tot system).[18] Although some farmers do not allocate alcohol[19] a UNISA study found that 73 percent of farmers surveyed supplied liquor to workers in their employ; just under half were given alcohol daily (Theron, 1976:144:7:36). In the words of one farmer, De Jongh, who owned the farm Vlakkeland, five km from Paarl:

> I never pay children who work for me less than R1.50 a week. Women receive R2.50 and men never earn less than R5. I'll be quite frank. I give them a little wine in the morning and two bottles each during the day because I like to keep them happy' (*Sunday Times*, 24 February 1974).

This and other evidence (Graaff, 1976:2) points to a change in ritual surrounding wine rationing and a possible reduction of the quantity received. For whereas in the past it was common for workers to be given nine to ten *dops* in the course of a working day,[20] it would seem that more farmers are inclined to give out wine at the end of the day or week. In 1983 Johan Olivier, an 80-year-old ostrich farmer from Oudtshoorn, stated: 'We still give them (his 25 labourers) a *sopie* (small tot) every evening ... otherwise after sundown they leave you. Most of them wait until 10 o'clock at night until we come round to give them the liquor' (Buirski, 1984:8). What this also shows is that wine rationing is not confined to the grape growing areas, as is often claimed (e.g., Antrobus, 1984:32). Nor, it should be added, are such rations given to adults alone. Children working on the farms are also supplied with wine whatever their age.[21]

Wine is not listed as part of the payment in kind farmers make to workers, as it has been illegal to do so since 1963.[22] But it is rather a moot point whether farmers do or do not calculate it as part of the payment made to workers.[23] Workers see it as a substitute payment in lieu of cash and most favour its abolition, preferring a cash wage increase (UNISA Survey, 1975 in Antrobus, 1984).

Restructuring has thus seen a contraction of the wage in kind to the extent that food rations provide the primary and often the sole content of this form of payment. At the same time, the size and the content of the food payment has altered little or even declined over the years. At present it falls well short of meeting the elementary food requirements of workers in commercial agriculture. All these reductions in payments in kind have seen a growth in the proportion of farm workers who receive no non-cash wage at all.

> Food on the farm is shop price, meat is shop price. You have to buy everything you want. The farmer gives you nothing ... Things were a bit better then years ago because then they used to give you meat and meal and sugar for free. But now everything has changed. You have to buy everything out of the money he gives you, so he keeps all the money himself. It must all go back to him. This all happened about eight years ago (mid-1970s). All the farmers changed. They stand together, they eat out of the same spoon (Schmidt, 1984:44).

With few exceptions, most 'casual' or 'seasonal' workers, whether they are drawn from the workforce resident on the farms, from the labour reserves in the 'homelands' or from the segregated ghettoes of 'white' towns, receive no food rations at all. It is commonplace that workers must make and bring their own food if they are resident on the farm or travel between their homes and the farms on a daily basis. Or they have to buy their food from the farmer, an obligation often imposed on those who stay on the farms for the period of their employment. Thus, in 1982, children working on the white-owned farms near Groblersdal to help support their families, sleep at home, their mother says, and a farm lorry fetches them every morning and returns them at eight at night. They get R2 a week and from this they have to buy their food as no food is given to them at their place of work. As a result none of the money paid to them can be saved (James, 1983:53).

Nor does migrant contract work automatically mean that such workers receive food as part of their pay, as the contract of Masingayi Xhalalegusha reveals. Hired to work on a company-owned poultry farm, the terms of his contract were: 'period of contract — one year; no rations supplied; an eleven-hour day and a seven-day week; rate of pay — R6.50 a week' or a wage of 8.4 cents an hour.[24]

Likewise, although 'full-time' on-farm male workers are relatively more likely to get a food in-kind payment, a substantial (and growing) proportion do not. Surveys of ex-farm workers who have been relocated into the reserves reveal that a substantial number received no food payment. This applied to at least 32 percent of those now living at Sada, for example (SPP, 1983: Vol.2,211), and to a substantial number of ex-farm and labour tenants from northern Natal living at Mzimhlope, for whom the greatest hardship and most strongly resented feature of their eviction from so-called 'white farmland' is their loss of land and livestock, rather than rations (SPP, 1983: Vol4, 357). The advanced nature of this process for 'full-time' workers (in some areas at least) was revealed indirectly in a 1983 study of malnutrition on the vineyards and fruit farms of the Stellenbosch district (Vergnani, 1984:13).

> The argument that farm workers receive food as part of their remuneration does not hold water in Stellenbosch. Only 15 percent of the malnourished group (12.6 of 84 cases) receive food and this is usually only vegetables (e.g., cabbage) in season.

'Full-time' farm workers, too, are frequently forced to buy their food from the 'farm shop' or from rural traders.[25] Clearly, at the same time as food rations have become the primary, if not sole, form of non-cash wage payment in commercial agriculture, a growing number of farm workers do not receive this form of payment at all.

Housing[26] is a further form of non-cash payment that warrants consideration. It is particularly interesting that, as other forms of non-cash wages have declined, so the stress laid by farmers on the benefits of farm housing to agricultural workers has grown. This raises two points:

i) It has long been claimed by farmers that workers get 'free housing' as part of their pay. This stemmed from the rationale that farm workers, in building their dwellings on the farmer's property, were either making a saving or being paid in kind. Either way, housing allegedly boosted workers' incomes beyond their face value. The provision of 'good' housing is viewed as a key and cheap way to realise the goal of 'stabilising' the agrarian workforce around a nucleus of on-farm workers. As an eastern Cape citrus farmer saw it, it 'provides the farmer with what a home-owning middle class provides to a nation — a vested interest, an acceptance of the status quo that is both desirable and financially possible (Aires, 1976). In other words, their new-found readiness to call for, if not install, 'decent'

housing reflects a change in the way they perceive how they should go about securing a supply of labour adequate to their needs (increasingly in qualitative rather
than in quantitative terms). Perhaps with the exception of some employers of
migrant workers, a small number of farmers first began to build housing for some
workers in their employ only in the 1960s. Their numbers have grown, albeit slowly
over the years, and it is this shift which is the source of the claim behind 'free
housing' under restructured terms. They contend that farm workers live 'rent free'
in accommodation built and provided by the farmer.

ii) But what substance do these claims have?

● In theory it is possible to include housing as a payment in kind where farmers
have made specific accommodation provisions. But allowing farm workers to build
houses on white-owned farm land has never represented a form of payment to
the worker. This is not to suggest that it is not a social condition of employment
in the sector. In the particular conditions of national oppression in South Africa,
where the location and residence of the African majority is restricted and controlled by the pass laws/influx control/reserve system, it has been one of the forces
driving Africans into farm work,[28] because it enabled them to work and at the
same time live with their families. Restructuring, and particularly the expulsion
of over one million Africans from farm land, has altered these conditions so substantially, however, that they no longer hold true in general. And where they still exist
the worker has indeed paid rent. Rather than being a recipient of housing as pay,
the on-farm worker family has had to (and still does) pay in part or all of the labour
of its members. These terms are integral to the conditions of 'full-time' farm service.

● In practice, restructuring, and particularly the changes in labour forms in the
sector, have had a direct bearing on the question of housing for farm workers.
Notwithstanding the fact that proportionately more farmers are building accommodation for some sections of the agrarian workforce, the process has generally
served to relieve farmers of the onus of providing housing for their farm workers.
This has occurred in one of two ways.
Most farmers continue to make no provision for 'seasonal' and 'casual' workers
who have to be accommodated on farms for weeks or months at a time. Generally
these women, men and children are housed in sheds, outhouses or barns (Bekker,
1982:14) or with 'permanent' workers resident on the farms. Others are forced
to build their own shelters[29] or to sleep in the open. At the same time, the growth
in the practice of trucking workers to and from the villages and towns on a daily
basis — so-called 'commuting' — means that farmers are relieved of the responsibility of providing accommodation altogether. This is increasingly preferred by
them and is only tempered by the distances they have to travel to get labour at
the wages they are offering. When these are too great, the cost in time and in
money makes daily transportation impractical and uneconomic.

For farm workers, whose options are limited by whether farmers will allow them
to remain on the farms at night, commuting adds hours to an already extended
work day. Travelling to and from the farms in open lorries and trailers is rough,
cramped and often dangerous,[30] and has resulted in injury and death.[31] More

importantly, in some respects, it puts an additional squeeze on farm workers' wages — since they are charged for the transport. Either this payment has to be made for every trip they take, or, less directly, the costs of transport are deducted from their wages or treated as a payment in kind.[32]

At the same time, by returning home each day workers are removed from the direct control of their employers in their non-working hours. They are not separated from their families for long periods and they do not have to live with strangers in compound conditions. These considerations often outweigh the cost of travelling. Some workers in 'full-time' employment have moved into nearby towns or villages when this has been possible.[33] As bad as housing conditions are there, they are often better and certainly no worse than those on the farms.

The other way by which the onus of providing accommodation for workers on the farms has been shifted from the farmers is, paradoxically, in its provision. On the one hand, the majority of farm workers living on farms have had to build their own housing. Antrobus (1984:138) shows that 70 percent of farm workers' houses in the Albany district survey were built by the workers themselves. This probably applies to most parts of the country, with the exception of the Western Cape and the Natal sugar belt. This means that many farmers, as in the past, simply ignore the housing question for farm workers living on their property.[34] The burden is borne entirely by farm workers.

On the other hand, whilst the state and a growing number (albeit still a minority) of farmers have increasingly been more ready to acknowledge that some farm workers — at least those resident 'permanently' on the farms — should be 'decently housed',[35] generally they have been unwilling to make the financial outlay. The state, in turn, has been restrained by considerations of cost and, even more, by its general policy on the provision of housing for Africans with respect to both location and subsidy. It has acted to restrict and control the number of Africans on the farms, and has used housing to regulate their presence there. On the sugar estates, for example, millers-cum-planters may not house more than three percent of their African workforce as married men,[36] and generally labour control boards limit the number of families allowed to reside (and therefore be housed) on a particular enterprise. At the same time, the white minority state has tried to minimise the subsidisation of African housing, wherever it is located. As the SAAU pointed out (in an expression of its conviction that workers' housing was not the farmer's responsibility), none of the meagre budget allocated for the housing of Africans is earmarked for farm workers (SAAU, 1978:73).

The state does have a scheme, however, in the form of loans to farmers to assist them with the construction of workers' houses. This lame attempt to help resolve the housing problem in the countryside by transferring responsibility back to the farmers was introduced in 1974 with Coloured farm workers uppermost in mind.[37] Most applications for and most grants of loans go to farmers in the Western Cape. In 1977 they represented 55 percent of the 326 applicants and 55 percent of the 192 granted loans. And as the Minister of Agriculture made clear when explaining why some applications in the Western Cape were rejected:

In a few cases loans have been requested to house families of black (African) labourers in the Greater Western Cape Province where loans are granted for the housing of the families of Coloured farm labourers only. (Hansard, 16 February 1978: Col.180).

In that same year, only three loans were made to farmers in Natal, 34 in the Transvaal and 30 in the OFS, with a stipulation as to the number of houses they were meant to build. In 1982, the Minister of Finance announced that 'loans for black (African) housing have been discontinued'.[38] This is not to suggest that Coloured farm workers fare particularly well with respect to housing, although their poverty is somewhat less acute than that of African farm workers. Writing of Calitzdorp near Oudtshoorn in the Little Karoo in 1983, researchers report that:

> Housing for rural Coloured people is very varied ranging from mud huts to modern small bungalows, while some farmers accommodate their workers in the more commodious solid structures built in earlier days by small-holders, sharecroppers and *bywoners* (tenant farmers) and later deserted. Few houses are supplied with piped water and in a well-watered district it is very rare to find a water tank near workers' dwellings ... Wood is the main fuel and candles and paraffin lamps supply light (Horner and Van Wyk, 1984:62).

For the most part, restructuring has enabled the majority of farmers to shift responsibility for the provision of housing in the sector to the workers who have had either to build their own housing or to find accommodation in the towns or villages. The farmers have also tried to pass the burden to the state, which has evidently been unwilling to take it on.[39]

Housing for workers who do not live on the farms or who live in accommodation which they have built on farm land cannot be included as part of their income, although it is a consideration when assessing the cost of living. The accommodation built by farmers — with or without state loans — is what has to be looked at as a non-cash wage form. It would be inaccurate to presume that the few houses built per year with state loans represent the total housing constructed by farmers for workers resident on the farms.[40] Most farmers do not apply for loans, but some have built housing or compounds at their own expense to accommodate workers in their employ.[41] But even allowing for this, the number involved affects the housing conditions of only a minority of farm workers, especially since the quality of the housing built is constrained by the amount of money farmers are prepared to lay out for the purpose. The standard design — considered the best of farmer-constructed housing for farm workers — has a steel frame, four rooms, concrete floor, no ceiling, asbestos or iron roof and possibly only one internal door.[42] Since construction costs are calculated by meterage, the tendency is to make these dwellings very small. On a farm producing maize, beef, milk and potatoes in the eastern Transvaal, for example,

> until recently most workers had to build their own houses, getting no help from the farmer. Recently, farm F has built location-type houses and the farm population is required to destroy their present dwellings. They are unhappy about this because the new houses are much smaller (Seleoane, 1984:28).

Virtually none have electricity and few have internal water.

The other major type of dwelling built for farm workers is the compound — a barrack-like structure made up of one or two stable-like rooms or several small ones adjacent to one another with common ablution facilities if these are provided, for often toilets, washrooms and even water are not. So, for example, in the eastern Transvaal ten girls (ten to fifteen years of age) working in the fields were housed in a compound without water, light, heating or ablution facilities. They slept on cement bunks and the blankets they used they had brought from home (Anti-Slavery Society, 1983:23). In others, no beds are provided and workers are forced to construct their own from cardboard boxes or wood or otherwise to sleep on the cement floor.[43] Thus, on an OFS factory farm, for example,

> 'the conditions are very bad. We have made these wooden pallets to sleep on because there are no beds. There are some bunk metal beds in other hostels but these we have made for ourselves. There is no place to wash, no shower. We all bought these basins to wash in. There is no water from the taps in each hall and outside also. The outside water is very dirty. It is from the dam. When the water inside finished we drank that dam water even though we were not allowed to, but what could we drink?' (Barrett et al., 1983:66).

Many workers share the rooms, depending on their size and the number of workers to be housed. This invariably means cramped conditions and a lack of privacy. At the De Hoek sawmill, eight men shared a room (*Post*, 19 November 1979). On another company estate in the north-eastern Transvaal, there were two compounds on the farm. Men were housed two to a room, women three or four per room and 'the number of children per room depends on the size of the children'. This estate also had 47 two-roomed houses for the men allowed to 'live with their wives' (Young, 1979:56).

It is this type of construction and these conditions which are the substance of the housing component of payment in kind. As things stand, they represent a negligible contribution to the wage of a minority of workers.

The cash content of payment in kind

Lastly, with respect to the shift to a cash-based wage system in the process of restructuring, we see that even where wages take the form of payments in kind, if they are not immediately consumed, they in fact conceal a cash content. In other words, most workers try to convert a substantial part of the goods they receive into cash. This is clearly evidenced by practices recorded on maize farms, where both 'full-time' and seasonal workers transformed a part, if not all of their maize wage in kind into cash.

Often, especially for 'casual' work, this conversion entails a further (and often considerable) expenditure of time and labour for very meagre returns. So, for example, in 1981 in Pasha village in the Lebowa 'homeland', the majority of the women were working for one farmer, and all were being paid in tomatoes.

> A tin of tomatoes for a day's work means that people have to rely on barter as a means of getting food ... Tomatoes as a means of exchange had become

totally devalued. Women were having to exchange a ten litre tin of tomatoes for about 15 or 20 cents worth of mealie meal because there was such a glut (Buirski, 1984:7).

Others living at the Bothashoek relocation settlement in the same reserve were working on the surrounding white-owned farms for reeds. These reeds were then woven into mats and sold. One woman said it took her two to three weeks to weave the bigger mats. So that 'If she is lucky, she sometimes makes R20 a month, but usually this figure is nearer R10 or R15' (Yawitch, 1982:63).

These examples also show that, although the cash value of wages in kind may be greater than direct cash payments for casual work, such calculations do not take into consideration the labour expended to convert the goods into money. Farmers ignore the work that goes into this conversion when giving goods a money value. And workers have little choice. Their labour is undervalued, whichever way, and their efforts are concentrated on the struggle for survival.

To summarise, restructuring has changed the form wages take in commercial agriculture. There has been a steady shift to a cash-based wage system which has meant;

- that generally workers who receive some form of payment get part of it in cash;

- that the content and composition of the non-cash payments they receive have diminished and changed, now primarily taking the form of food or food rations;

- that the part payment of wages in non-cash forms generally applies to adult men who work 'full-time' and are resident on the farms, and to migrant workers on contract, also usually men;

- that women and children and workers employed 'part-time' are less likely to receive payment in kind, and when they do it is a fraction of that received by male 'full-time' workers;

- that many workers in commercial agriculture receive no form of payment in kind at all;

- and that wages in kind conceal a cash content.

This is not to suggest that payment in kind is not important to the subsistence of agricultural workers, given the inordinately low level of wages in the sector. Rather, it is to argue that the primary component of wages in the sector takes a cash form. And that it is this cash wage which is the key indicator of wage levels in the sector.

Cash wages — their material form
Generally speaking, farmers tend to pay cash wages in rands, i.e., in the local expression of a universal equivalent. However, there are some farmers who do not pay in currency. Instead, they substitute tokens for money which are exchangeable in their stores or in local stores with which the farmer has an arrangement. The extent of this practice is not known, but that it does occur can be seen

from a survey in Oudtshoorn (Western Cape) in 1983, which found that, for example,

> Gerrit le Roux, a wealthy wine and ostrich farmer in the De Rust region of the district, pays his labourers in 'good for' once every two weeks, because it is too much bother to give cash. A 'good for' is a locally accepted bill of exchange which labourers may exchange for cash or commodities at a nearby café or trading store. In the case of Le Roux's farm, the nearest cafés are in De Rust, some five km away (Yawitch, 1982:58).

Now whilst this form of 'cash' payment relieves the farmer from directly paying out currency, it binds the worker to the farmer's store or local trading stores where the arrangements for these exchanges can be realised. It restricts their expenditure options and it is likely that workers have difficulty converting the tokens into cash rather than goods.

To summarise, farmers pay in cash, or in kind, or in combination, according to which form is the least costly to them and enables them to exercise the greatest authority and control with the least responsibility.

Methods of payment

Having established the material forms that payment to black workers in commercial agriculture takes, we need to examine the methods of payment which characterise the sector. The introduction of this aspect of wages is a departure from general practice in the literature of wages in commercial agriculture, which tends to treat all aspects of wages statistically without analysing their forms and even less so the methods by which they are made. Such an approach presumes these to be conventional (for capitalism), and relatively uniform. But in the conditions which prevail in South African commercial agriculture, this is not the case.[44] Therefore, any analysis of wage levels has to take into consideration not only the forms wages take, but also the methods by which they are paid. These are numerous and far from standardised. They affect the level of wages in a way which is concealed by figures averaged out to monthly or annual totals (as low as these are) and obscured by presumptions that agricultural workers' wages are paid at frequent and regular intervals of the year in a fixed form.

By methods of payment is meant the way the wage rate is determined, the intervals of pay, whether workers are paid directly or through an intermediary, and the sanctioning of workers through wage manipulation. The problems of assessing payment methods are several. First, it is an area which has been little studied and the information that exists is there more often by chance and inference than by design. Second, although each of these aspects is treated separately, this is essentially an heuristic device. In practice, not only are they interwoven in particular combinations, but it is this very combination which carries with it the full weight of their implications for wage levels. Third, each has been affected by restructuring although the impact of the process is far from uniform. Fourth, methods of pay differ somewhat for full- and part-time workers. Last, they are also affected by and affect the composition of the wage. In this context my analysis is qualified by the limitations of the material base on which it has had to be drawn. It will undoubtedly be refined by further research.

Determining the wage rate
One of the most important consequences of restructuring for wage determination and methods of pay has been the growing trend on the part of employers in the sector to link wages to output. Whereas prior to restructuring wages tended to be fixed (however arbitrarily), from the 1970s farmers have increasingly tended to manipulate the wage base. Although many workers are still paid on a fixed rate basis, it has become more and more commonplace for most farmers to operate some form of incentive scheme. The essential reason underlying this development 'is to increase daily output so that the number of employees can be reduced and thereby labour costs reduced' (La Borde, 1980:6.9). Incentive schemes operated by farmers vary both in their main content and in their particular combination.

Bonuses
Some farmers make a fixed payment to 'full-time' workers plus an annual bonus. This is an additional lump-sum made either at the end of the agricultural cycle or at the end of the calendar year as a so-called 'Christmas bonus'. The most outstanding example of a 'bonus' payment scheme related to a production cycle is that practised on farms producing maize.[45] Here workers receive a very small part of their cash wage at regular intervals, and the bulk of it comes after the harvest in one lump payment. De Klerk (1984:22) found that just under 58 percent of 'full-time' workers in the study were paid 20 percent or less of their total cash wage at intervals over the year. Once a year, at the end of the agricultural cycle in August or September, they were paid 80 percent of their cash wage as a lump-sum bonus. In fact, for 98 percent of the workers, half or more of their total cash wage took this form. For half the workers the annual bonus represented up to 70 percent of their total wage, including the food ration. When averaged out

> the average permanent wage rate estimated by the author was a little under R150 per month, of which just under half took the form of food, just over a quarter an annual bonus in cash and/or kind, and the rest in regular cash payments.[46]

Thus, through this type of bonus scheme, maize producers are able to defer a substantial proportion of workers' wages to the end of the season. In fact, it is possible to go further and argue that this method of payment is nothing less than a disguised form of credit, advanced *by workers to the farmer*. Although it affects thousands of workers and is not confined to maize, this practice is not entirely typical of many branches in the sector. Bonus schemes are less extreme and more discretionary. The practice of farmers in the Langkloof valley in the Western Cape, for example, is more typical (Bekker et al., 1982:18). In a survey of deciduous fruit producers, approximately 80 percent of the farmers said that in addition to paying a fixed wage to 'full-time' workers, they also pay a 'piece-work' bonus at the end of the picking and packing season equal to two weeks' pay, i.e., R18 for women and R26 for men (1980). The authors write that

> in addition, most farmers either pay a Christmas bonus or a bonus to workers who have worked regularly during the year (i.e., a selective bonus). This incentive bonus was also estimated to be roughly equivalent to two weeks' wages.

This meant that 'full-time' workers received between 4 and 7.7 percent of their annual cash wage (R676 for men, R468 for women) in the form of lump-sum bonuses and their pay, although small, was more evenly spread through the year. In fact, it seems to be generally the case that bonuses represent a very small amount of the worker's income. On a company farm in the Transvaal, the bonus was put at ten percent of the gross annual wage of 'full-time' workers (Young, 1979).

Table 5.2
Incentive payment schemes reported by farmers in the Albany District — 1977

Worker	Reason	Amount
Tractor driver	every hour driven	2-5 cents
Shepherd	lamb weaned	1-10 cents
Shepherd	Angora kid weaned	15 cents or less
Herdsman	calf weaned	R1.00
Herdsman	cow calved	R1.00
Herdsman	night injection	R2.00
Herdsman	sales bonus:	
	— weather	50 cents
	— grade bovine	R2.50
	— stud Hereford	R5.00
General worker	killing predators	R2.00 (bottle of brandy)
	killing jackals	R5.00

Source: Antrobus, 1984:127.

What Table 5.2 shows is that farmers tend to link incentive payments to an aspect of production. In fact, whilst 40 percent of farmers in this survey reported giving no 'traditional' bonus, only 25 percent made no form of periodic extra payment. But the size of these is pitiful. In total, the amount paid through such incentives averaged less than R20 per year in the district.

Bonuses as deferred payment as well as an incentive scheme are confined to 'full-time' workers. This is not to suggest that all workers employed 'full-time' get bonuses, nor does it imply that those who receive such payments are treated equally. On the contrary, within such schemes there is a hierarchy of reward, which relates to both skill and authority. On the wattle plantations, for example, 'full-time' timber workers are paid monthly bonuses. Chain sawyers are paid a bonus if their chainsaw has used below a certain quantity of cutting chain (a major cost saving), the cutting bars have lasted well, general maintenance costs are low and their team's production has been above a certain level and whether the chain-sawyer is always fully equipped with protective clothing and tools while working.

First-line black supervisors (*'indunas'*) earn bonuses depending

> *inter alia* on the standard of team discipline, the condition of the produce of the gang (work team), uniformity of work and the condition of the field after the team has completed work (La Borde, 1980:6.2-6.12).

Clearly, then, for most farm workers incentive bonuses are both discretionary and conditional, and the percentage they represent of the total wage is both small and variable. Any figure that is given represents the maximum possible under the best circumstances.

Piece rates in combination

Aside from an incentive scheme built around bonuses, with restructuring the wages of many farm workers have come to be determined by worker output which is calculated according to the task, piece or quota of work to be performed within a specified period. Although the extent of the practice is unknown, some farmers pay workers in full-time employment by piece rates. In the Albany District, for example, one farmer was found to pay a small wage plus what he called bonuses for everything (Antrobus, 1984:127) — effectively a piece rate. Determining full-time wages by piece rates also appears to be prevalent on the timber plantations. Writing of wattle farms in Natal, La Borde (1980:6.2—6.12) states that from the point of view of plantation management

> increasing attention has been given to incentive schemes to extend the length of the working day. Extending the working day length combats the escalating direct overhead costs for labour per tonne of product.

Although he gives no indication of wage levels on these estates, piece rate payment stimulates the tendency to work overlong hours. It may result in higher pay, but this is at a price in workers' health and safety. It is therefore not surprising that the timber industry is reputed to have the second-highest accident rate in the country.[47] Paying 'full-time' workers according to a piece rate scheme, however, appears to be relatively less common.

Piece rates are particularly widespread in determining 'seasonal' and 'casual' workers' wages. Piece rates are set in one of two ways. Either a quota is fixed at a given rate, and all production above the fixed rate is paid according to output, or straight piece rates are applied, which means that the products are given a monetary wage value and the wage of the worker is determined by the number of products produced.

Many examples of this practice are to be found in all parts of the country. Table 5.3 gives an indication of the schemes in operation for different branches of production.

Table 5.3
Fixed rate plus incentive bonus schemes for workers in seasonal employment

Worker/Branch/Year	Fixed Rate (R)	Incentive (R)	Wage (approx.) (R)
Sugar cane cutter, Natal, 1977	2/day	1.50[1]	52 — 91/month
Fruit pickers, Elgin/Hex River Valley — 1976	1.05/day	0.95[2]	32 — 40/month
Citrus estate, Transvaal, 1976	6/15 days presence	½ c/bag picked	9.75 for 15 days
Tea pickers, Sapekoe (Tvl) 1979	20/month	4½c/kg	28/month

1 — average, estimated by employer's labour recruiting organisation (SILO).
2 — maximum.

Sources: *Financial Mail*, 17 June 1977; Petersen, 1976; Graaff, 1976; Godet, 1976; *Post*, 7 August 1979.

It reveals that approximately 40 percent of seasonal workers' cash wages paid on a piece rate system is not fixed, that is, it varies according to their productivity. Often the basic quotas are set too high, making it impossible for workers to achieve a reasonable bonus. And frequently workers are not paid in full for the number of pieces they produce.

The experiences of workers on the Phaswana Coffee Project in 'independent' Venda (Northern Transvaal) give an insight into the problems these incentive schemes create for workers. Owned by the Venda Development Corporation and Sapekoe (both parastatals), the estate employed 'casual' workers to dig a quota of pits (each about a metre deep) a day. Men were paid R1 a day to dig 108 pits and women 70 cents for 72 pits (1979). Their rate of pay was a maximum R23 (men) and R16.10 (women) a month. However, since their daily tickets were not checked unless the exact number of pits were dug, it was hard to achieve even this poor wage. Furthermore, the incentive rate of pay (R1.20 and R1 for men and women respectively) for a quota half as large again as the one they were now forced to reach could only be achieved by working at full speed all day, that is, from 6.30 a.m. to 4 p.m. every day including rainy days. If injured, they lost their pay and had to foot any hospital bills. Many workers became ill with back complaints and swollen hands. These grievances led to a work stoppage where workers demanded a reduction in the quota and a pay increase (*Post*, 18 December 1979). The response of management was predictably recalcitrant. They refused to lower the quota of pits to be dug each day, although after several months workers were given a R6 increase plus 25 kg of maize meal every two weeks and a number of pills for round worms.[49]

Piece rates only
The other piece rate system in operation provides no basic wage at all. Historically, this has long applied to sheep shearers. In the Karroo in 1984:

> The farmer sets the price — 25 cents a sheep or a goat. It was first 10 cents, then 15, then 20 and last year it was 25. But we have to be satisfied with the

bosses' price. What can we do? There are four teams in Rietbron alone.[50]

In an earlier study it was stated that a competent hand shearer could shear 50 sheep a day (Kooy, 1976). However, in the team interviewed in Rietbron, the youngest and by common consent the fastest shearer reported that he had only managed 31 sheep the day before. In fact, in summer, working from 6 a.m. to 7 p.m. during *'die lang dae'* (summer), shearers manage to shear an average of 25 to 35 animals a day. 'This means that we earn betwen R6 and R9 a day, on average 3 to four days a week ... the only extra income we receive is the *slagding'* (slaughter animal) (Wentzel, 1984: 86). At best that makes a weekly cash income of R36.

Machine shearers are able to shear more sheep in the same period — 250 to 440 a week. This makes wages of between R60 and R110 a week possible, at least in theory. But in raising their output, either the length of the period of employment is shortened, since the number of sheep to be shorn is finite, or the number of shearing teams is reduced, generating unemployment. In practice, restructuring has led to a combination of both these trends, which offsets the high wage level suggested by these calculations. If workers' earnings are raised, this is usually at no extra cost to the farmer, but rather at the expense of other workers. The practice at the maize harvest of paying seasonal workers a proportion of the crop is effectively a variation on this form of piece rate payment. Instead of fixing a rate for each bag of maize gathered by gleaners *agter die masjien* (behind the machine), or hand harvested, the rate of pay is set as a proportion of the total quantity of bags gathered. For reapers this means maize harvested, whereas for gleaners the proportion is of the amount gleaned. On a Southern Transvaal farm in the late 1970s, seasonal workers hired to glean were paid 6 bags for every 100 gathered, or the cash equivalent (Young, 1979). De Klerk estimated that the rate in the Western Transvaal in 1981 was 8 to 10 percent of the glean and for hand reaping 4 to 5 percent of the harvest (De Klerk, 1984: 13). Whatever the rate, it is determined by worker output within a given set of constraints — the size of the harvest and/or the rate of wastage by the combine harvester.

In addition to these two instances, this type of piece rate system is used to set part-time wages on farms producing other goods. For example, inferring from La Borde's study of the wattle industry in Natal, it is probable that this system is used on the timber estates. He reported that because of bad organisation bark gatherers experience difficulty in obtaining sufficient bark to realise a basic wage. (1980: 7.9).

Similarly, in the Albany District 'gangs' of women 'part-time' workers who work the year round clearing bush and eradicating noxious weeds, are paid piece rates. (Antrobus, 1984: 89). Not all these schemes to stimulate output are successful. To wit:

> 'We used to have a lot of trouble meeting our daily (and) weekly picking quotas. We'd tried piece work and other incentives unsuccessfully. We also tried strict supervision and harshness to no avail.'

Farmers then have to devise other schemes in order to manipulate workers and counter what is essentially a form of worker resistance. In the instance cited above, the workforce was divided into two teams. Workers were given a weekly target to pick. If they did not finish, they had to work on Saturday. The farmer reported that not only had they not had to work a single Saturday, but that he was able to use a workforce 70 percent the size of the one used in the previous season for a similar sized crop. (Aires, 1976: 14).

Generally, the available evidence (which, it must be stressed, is not particularly sensitive to this question) tends to suggest a piece rate tied to a quota system as the most prevalent way by which farmers determine 'part-time' wages, for harvest-type work at least. Given the low level of wages, this is perhaps one of the main means by which they can raise output without direct compulsion, and at the same time limit the size of the workforce. For workers, whom farmers accuse of laziness and tedium, there is little point in working long hours at breakneck speed for invariably meagre rewards. Payment by piece rate is not designed to yield high wages. So, notwithstanding the fact that farmers are able to raise productivity and profits with these schemes, they often do not work on their own. Invariably they have to be coupled with a range of penalties, if not direct coercion. For workers, earning a wage by piece rate means that many, if not all workers 'battle to buy the rudiments of a balanced diet which means that they become more incapacitated and less able to produce piece work output which earns their only incomes' (Levetan, 1984: 108).

Flat rate

Finally, 'part-time' workers who are not paid on piece rate (but earn an income), are paid on a flat rate basis which is fixed by the day, or the job, or the week. Although the way of determining the wage is unchanged in some respects from the *itago* system where workers are hired 'casually' for the day, even this form of calculation has been affected by restructuring, and specifically by rationalisation and the drive for productivity. Where workers are hired to assist others employed on a piece rate basis, they are paid a flat rate because their pace of work is set by the piece rate workers. This applies to the *dagsmanne* ('day men') hired on the shear to do jobs ranging from floor sweeping to fleece throwing and wool sorting (both the latter are in fact skilled jobs) (Kooy, 1976: 1). Similarly, the children and young women who 'comb' behind the fruit pickers' bags are also paid a flat daily rate *(Post,* 23 July 1979). However, where the workers' pace is not set by other workers, for example, on jobs like weeding, hoeing or clearing irrigation canals, workers increasingly have their pay tied to a specified quota of work which the farmer expects them to have completed in the period that they are hired for. Sometimes this is implicit, but often farmers stipulate that day rates are tied to completing the task. Thus, even in seemingly unchanged methods of determining pay, workers' wages are affected by the process of restructuring.

In short, the impact of restructuring on the way that wage rates are determined has increasingly linked pay to some form of incentive scheme in order to raise productivity. Whilst for workers employed 'full-time' this has generally tended to take the form of bonuses, for those hired to do 'part-time' work the trend is to link most if not the entire wage output through piece rates and quota schemes. This has meant that workers have had to work even harder to earn the same, if not even lower wages.

Intervals of payment

The second aspect of methods of payment concerns the intervals at which wages are paid to farm workers. The basic problem with the material on this question is that it often indicates the time intervals over which workers' payment is calculated, but this does not necessarily mean that payment is made *at* these intervals. Nevertheless, it is possible to discern some pattern in the variety of practices. And it would seem that these on the whole are shaped by methods of payment to workers in 'full-time' employment.

'Full-time' workers

At the most general level, the only farm workers who are paid a part, if not the whole, of their wage at regular intervals over a sustained period of time are those who are employed 'full-time'. This payment is most regularised, frequent and most evenly spread in the Western Cape, where 'full-time' workers are most likely to be paid their wages at weekly intervals — this applies to payments both in cash and in kind. For 'full-time' workers in the rest of the countryside, the intervals of payment are generally less frequent, particularly when it comes to the cash part of their wage. On the whole they tend to be paid monthly.

There are, however, many exceptions. So, for example, even in the Western Cape, where comparatively speaking conditions are more standardised, many workers experience longer than weekly gaps between payments. For example, Gerrit le Roux, the Oudtshoorn farmer cited earlier, preferred to pay workers fortnightly. But, worse still, there are farmers who stretch the gaps between cash payments beyond the already long monthly intervals. Thus, in the Albany district survey, one farmer paid workers their cash wage every three months and another once every six months (Antrobus, 1984: 104). On the maize farms studied by De Klerk, where most of a worker's pay came as a deferred lump sum once a year, as much as 14 percent of the 'regular' ('full-time') workforce received between nothing and 10 percent of their total wage as a regular weekly or monthly cash payment (De Klerk, 1984: 22).

In general, the regularity and frequency of cash payments has not kept pace with the shift to a cash-based wage system. Monthly payments of very small amounts of money explain in part the inordinate significance of food rations to farm workers. This is not only because of the proportion they represent in the total wage, despite their very frugality, but also because they often provide the basic subsistence on which 'full-time' farm workers and their families are forced to rely. It is therefore not surprising that farm workers are reported to be acutely aware of food rationing practices on local farms, sometimes reason enough for them to remain on a particular enterprise. (Levetan, 1984: 108).

Food rationing is not necessarily more frequent. Many 'full-time' workers are also paid food in kind once a month. However, often both farmers' perspectives on the food ration — that is, that food is the 'real wage' and that the cash wage is essentially 'pocket money' — and the perishability of some of the food ration means that at least some of it is likely to be paid more frequently. In the Albany district, for example, milk was allocated daily, groceries (mainly mealie meal and salt) weekly or monthly, and meat at less frequent intervals (Antrobus, 1984: 109). But given the low and declining content of food rations, as well as the fact that for many rations only come once a month, food, like money, simply runs out. As a farm worker in the Eastern Transvaal explained bitterly:

> 'We receive 50 kg of mealie meal per month, regardless of the size of our families. If this runs out before the month ends the farmer refuses to give us more … of the 50 bags of mealies we receive every year we sell only 35 and retain 15 in order to provide for such instances' (Seleoane, 1984: 19).

This is a frequent, grim reality for 'full-time' workers and their families. Indeed its existence is even reflected in farmers' behaviour. Some go to quite considerable lengths to try and resolve the problem without, of course, paying more. Thus, a farmer reports:

> We used to give a bag of maize a month, but it was finished in two weeks. Presently, we ration 35 lbs (16 kg) of mealies (maize) or mealiemeal per week which totals less than a bag and we have no problems.

And in the words of another:

> 'I ration on Mondays after the visitors have left. It is not a good thing to ration on a Friday because whatever they have they share — even if it means they go hungry for the rest of the week' (Antrobus, 1984: 110).

These manipulations highlight the general unwillingness of farmers to raise wages, even when the poverty these generate is so patently evident. They are even able, perhaps unwittingly, to lower wages still further, although it is unlikely that they interpret the reduction of rations as a wage cut.

Despite all their efforts, farm workers are unable to ensure against the inevitable fact that the food will run out. What is clear is that the longer the intervals between payments, the more the poverty of their wages is aggravated.

'Part-time' workers

The position for workers employed 'part-time' is, if anything, worse. They can never be sure of employment, so the frequency of their payment is surrounded by uncertainty. This mitigates against any advantage that might allegedly be attached to being paid at the end of the job. In fact, only some farm workers who are hired on a daily basis are also paid on a daily basis, e.g., seasonal workers drawn from the population resident on the farms who work on the maize harvest (De Klerk, 1984: 26). Many 'part-time' workers are paid at weekly, fortnightly or monthly intervals. This applies even when the job may have been completed earlier. A survey of the Letaba District (Northern Transvaal) found that only one percent of 'casual' workers were paid daily. Pay intervals for the rest were roughly equally divided between weekly (30.4 percent), fortnightly (30.4 percent) and monthly (27.8 percent). (Smit and Herbst, 1983: 65).

The frequency of cash pay for workers whose 'part-time' status is a disguised form of 'full-time' employment — contract migrant workers or so-called 'commuters' who travel between the farms and the reserves daily but who are not recruited daily — differs little from that which governs the pay of 'full-time' workers. In the Letaba district, 75 percent of contract workers were paid their cash wage monthly. The intervals governing rationing practices, however, seem to vary more widely. On the sugar plantations, for example, migrant workers on contract are allocated daily food rations (at least on working days) in the form of meals. But workers who 'commute' tend to get weekly, fortnightly or monthly rations if they receive them at all. In the survey of Mtubatuba/Hluhluwe district (Natal), where giving rations seemed quite common, 60 percent received weekly rations, 24 percent fortnightly and 16 percent monthly (Daphne, 1982: 6). Cash wages were paid monthly. Workers employed seasonally on the timber, cotton and tea estates are also generally paid cash monthly; their food rations range from daily meals to fortnightly or monthly allocations of maize or mealie meal.

For sheep shearers, payment is at the end of the shear, or sometimes weekly if the job is expected to last over several weeks and the farmer is willing. He often makes the money out as a loan (an advance payment), an aspect of pay practice which will be looked at in Chapter Six. Similarly, seasonal workers working on the maize harvest are paid in kind only at the end of the harvest, although they are sometimes also allocated food in the form of a daily meal.

Once again, as the assessment of the OFS factory farm workers so demonstrably underscores, food rations — their presence and more often their absence — have a direct bearing on the existence of workers employed 'part-time' in seasonal or 'casual' jobs. This is because their cash payments (the larger and more often sole part of their meagre pay) are often delayed for days or weeks after they have completed the job; they come at intervals between which they have little or nothing to live on; and they come in too minute amounts to make much of a dent in the problem of trying to feed themselves, let alone their families.

Clearly, the intervals between payments for most farm workers aggravate the problems they face because of low wage levels in the sector. The infrequency and uncertainty surrounding employment for many workers hired 'part-time' makes their position even worse. Their problems are compounded by even lower wage levels and the frequent absence of food rations. Restructuring has not had any markedly beneficial effect on the frequency with which workers are paid. If anything, the decline in food allocation has meant that they are given little or no relief during the long period between payments.

Payment through intermediaries

Figures given for levels of pay in the sector need to be further qualified by another aspect of methods of payment — whether workers are paid directly or through an intermediary. In essence, the argument is that wage levels are affected where workers are paid through intermediaries and that the implications differ according to the intermediary channel. Whilst paying through intermediaries is not new, restructuring has generated and expanded indirect payment practices for some sections of the agrarian working class.

This problem is far from theoretical, but at this point in time it has to be treated at a somewhat abstract level because it is an area of information almost completely overlooked by researchers. This, indeed, underlines the necessity of raising it (however tentatively) in the hope that it will stimulate research so that we can know the extent to which it does shape wage levels in practice.

Many farm workers are paid directly. However, there are workers on the farms who receive their pay through an intermediary — a so-called middleman. These indirect channels of payment affect at least three groups of workers and take slightly different forms. In the first group — worker families resident on the farms — family members who are dependants of the 'full-time' worker have their pay channelled through him (rarely, if ever, her) as the recognised household head. Even family members who are employed 'full-time' alongside the household head may be paid in this way, especially if they are women, but invariably the brunt of this system is borne by the women and children employed 'part-time' and treated as his dependants. This form of intermediary payment is not detrimental to household income, but it does reinforce the subordination and dependency of women and children within the family. Although they are workers, they often do not receive their wages personally or as individuals.

The second group affected are migrant and casual workers recruited from the labour reserves and not resident on the farms. While some farmers recruit workers themselves, many employ an agent or agency. Practices range quite considerably. Many farmers have an informal arrangement involving workers already in the employ of the farmer — most usually foremen ('boss boys' or *indunas*) — whose job includes recruiting workers. Either they look for workers from the locality, or they are sent to recruit 'contract', seasonal or 'casual' workers from the towns or bantustans. Others employ semi-formal agents such as traders, headmen and school teachers, who live and work in the areas where farmers recruit their labour. Lastly, there are the formal labour agencies, including state labour bureaux (not particularly popular because of the bureaucracy and inefficiency of their operations), farmer co-operatives and private labour agents. Recruited workers are paid both directly and indirectly through the intermediary who recruited them, although the extent of each method is unknown. Of particular concern are the indirect payment practices. These are most likely to influence wage levels, as the income of recruiting agents or agencies is often met (at least in part) by deductions made directly or indirectly from workers' wages. Practices are likely to vary considerably and the available evidence only hints at the range.

Thus, for example, ten girls working in the fields of a Transvaal farm were not sure how much they were earning because their pay was being sent to Pogietersrus where they were recruited. Their uncertainty was compounded by the fact that, although they had been told that they would be paid 60 cents a day, if they wanted soap or bread the farmer 'gave them credit', which he then deducted from their pay. The passes of those who were old enough to carry them had been taken by the contractors, so they could leave only on pain of arrest. (Anti-Slavery Society, 1983: 23). An earlier instance, reported in the press, cited the case of five women who fled from a potato farm where they had come as contract workers. Not only were they exposed to considerable ill-treatment including starvation and assaults with a sjambok, but they reported a R10 per month wage which was 'often paid the headman on the farm and which they never got' (*Weekend World*, 17 April 1977).

In the Hex River Valley the most common form of recruitment was through 'a middleman of sorts'. These were agents-cum-team-leaders who generally were paid a higher wage than team members. Recruiting teams through individuals is also the practice for getting in the maize harvest. But whereas the research on Western Cape fruit farms implies that workers are paid as individuals, during the maize harvest the team is paid as a team — usually a lump sum in kind at the end of the harvest. De Klerk writes that, while some farmers paid foremen an additional fee in cash or kind for organising the team, the income of most was met from the proportion on the crop payment. This meant that 'foremen almost always received a larger-than-average share, but whether the balance was equally divided amongst the rest of the team, or whether some differentiation was made on the basis of sex and/or age was not clear' (De Klerk, 1984: 13). In the Hex River Valley case, that a large proportion of seasonal workforce returned annually to the same farm suggests the possibility, at least, that some form of 'commission' was taken from their wage for the team leader (Godet, 1976). And even if it was not, it seems unlikely that the farmer did not take recruiting costs into consideration when setting their pay rates.

Similarly, the tendency to recruit shearing teams through agencies has grown with restructuring. Thus, in the George district

'Dryland sheep farming is the only employer of contract farm labour ... Lesotho sheep shearers move through the area under contract to the farmers co-operative for six months of the year (Levetan, 1984: 37).

In the Hanover district

Instead of hiring shearing 'gangs' locally together with extra labour required for wool sorting, baling and allied tasks (a substantial minority of) farmers now employ contracting firms who supply full teams to shear, class and sort the wool on the Australian pattern (Archer and Meyer, 1984: 49).

Whilst the authors suggest this is more costly, implying that farmers meet some of the agency costs, what needs to be looked into is by how much this affects wages paid and whether agency income is taken from the workers.

This form of indirect payment is inseparable from the restructuring process. Specifically, it is tied up with the reorganisation of the division of labour and the migrantisation of the farm labour force, since many, if not most, farmers are forced to recruit a part of the workforce from the non-resident working population. And although the wages of all migrantised workers are affected, it is women and children who are hardest hit since they form the majority of recruited 'seasonal' and 'casual' workers.

Payment for and through the recruiting agent or agency is perhaps the most important form of indirect payment, in terms of depressing workers' wages. Workers are aware that the livelihood of such agents is borne by them: 'I was contracted to work here by Rantsane in Sterkspruit. He is a black person with an office near here. He earns nicely because he earns on account of us' (Barrett et al., 1985: 66).

The third group of workers affected by indirect payment methods are 'full-time' workers who are too old, ill or disabled to work. As a form of indirect payment pensions have a very limited significance as very few farmers even bother to pay. This ties in with the policy practice of expelling these sections of the workforce from farm land into the towns and particularly into the reserves which is amply testified to by ex-farm workers 'resettled' in the reserves. The majority of farmers simply evict such workers (SPP, 1983: Vol.2, 213; Vol.4, 80) and in this way absolve themselves from supporting these men and women who have laboured for years, often all their lives, for them.

In the latter period of restructuring, however, it would appear that some company estates at least make provision for workers with long service. In his study of agribusiness in the Transvaal, Young (1979) found that in addition to a contributory pension scheme introduced in 1976 'for selected African workers', workers who did not belong to it, but who were employed for more than five years, were allocated a lump sum of R150 per annum for each year of completed service.

> This lump sum is paid to the Bantu Affairs Commissioner in the area where the worker is retiring. The Commissioner may then, at his discretion, pay some of the amount in a lump sum ... while keeping the rest to pay a monthly allowance.

In this form, part of the worker's pay is channelled through an intermediary, not of his choice, who is vested with control over both the amount and intervals of payment of income.

Indirect payment of workers opens up extensive avenues for corruption. Although this is not the intended object of employing intermediaries, it is inevitable where labour is both forced and rightless and where employment is a scarce resource. It is yet another way in which the meagre wages of workers on the farms are further depleted. It also places some workers in an ambivalent position, not least of all because their wage often depends on what they can exact from other workers. This aspect, in fact, is closely tied up with the fourth element of methods of payment in commercial agriculture — namely, the endemic practice amongst farmers of defrauding workers of their wages.

Fraud and compulsion as a method of payment

Most workers in commercial agriculture are defrauded by the farmer of at least part of their wages, if not systematically then intermittently during their employment. It is not usual in the literature to raise the problem of fraudulent pay practices in a discussion of wages. When it is, it is in the context of a problem reserved for a discussion of general social conditions. They are presented as deviations from the norm, the outcome of conditions on a particular enterprise and a result of the personality traits of some farmers.[51] Whilst it may be all of these, it is also more, Not only are such practices not new to the sector, but, more importantly, they are not exceptional. On the contrary, cheating black workers out of their wages is endemic to payment practices in 'white' agriculture and stems from social relations which are based on a compelled and oppressed labour force. The persistence of such practices under restructured terms, albeit often in new forms, reinforces the main contention here that these relations have been reorganised rather than transformed by this process. In other words, it is yet another indicator that direct and indirect compulsion continues to govern social relations in the sector.

Although how workers are cheated of their wages encompasses a seemingly limitless variety of practices, essentially these fall into two broad but not necessarily mutually exclusive categories. The first includes those practices which entail straightforward fraud. The second covers those which deprive workers of a part of their wage as a penalty, or as a means of compulsion, i.e., a negative incentive scheme which operates through wage sanctioning.

Although straightforward cheating persists, the tendency to drive and control workers under threat of wage sanctioning, and to impose wage penalties for 'transgressions', is much more widespread. Its growth is a direct outcome of restructuring.

The apparent rationale underlying the latter category does not make it any more legitimate. Nor, for that matter, is it even legal. By law a farmer must pay a worker his full wages. He may not deduct money from the wages for damage done. The reason for this is that the worker will only be liable for the damage if he has been negligent and this must be proved in court. Where a worker owes a farmer money (e.g., for food bought) this may be deducted from wages. The farmer may not deduct money from the worker's wages on behalf of somebody else to whom the worker is in debt (Benjamin, 1984: 99).

But of course the illegality of all these practices (as in common cheating) has little bearing on their extent or persistence, as the following examples so clearly testify. What it does confirm (if such confirmation is needed) is that the law that is enforced in the South African countryside is one which categorically affirms white power and bourgeois authority so that the laws against blacks are enforced with extreme vigour on the one hand, and on the other hand the protection that the law is supposed to offer them is ephemeral (Haysom, 1984: 51).

Fraud

When it comes to robbing workers of a part or even all their wages, it appears that no category of workers, no form of payment, no branch of production and no region in the country is unaffected. This is not to suggest that all, or even most, farmers defraud their workers so blatantly. The weight of the evidence suggests, however, that quite a few do.[52]

In terms of the implication for wages, one might begin by considering the claim of De Klerk (1984:6) that lump-sum, annual payments in kind (in the form of maize) present little difficulty for wage calculations 'because they are usually converted into cash by being sold along with the rest of the crop. On receiving payments for deliveries made to a co-op, farmers simply passed on to workers the cash value of the weight of grain delivered on their behalf'.

This is a deceptively smooth, even idyllic portrait of relations, which, of necessity, has to be qualified by conditions on the ground, for some workers at least. The experiences of a farm worker in the Middelburg district in the Eastern Transvaal vividly exposes a very different reality. He sells 70 percent of the mealies he is paid at the end of the harvest. He explains that the farmer

'actually cheats us even on this front. He transports the mealies on the OTK (Eastern Transvaal Co-op) and sells it on our behalf. He always tells us that the value of a bag is R7.00. Now we expect him to give us R245.00 for 35 bags but he always gives us R200.00. We went to the OTK to inquire how they make their calculations and found out that a bag of mealies is actually sold at R8.00' (Seleoane, 1984:20).

The farmer systematically cheated them of just under 30 percent of their annual bonus.

Workers have no guarantee that they will be paid when they are hired.[53] Sometimes they lose not only their pay, but also their possessions, even their tools of trade.[54] And even when they are paid there are often discrepancies between the amounts they are promised and the wages they actually receive.[55] Farmers also rescind part of the wages they have paid, especially when it comes to so-called 'wages in kind'.[56] Indeed, withholding pay is a means by which farmers can evict workers without directly forcing them off the farm.[57]

Any and every pretext is reason enough. Sometimes they are provided by changes arising from the restructuring process, and sometimes not, but whichever, workers are simply cheated of their pay. Invariably these frauds do not come to the attention of the public simply because of the enormous difficulties workers face in challenging farmers on these or any other grounds organisationally, or even at less effective levels, through the courts or media. This, of course, applies to the other category of fraudulent pay practices as well.

Compulsion

In contrast to the blatant robbery of the first category, that of fraudulent pay practices is intimately linked to the restructuring process. These are widespread, commonplace and applied by most, if not all, farmers in one or more situations. Furthermore, few farmers consider their behaviour negatively. Quite the opposite. They feel themselves to be morally and socially justified in applying wage sanctions to discipline and control workers, since they presume that their colour and their class vest them with both the right and the duty to assert magisterial power over black people present (in whatever capacity) on their property. Physical assault and abuse remain an inseparable and 'natural' part of these paternalistic assumptions. In the past violence was the primary, if not sole, instrument of asserting control and authority over farm workers. With restructuring, however, farmers have increasingly used wage sanctioning (often still coupled with physical violations of the person) either to punish workers for their behaviour or to control and stimulate their output. In other words, restructuring has brought about a change in the moral content farmers attribute to the role of wage payments.

All payment schemes, in fact, are coupled with a parallel system of penalties. Workers find their wages reduced through deductions — fines — for a whole number of reasons. Although these are applied in a variety of situations, essentially they fall into two groups: compulsion in relation to work performance and compulsion as a condition of social relations.

Compulsion in relation to work performance

The first group of wage penalties are those which are imposed on workers for their performance and productivity. So, for example, at the same time as deciduous fruit and grape farmers in Elgin district (Western Cape) introduced payment by incentive for pickers (mid-1970s), a bruising rate was set at two percent, above which workers would have money deducted from their wage packets (Petersen, 1976:9). Similarly, workers in animal husbandry may receive bonuses for successful calving and lambing — on the one hand. But on the other, whether they do or not, when these operations are unsuccessful, or a task is not done as the farmer anticipated (he feels the worker has been 'negligent', or has not behaved with 'enough responsibility', or is simply angry because he has lost an expensive animal), the worker's wage is duly 'adjusted' (Seleoane, 1984:33).

Where pay is determined by a base quota rate, should the worker not meet the target set, either part or even the whole of that day's wage can be lost as a penalty.[58] In instances where no quota or piece rate sets the pace of work, the threat of losing part of the wage promised hangs over workers as a means of driving them forward. This is graphically illustrated by the experience of workers picked up in the district of Victoria West (Cape) in 1982, who found themselves tricked into working on a potato farm. They began work at 5 a.m. and at 8 a.m. had to take their breakfast standing because there was no time. Lunch at 1 p.m. was another standing meal and there was not enough time for them all to get water. At 4 p.m. they were given another 'rest' and they finally stopped work at around 8 p.m. in the evening. The farmer — 'baas' — was ever-present and he shouted and threatened them all day long. They were told, 'you must harvest the potatoes like chickens picking mielies in the yard', and that R1 would be subtracted from their R3 daily wage if they so much as stood still.[59]

The investment and use of costly capital equipment has added to the burden of work performance penalty. The reluctance of farmers to train workers to handle machinery (as discussed in Chapters One and Four) is inversely matched by the demands and expectations they put on untrained workers who have to handle these machines.[60] Should anything go wrong, more often than not the worker has to pay. Indeed, the extremes to which farmers go in this respect are shameless. In one instance a tractor driver on a farm in the south-eastern Transvaal was expected to meet all the costs of breakdown, etc. from his R20 per month wage (*The Star* 5 October 1974). In another case, a farmer asked a child by the name of Madidi if he 'wanted' to drive a tractor. He was untrained. Unable to control the machine he drove it into the river. The accident led to the boy's death by drowning. The farmer later alleged that he had driven the tractor without permission and, unperturbed, demanded a goat from the boy's family 'in compensation' (Anti-Slavery Society, 1983:34). More usually, farmers try to ensure the maintenance of their equipment by penalising workers through summary fines for breakdowns, 'negligence', etc.[61]

Compulsion as a condition of social relations
The second group of penalties incurred by farm workers relate as much to the assertion of authority and control over all aspects of workers' behaviour by farmers as they do to the work process itself. In a sense they are measures more often taken to underline and reaffirm power relations in the sector than actually to ensure work continuity and output.

It would seem that when it comes to withholding workers' pay, nothing evokes generalised disciplinary reaction from farmers like absenteeism defined in the broadest possible sense. The failure to 'report for duty' for whatever reason invokes a categorical response from farmers. Whether worker absence without the permission of the farmer is due to the state of the worker's health, family and social obligations, the general lack of free time accorded to workers who are treated as 'on call' at all times, etc. — farmers perceive it as an act of defiance, a challenge to their authority which must be punished. In the past, the form of punishment was most likely to be verbal and physical abuse. With the shift to a cash-based wage system, however, farmers increasingly have recourse to 'fining', i.e., simply withholding some of the wage. This does not, of course, imply that wage sanctioning has generally superseded verbal and physical violence against workers. In most instances these penalties are simply coupled together.

Few farm workers are not penalised for illness through pay deduction.[62] 'Part-time' workers, even if they are taken on for fairly lengthy periods, automatically go unpaid if they fall ill, since their pay is calculated by the number of days worked and/or their output. Contract migrants, who are de facto 'full-time' workers, may be covered for a stipulated number of days in the period of employment, in which case their cash pay will not be reduced by deductions, although their rations may be. Generally speaking, only a fraction of 'seasonal' workers get sick leave. That the majority lose pay through illness, however, is more related to the labour form than the methods by which wages are paid.

For 'full-time' workers, these two aspects are more closely tied together. Although in the process of restructuring an increasing number of farmers have included paid sick leave in the terms of employment, they are still in the minority, and such provisions do not enter into the reality of most farm workers' lives. On the contrary, more often than not the pay of 'full-time' workers is simply docked when they are sick and can not work. In fact, because of the belief widely held by farmers that the workers sham illness, often their disciplinary measures take on an even more severe form. Seleoane's finding (1984:22) that workers on a farm in the Eastern Transvaal were dismissed and evicted when they became sick 'too often', even though they were allowed no annual or sick leave, and deductions were made if they did not come to work for any reason, is far from exceptional.

Even where sick leave is granted, there is some *idée fixe* amongst white farmers which dispels all reason. Monday is not a day in the week on which a worker can report ill. 'Monday illness', in the common wisdom, is a direct result of weekend 'excesses' — i.e., drinking — which is not countenanced by the 'moral and upright' farming establishment, despite the fact that at least some of them pay their workers in alcohol.[63]

Other forms of 'absenteeism' which arise from intolerable working conditions — *inter alia*, low and no pay, long hours of work and little or no free time — inevitably solicit punitive reactions from farmers, including pay penalties. The following example of conditions on a maize and livestock farm is fairly typical:

> The farmer keeps a record of all the family members living on the farm, an attendance register for all the members who are employed and a roster for people required to work on Sundays and on public holidays and a penalty for failing to work when on call. The form of penalties varies according to the age of the defaulter. For the older worker it almost invariably takes the form of a salary adjustment while for the younger workers the salary adjustment is coupled to corporal punishment. Two sjamboks hang on the wall of the farmer's lounge

... He narrates unsolicited that on Sunday 21 November 1982 he used one of them on Lucas for failing to report for work on that day.

The farmer's wife commented:

> My husband did the correct thing under the circumstances ... If this kind of thing is allowed the other boys will think that they can disregard the boss's instructions (Seleoane, 1984:39).

Furthermore, few farmers acknowledge overtime in commercial agriculture. In the euphemism of Antrobus (1984), 'Farmers always reserve the right to ask their staff to work on Saturday afternoon or at any other time over the weekend in an emergency' — or after hours on normal working days, for that matter (whether workers are then given any choice is rather academic). The rewards are few — 'a tip of sugar, or coffee or a rand' — if any. The loss of free time is great and the penalties even greater, as the instance cited above underscores.

Harsh conditions often drive workers to run away, forfeiting the money owed them for their labour. On top of that, in the case of resident worker families, the farmer can and does take a whole range of retributive actions. Fairly typical are the experiences of one family in Natal. The mother of the children working on the farm recounts:

> If your child runs away you are fined a goat before he can be taken back. My son ran away because he said he was hungry. I took him back immediately. When I arrived, the Schroeders said I'd have to buy forgiveness with a goat, which I did. The second row which I had was when he complained that my girl burnt the *putu* when she cooked. So she ran away. She was 16. I took my daughter back and he said this girl was very cheeky, that she burnt the *putu* deliberately, and that he was not prepared to take her back unless I paid him R60. I gave him a goat (R40-R45) and R20 ... The farmer now has a huge herd and when we go there we can always see our goats by the earmarks. We do all this because we love our homes and are prepared to stay, especially as there is nowhere else to go.[64]

On many occasions, having 'bought forgiveness' for alleged misdemeanours, workers and their families are then served with eviction notices (Anti-Slavery Society, 1983:34) anyway, exposing the depths of insecurity under which workers in commercial agriculture labour.

As far as keeping time and absenteeism are concerned, in the past this invariably meant workers faced verbal and physical abuse. With restructuring, especially since the 1970s, workers increasingly have their pay docked as well.[65]

Wage sanctioning as an instrument of control is not restricted to absenteeism, lateness, 'negligence' or any other seemingly rational 'misdemeanour'. Any alleged offence can be and often is punished. There are innumerable situations in which workers, however unwittingly, seem to 'give cause' to farmers, as the following examples graphically highlight. In 1979, a worker and his family on a farm in the Weenen district (Natal) were served with an eviction notice. The farmer alleged that he had not been informed that some implements had been stolen from his farm.

The worker protested that it was not his job, he was not the 'baas boy' and, besides, he did not see the thieves. The farmer said that, if he wanted to remain on the farm with his family, he must pay an ox. So the beast was taken for an offence with which the worker had no connection, other than that he worked on the farm (AFRA, 1980-84: Reel III). With it, went a sizeable chunk of the worker's income, since he earned a mere R6 cash per month and running livestock was part of his payment in kind.

In another instance, in 1984, a farm worker who usually earned R55 a month found that at the month's end his pay had been reduced by R20 because a relative had left the farm. The farm owner was trying in this way to pressurise the relative to return. When questioned about her actions, the owner of the farm threatened 'to fire the boy (!) immediately. If he was not happy he should leave' and 'that was all she could afford' (AFRA, March 1984). The life of every farm worker is replete with such experiences, which differ in detail but revolve around the same issues — rightlessness, landlessness and compulsion. Penalties range over several forms: directly defrauding workers of their wage; imposing pay penalties by deductions in cash, kind, or both; levying fines on workers, who have to pay the farmer, etc ... Automatic deductions remove any say, however minute, that workers may have over the validity of the action taken by the farmer. But the alternative practice of demanding that workers pay the farmer when penalised is hardly better. Qualitatively, the differences between these penalties are very limited. Whatever the cause for penalising workers through wage sanctioning, these actions serve to generate insecurity and reduce workers' wages.

More important, however, is the connection between controlling workers and stimulating production through wage sanctioning which the shift to a cash-based wage system and production-related payment schemes has brought about. Wages are not only a 'reward for labour'. In the conditions of national oppression and social exploitation which characterise commercial agriculture in South Africa, they are also openly and assertively used by farmers as an instrument of control. The earnings of black workers are not had by right, but given and taken as white farmers see fit. As such, sanctioning workers through withholding or withdrawing their pay reflects the general social conditions in which an analysis of wage levels has to be framed. At the same time, it has a direct material bearing on the question of pay because, in yet another way, it serves to create a gap between the real wage received by the worker and the one the farmer claims to pay.

One further point needs to be made. The focus has been on pay sanctioning as an aspect of methods of payment in commercial agriculture and their implications for wage levels. It should be borne in mind, however, that it forms an integral part of a system of penalties, not directly related to wage levels, which entail systematic verbal and physical violence against farm workers by farmers. If anything, they represent the milder side of punitive reaction in the sector, given that not a single year passes without several farm workers losing their lives at the hands of white farmers, and that not a single day passes without some farm workers being subjected to abusive language and physical beatings.

This section has shown that methods of payment have a direct bearing on wage levels in commercial agriculture. They act to depress wage levels, so that average figures often represent a wage that is more theoretical than actual. The full extent of the discrepancy is impossible to calculate without more in-depth research. Restructuring has generated changes in the methods by which farmers pay workers. In some respects, these have not kept pace with other developments, such as more regular payment intervals and the change to a cash-based wage system. In other respects, through pay practices, farmers have been able to take advantage of the shift to cash wages to stimulate output and extend and assert their authority and control. Sanctioning workers through wages has added to the arsenal at the disposal of farmers to coerce workers to labour in conditions of super-exploitation.

There is little indication that changes in the method of payment have brought any relief to the position and condition of workers in the sector. Indeed, if anything, they have opened up new avenues by which the pathetic wages of workers can be further reduced. They have also provided additional channels through which farmers can assert authority and control.

The changes that restructuring has brought about in the forms of wages and methods of payment in commercial agriculture indicate a trend towards practices more typical of capitalist production relations, though these changes are far from uniform or complete. They show the very unevenness of production relations in the sector, despite extensive capital concentration, and they graphically express the context for forced labour and national oppression which is so integral to these conditions and which shapes new as well as old practices. Without a fundamental transformation of these social relations, it is clear that 'change' serves to reshape and reinforce the existing power relation although, at the same time, it brings out new contradictions. The changes in wage forms and methods of payment have contributed to the intensified exploitation of workers in commercial agriculture, which wage levels make so evident. This is the subject of the next chapter.

Notes

1. The wage value does not equal the total value of the labour power expended, but only the part for which the worker is paid.
2. This applies to all official and much unofficial research. The argument in recent 'progressive' literature that wages in kind cannot be counted as the wage reflects a questioning of what has been generally accepted as wages in the sector. This, however, has been expressed more as a moral argument than in explicit theoretical terms. See, for example, *The Farm Labour Project, 1982.*
3. The most notable exception is domestic service, although the mining sector also has a payment-in-kind component which derives from its roots in a migrantised workforce.
4. The non-payment of wages does not apply only to forced labour forms. It was also integral to the labour tenancy relation, where often the worker paid the farmer in labour rent for the right to live with his family on the farm, to keep livestock and/or till a piece of land.
5. This is generalised by the relations in agriculture which enable farmers to use the elements of nature which they have appropriated as their private property — land, fuel etc. — as a cash substitute which entails no economic outlay on their part.
6. SAIRR, 1939:18. Writing of conditions in the late 1930s: 'Married men usually received 1-2 morgen of land for ploughing. Single men did not ... And grazing, although generally allowed in most parts of the OFS, was much more restricted than thirty years earlier, for

example.
7. Native Economic Commission, 1930-1932. Not all farm workers received all of these items or received them in equal proportion, nor were they constant over time. Part of the deterioration in conditions in the sector is tied up with a decline in payment which, *inter alia*, meant payment in kind, given that this form was the base on which wages in the sector were organised.
8. Reference to the extremely undernourished conditions of farm workers and the general absence of meat in their diet is made in evidence to the NEC (Ibid., Addendum, para. 108), quoting from a report by a District Surgeon who had written:

> The farm labourer in my experience is badly nourished. I have a recollection of a number of post-mortem examinations which I performed on Natives on farms and they had hardly any superficial fat on their bodies. You found hardly any subcutaneous fat and their bowels were very thin ... It seems to me that a Native ages a great deal earlier than he should. A Native in his fifties is pretty well worn out ... To my mind it is entirely a question of nourishment ... If you have a diet of mealie-pap without fat the balance is all wrong, and that is the cause of it ... An increase in the meat diet would undoubtedly give them better health (*South African Journal of Economics*, 1935: Vol.III, 72).

This evidence has a direct bearing on contemporary conditions and the general absence of health of farm workers today.
9. As the author (anonymous) of the work on farm labour conditions in the OFS in 1939 incisively asked — 'Does a farmer buy an extra 20 morgen for his workers when he buys a farm?' SAIRR, 1939:21.
10. SPP, 1983: Vol.4, 357. Mzimphlope is a remote and inhospitable resettlement location in Northern Natal.
11. SPP, 1983: Vol.2, 212. Sada is Ciskei's oldest and largest resettlement camp and is located in its coldest and driest parts. Respondents report a general lower level of access to land than those in Natal.
12. Antrobus, 1984. Only 51 percent of the 'full-time' workforce had access to arable land. De Klerk (1984:9) found that workers only had access to vegetable plots on 38 percent of the farms, and in the Eastern Transvaal, arable land was granted on 62.5 percent of the farms (Seleoane, 1984:42).
13. SPP, 1983: Vol.4, 357. The differences in the extent and type of stockholding in the two areas, as well as in the extent of payment in food rations, reflects a difference in in-kind wages which developed around labour forms in the sector. In this respect, it would be interesting to know if the crushing of the peasant base in Natal has in fact meant that the shift to cash-only wages is more advanced than in other areas where, for example, food ration payments were more widespread.
14. Strict limitation and control of livestock in the bantustans has meant that most evicted farm workers have been forced to sell off their animals to white farmers at often ridiculously low prices. Others have had their animals impounded or even confiscated by the state.
15. *Post*, 19 November 1979. The complex consists of a saw-mill, five plantations and a garage. The press report is somewhat ambiguous, since workdays can mean the days on which the plantation is working or it can and probably does mean the days when the worker worked, that is, no rations when the worker is off due to illness, etc. Furthermore, in 1972 timber plantation employers estimated the cost of food rations reached a mere 54 to 85 cents a week or 26 to 53 percent below the paltry amounts of R1.15 recommended by the South African Timber Growers' Association two years earlier (Race Relations News, January 1973). Comparing their conditions at De Hoek, workers said that prior to 1972 the place was terrible. La Borde (1980:1.2) indirectly confirms the continuing bad state of affairs that prevails on many timber plantations. He argues that skill shortages can be attributed to 'unattractive working conditions' amongst which he lists low wages, 'unsuitable housing and bad diet'.
16. Archer and Meyer, 1984:14. In Hanover District the rate was one *slagding* per 1,000 sheep shorn.
17. This also affected other forms of payment in kind. Thus Antrobus (ibid.) noted 'one feature of livestock ownership that was surprising to find was that workers in the almost exclusively livestock area of Upper Albany should possess fewer grazing animals than those in the more

mixed farming areas'.

18. The only other province in which alcohol as pay in kind was specifically mentioned in terms of the law was the OFS, where a quarter pint of spirits or one pint of other liquor a day was stipulated as permissible pay for black male adult workers (*Survey*, 1961:148). What this suggests is that alcohol as pay was probably commonplace in the OFS in the past, and it is also probable that some farmers continue with the practice, although the extent of this form of pay is unknown.

19. It is not really possible to judge from the figures the full extent of the practice, let alone whether it has declined or not.

20. Graaff, 1976. He describes former practices as involving: 6 a.m. *inval dop*; 7.30 a.m. *voorbrekvis dop*; 8 a.m. *nabrekvis dop*; 11 a.m. *elfuur dop*; 12.30 p.m. *voormiddag dop*; 1.30 p.m. *namiddag dop*; 4 p.m. *vieruur dop*; 6.30 p.m. *uitval dop*; plus two bottles to take home at the end of a 12½ hour working day. Regrettably, he is not specific on how recent or commonplace this routine was.

21. Theron, 1976: 144:7:33, and Leon (personal communication) 1985.

22. Until 1963 the Liquor Act authorised farmers to supply a certain prescribed quantity of wine per day to a farm worker as part of his or her wage. In 1963 this clause (Section 96) was repealed and the supply of liquor to farm workers as part of their wage was prohibited. Ibid., 144:7:3:7:/9.

23. Antrobus, (1984) at the same time as he makes the misguided assertion (fn 50), informs that 'machine boys' — workers who are hired on contract to drive and service the combine harvesters — are paid R1 a day and half a bottle of brandy.

24. *Cape Times*, 15 August 1972. The terms of this contract were revealed in court where he was appearing on charges of refusing to 'obey a lawful command to work' because he had washed his one pair of trousers the day before and they were still wet. He was found guilty and sentenced to R20 (40 days) conditionally suspended for two years.

25. Graaff, 1976. The compulsion here is indirect. It derives from low wages, the long hours of work and the absence of free time, the lack of transport and the control of movement of black people in the countryside, etc.

26. The question of housing for farm workers is an aspect of a more generalised and acute housing crisis that has been generated by the terms of colonial capitalist exploitation in South Africa. For the present purposes, the problem is confined to its relation to wage forms and levels in the sector.

27. This is not to suggest that both these lines of reasoning are not used at one and the same time by farmers to justify the low wage levels generally found in the sector.

28. This has a bearing on all sections of the black population, whose social conditions are shaped by those under which the African majority live.

29. At Anglo-American's De Hoek saw-mill, for example (*Post*, 19 November, 1979).

30. In contradiction to the opinion that 'travelling comfort matters but little and the rough ride in trucks and trailers seems to be looked upon as an entertainment rather than a deterrent' (Godet, 1976).

31. For example, in 1980 a 15-year-old girl fell off the lorry of a Weenen farmer. She was taken to hospital with head injuries, but received no compensation. A similar accident occurred in 1976 when a 14-year-old boy died as a result (AFRA, 1980-84: Reel III, Sibiso memo). In 1979 workers returning after harvesting in the OFS froze to death on the back of the lorry (*Cape Times* 29 July, 1979). In 1981 a lorry transporting women and girls to the Weenen fields was overcome by floods on the Mngwenya River. In jumping to safety five of them, aged between 11 and 20, drowned (AFRA, 1980-84, Reel III, Sibiso memo). Many more examples could be cited.

32. In 1973 farmers calculated the costs of a round trip to be 25 cents per worker (*The Star* 22 February 1973). In a study of workers in the Letaba district (Northern Transvaal), 52 percent of workers who remained on the farms during the week did so because of the costs and the difficulties of transport (Smit and Herbst, 1983: 72, Table 3.24).

33. Bekker et. al., 1982:11; personal communication F.M.:1981.

34. This is not without its contradictions or consequences for workers or farmers. An Albany district farmer recounts: 'They used to ask off every time it rained — sometimes for up to

a week — because their huts were falling to bits. Now since giving them the iron off the pig runs they never seem to ask off' (Ibid.:139).

35. What farmers mean by 'decent' is qualified by their racist assumptions.

36. Potgieter, 1976. This restriction does not apply to 'private' farmers. Here the numbers are regulated by labour control boards.

37. Theron, 1976:143:2:30 goes so far as to suggest that it was 'a scheme for the construction of housing for Coloured farm workers'. It was actually introduced under pressure from Western Cape farmers.

38. *The Star*, 22 July 1982. Under the loan scheme until 1980 the number of houses considered for financial assistance per applicant was four a year. It was then raised to ten. Maximum loans in 1981 were R2,900 for a three-roomed house and R3,800 for a four-roomed house. An additional sum of R200 could also be lent for water and electricity respectively. The rate of interest on the loan was a mere one percent (SAAU, 1981:59).

39. The feebleness of the loan scheme is an expression of this reluctance.

40. It is hard to put any figure to the actual number built. In 1978, presuming that all those farmers who took loans built four houses only, then a total of 928 houses were built at a cost of R1,391 each. (These figures are calculated from those given by the Minister of Agriculture cited in *Survey, 1979*:236.

41. An important reason why farmers do not apply for loans is that they have to mortgage their properties in order to take them out — which they are not prepared to do for workers' housing. And they are constrained even further by the consideration that, if they want a loan for other things, they may be prevented from getting one because of the existence of the housing loan.

42. Evans, 1976. In the Viljoenskroon District (OFS) in 1976 this type of housing cost approximately R2/sq foot (about R1,260) 'using unskilled labour'.

43. On large-scale sugar plantations in Natal, for example, *Rand Daily Mail*, 19 December 1977.

44. I am not arguing here for the uniqueness of the South African condition. This is a general feature of the historical development of capitalism.

45. This practice predates restructuring, although it differed then from now in that where income came in bi-annually or annually, workers were paid only twice or once a year (SAIRR, 1939:24).

46. De Klerk (ibid.:19) expresses reservations about his findings on wage levels. He found the mean annual wage to be R1,777 in 1981 for 'full-time' workers, which is very high, and at least 43 percent higher than a 1981 survey by the state's Department of Agriculture which gave an average all-found wage in the Western Transvaal of R1,019 per year.

47. Most of these are related to fatigue, stress and the loss of concentration which arises from working very long hours with heavy chainsaws. Extended exposure to the vibrations of chainsaws also makes work a serious health hazard. Occupational diseases include Reynaud's Phenomenon, caused by such excessive exposure. The extent to which workers in the sector are affected by these and other work-related illnesses is unknown.

48. The figure for tea pickers is calculated on the presumption that the basic wage of R20 a month did not change between August and December of that year.

49. It is unclear if the R6 was an across-the-board monthly increase applying to women as well as men.

50. Wentzel, 1984:85. In Hanover District where there were two shearing teams, the going rate was reported as 30 cents a sheep (Archer and Meyer, 1984:14).

51. The situation and arguments are analagous to those presented about violence perpetrated by farmers against farm workers, which, like defrauding, is endemic rather than exceptional.

52. See especially AFRA, 1980-84; SPP 1983, Vols 1-5; the conference papers of the Second Carnegie Inquiry into Poverty and Development in Southern Africa, 1984, some of which have been used in this text, etc.

53. For instance, a farmer in the Excelsior district (OFS) who went bankrupt at the end of 1979 had not paid workers since January of that year. When the new owner took over the property, his first action was not to pay the workers the money owed them. Rather, it was to expel all 20 and their families on 24 hours' notice. They had worked the year for nothing and had lost the homes in which they had lived for generations (SPP, 1983: 156, Vol.3).

54. In Hanover district, for example, Archer and Meyer (1984:59, footnote 4) reported a shearing

team who had just lost their jobs, because the farmer refused to fetch them from town. They had worked for a week without pay and all their clothes, blankets, cooking utensils and, most importantly, tools were still on the farm.

55. There are many examples which can be cited. For instance, young boys and old men who were promised 'R3 a day for work on an egg farm' found themselves picking potatoes from dawn to dusk for between 50 cents and R1.50 a day (*Rand Daily Mail*, 1 May 1977). Women picked up from the Atteridgeville labour office (Pretoria) were promised R35 for five days' work when they were recruited. Instead they ended up being paid between R1.10 and R7.50 for their week's labour on a farm near Brits (Western Transvaal) (*Sowetan*, 15 March 1984).

56. For example, the dipping of cattle is compulsory and often farmers dip the animals of workers along with their own. They do not necessarily charge for this at the time. However, should a worker want to leave then he has to pay for the number of occasions the animals have been dipped (Seleoane, 1984:14).

57. Seleoane (Ibid:22), for instance, reported the case of a farmer who stopped paying wages, withheld rations and waited until the necessity of survival forced the family to do 'the only sensible thing: pack up and go.'

58. For example, workers on the Phaswana Coffee Farm in the Northern Transvaal.

59. *Argus*, 27 January 1982. The only food these workers received was mealie meal and *pap*. One woman had come with her two-month-old baby, whom she had to shelter in the potato bushes while she worked. They had been told they would be 'housed in comfort' and returned home by truck after three weeks. They did not wait to discover if any of the farmer's other deceptions would materialise or not — they ran away back to their homes in the arid veld.

60. The crassness of white farmers effrontery is encapsulated in the widely-held ignorant view that 'no machinery is kaffir proof' (Antrobus, 1984:208).

61. Negligence is in parentheses, since although there are occasions where problems arise out of negligence on the part of the worker, it is in fact farmer negligence which is primarily responsible for the cost of machinery maintenance, the rate of breakdown and, most importantly, the many accidents, injuries and deaths suffered by workers.

62. Industrial diseases and injury is an area of social relations in the sector which still needs to be extensively researched. Although the question of health and safety at work cannot be looked at in any detail here, it is an aspect of social conditions on the farms which needs to be tackled as a matter of urgency, given that restructuring has served to aggravate and intensify the poor health base existing amongst the agrarian working class.

63. Aside from their other immoral behaviour like beating and cheating workers. Kandas Perries, for instance, had to spend a week in hospital after the farmer, who was the local mayor and an ex-policeman, had whipped her with two sjamboks at least 25 times. It was said in his 'defence': 'It doesn't help to speak to coloured farm labourers when they are drunk — you have to beat them. Sometimes you have to take the law into your own hands.' The farmer was fined R250 (*Sunday Times*, 17 July 1977).

64. AFRA, 1980-84: Microfilm, Reel III. The family were working under labour tenancy conditions although this was no longer a legal form of labour anywhere in South Africa.

65. On a poultry farm in the Cape, a worker reported that they were fined 20 cents every time they were late. They worked long and irregular hours and were treated as 'casual labour' (*Cape Herald*, 4 April, 1981).

6.   Restructuring: Wage Levels *c* 1980

The general picture of extremely low wages, which has historically characterised conditions in commercial agriculture in South Africa, is unrelieved by restructuring. As far as wage levels are concerned, the reality remains stark. In the words of the Farm Labour Project's submission to the state commission into employment in commercial agriculture:

> ... it can be baldly stated that the cash wage of farm workers is extremely low in South Africa ... Even taking into account payment in kind the wage structure is low. We can go further and state that the only limit as to how low such wages may be is starvation (Farm Labour Project, 1982:11).

This was not an insignificant finding in 1982 for by then restructuring in the sector was well advanced. Nor is it really surprising in the light of the above analysis. But to confirm that wages are low does not take us very far in understanding the effect on wages of the restructuring process. The question is whether retaining a universally low wage base reflects the full impact of the reorganisation of production relations in commercial agriculture. Is it that wages have remained low, or has restructuring led to an even further deterioriation in wage levels? Further, have the reorganisation of the division of labour in the sector and changes in the social composition of the workforce affected wage levels? And can any regional differences be discerned? By examining what 'low' means in the context of the second phase of restructuring, we can try to find some answers — first by breaking down wages according to the forms of employment in the sector; then, by drawing out from this essentially synchronic description, some patterns and trends, as well as their more general implication.

In certain respects, this is easier said than done, because one is immediately confronted by the problems of the information base. On the one hand, official statistics present enormous hazards for analysis. They have as many pitfalls as those upon which employments levels are calculated (see Chapter Two). Irregularly carried out, they are based on compilations of returns made by farmers giving cash and cash estimates of in-kind payments made by them to farm workers in their employ.[1] In addition to the problems of putting a cash value to in-kind wages, which under the circumstances inevitably means that they are maximalised, a key weakness is that farmers are only required to distinguish between two categories of employment — so-called 'regular' and 'casual'.[2] These classifications are not only vague but so broad as to make them insensitive to wage differentials between skilled and unskilled workers; between men, women and children; between workers resident on the farms and those who have been migrantised, etc. Since all these aspects are significant in assessing wage levels, the net effect of the global figures presented in official statistics is that they tend to both inflate and obscure levels of pay for workers in agriculture. Inevitably, they are a blunt and insensitive tool for analysis. All the more cruel is the irony that, despite this, they stand as a record of unmitigated low wages in the sector, which is confirmed yet again by the 1980 survey: average cash earnings for 'regular' workers (i.e., workers considered by farmers to be employed 'full-time') stand at between R26 and R33 per month in the Transvaal and OFS, and at R53 in the Western Cape (*Sowetan* 10.9.81). On the other hand, whilst field research is often more profound and therefore revealing, it also poses serious problems. Some of these arise from the inconsistencies of methods of investigation adopted by researchers; the different time-spans over which information is gathered; and, despite enormous advances over the past decade or so, from the fact that field research is still very uneven, both in the extent and depth of its coverage. In combination, these shortcomings make comparisons and generalisations difficult. Nevertheless the body of information they provide is far more useful in analysis than the official statistics. As such, it forms the base on which this chapter will draw.

In keeping with the argument of Chapter Five, the focus here will be on cash wages as the central indicator of pay levels in the sector. This is not to suggest that the cash wage equals the total wage, although often this is the case. Nor is it to argue that payments in kind are irrelevant to the incomes of farm workers. If anything, the opposite is true, given the depths of poverty they have to grapple with. But, rather, the focus is on cash wages because they form the kernel of the wage system, despite the existence of non-cash wage forms. They provide the most significant and adequate measure of wage levels.[3]

The structural divisions around which the workforce in commercial agriculture is organised are central to an analytic description of wage levels. Whether workers are 'full-time' or 'part-time', skilled or unskilled, men or women, resident on the farm or drawn from the reserves, Coloured or African, all intertwine with specific regional and sectoral characteristics, as well as the degree of capitalisation, etc., to affect wage levels.

The central demarcation between farm workers is whether they are employed as 'full-time' or 'part-time' workers. Within each of these categories further structural divisions centre on gender, age, skill, and residential location, some of which intersect, and all of which are hierarchically ordered. These divisions are further affected by regional and sectoral differences. The weakness of the information base, however, makes it difficult to treat these latter aspects with the subtlety argued for in Chapter One, for instance. As far as regional differences are concerned, the material will be grouped around broad geographical/administrative demarcations. Lastly, the lines between groupings are not necessarily always clear-cut or fixed, especially when they do not concern immutable characteristics such as gender, colour or age.

Wages of workers in 'full-time' employment

The primary divisions which affect the pay of 'full-time' workers are skill and gender. Whereas skilled labour is all but synonymous with working men, within the category of unskilled employment the sexual division of labour is a key line of demarcation. Each of these will be looked at separately.

A further problem which affects the wages of 'full-time' workers is the classification itself. This particularly concerns the position of migrant and casual workers who, in reality, are employed 'full-time' although they are not necessarily classified as such. In some instances the difference (or lack of difference) between these two is clear and evidenced in the wage structure — for example, contract migrants in the Western Cape or on the sugar plantations of Natal. In others it is not, especially when the time period for which workers are employed is not stipulated. Mostly this affects women workers, 'commuters' and also longer-term migrants. The position of these workers is deliberately made ambiguous with inevitably negative consequences for the terms and conditions of their employment. Dealing with this ambiguity is made doubly difficult by the way information about these workers is presented and particularly by the vagueness or even absence of definition. This poses problems for classification and therefore for the analysis itself. To try and resolve this, I have had to take into account the wage level itself. This is not a particularly satisfactory solution either, since seasonal workers can earn as much as people in 'full-time' employment in the month or more that they are employed. Short of more specific data, however, there seems no other way to overcome the problem more meaningfully.

Men in unskilled 'full-time' work

Table 6.1 represents figures from several reports on wages in the *Western Cape*. These figures cannot be generalised for the province. They only serve to indicate the types of wage levels to be found in the region.

Table 6.1
Cash wages for men employed as unskilled 'full-time' workers in the Western Cape

Year	District/Area	Farming Type	Ave. wage/week (R)
1980	Knysna (Langkloof Valley)	Deciduous fruit	13.00
1982	George	Vegetables (mainly for freezing	15.13
1980	George	Forestry (state)	32.21
1982	George	Forestry (private)	25.00
1983	Oudtshoorn	Ostrich (mainly)	24.70
1983	Oudtshoorn (Schoemanshoek)	Tobacco and fruit	12.50-15.00
1983	Calitzdorp	Unspecified	17.15
1982	Stellenbosch	Viticulture	17.00
1984	Stellenbosch	Viticulture	20.00-22.00

What the figures in Table 6.1 show is that unskilled men were averaging nominal cash wages of between R12.50 and R25 a week in the first four years of the 1980s. Only state forestry workers earned wages substantially higher than general farm workers (R32 in 1980). On privately owned forestry estates, although wages appear higher than in other branches of farming in the region, the difference was not as great. This discrepancy may not, in fact, be particularly accurate since the average for forestry workers is likely to be distorted by the inclusion of skilled workers' wages.

In the figures for Oudtshoorn, the difference between farming types seems substantial. Whilst it is probable that there are differences in wage levels, the size of the gap given in these figures would appear to reflect sampling problems more than conditions on the farms. The figures for workers on ostrich farms are based on oral evidence from mostly wealthy farmers who paid higher wages than those in the immediate neighbourhood (Buirski, 1984:5).

Wages could also drop well below the average. In the case of the survey of Calitzdorp farm worker households, the lowest wage reported was R8 a week, or less than half the average weekly wage (Bekker et al., 1982:18). Finally, to give an idea of the meaning of these wages in terms of hours worked, the case of workers in the Langkloof Valley reveals an average 45 hour week (the length given by farmers) during which they earned 28.8 cents an hour. Even if a food ration valued at a high R3.45/week was added, earnings rose to a mere 36.5 cents an hour in 1980 (Horner and Van Wyk, 1984: 59). Farmers are well aware and sometimes even acknowledge that they pay very low wages. As a manager of one of the grape farms in Stellenbosch explained: 'We pay quite low wages here(R3 to R4 a day) and our families can't afford to spare children from their share of the work. They need the money' (Nasson, 1984:27).

Turning to information on the *Eastern Cape*, Antrobus's study of the Albany district found that the average monthly cash wage paid to men in 'full-time' employment worked out at no more than R12.65 in 1977. Workers regarded as youths were paid an average R8.71 a month. Men 'just starting' got R12.37, which rose to R14.05 'after some service' and reached an average of R15.50 a month 'after long service' (Antrobus, 1984:100). This gradation of pay for 'length of service' shows how farmers resort to any and every pretext to depress workers' wages. If length of service was indeed the reason underlying the pay differential, the difference in pay between workers employed for 'some' or a 'long' period of time (whatever these terms mean) should be substantially greater than the paltry R1.45 (nine percent) a month.

In 1983, an investigation of one dairy and pineapple farm in the Salem area of Lower Albany found men working in the dairy section earning R40 cash a month. Those working in the pineapple fields earned a basic monthly wage of R23 to R28 with a production-linked bonus of R20 or R30 after an unspecified number of months (Manona, 1984:3). This example also highlights the effect of methods of payment on wage levels.

At the resettlement site of Pampierstad in the *Northern Cape* (1982), workers who had been relocated off the farms reported that before they moved they were earning cash wages of R9 to R19 a month, and one earned R20 to R29. Only one reported earning wages in kind as well (SPP, 1983: Vol.3, 115).

In the districts of the *Orange Free State* wages were little better. In 1976, wages in the Viljoenskroon district were given as averaging R15 to R20 a month (Levy, 1976:9). In Dealesville district, however, cash wages reached only R8 per month. The rest of the wage was made up of payment in kind — rations and the annual bonus (Maree, 1976:4). In a survey (1981) of farm workers resettled at the huge relocation camp of Onverwacht, residents who had come off the farms reported even lower wages: 63 percent earned less than R7 a month in cash; 28 percent earned between R15 and R18 cash a month; and the only respondent who 'earned' R60 a month turned out to be referring to the collective wage of the family. The author writes:

> One appalling extreme recorded here is that of a farm worker who had worked for twelve months a year for 24 years on a farm in the Reddesburg district and was paid R3 a month in cash and nothing in kind, but did have access to a small field (SPP, 1983: Vol.3, 169, 171).

Wages for unskilled men on the Highveld farms surrounding the town of Clarens averaged R20 a month. They worked a ten-hour day, except in season when the working day was 'considerably longer', and a five-and-a-half day week (Walwyn, 1984). In 1984, on this average, these workers were earning eleven cents an hour.

Part of the explanation for these exceedingly low cash wages lies in the fact that, at least for workers on maize farms, a substantial part of their wage takes the form of a deferred annual bonus paid at harvest end in August. Nevertheless, conditions on the farms in this province are notoriously harsh.

On *Western Transvaal* farms in the maize triangle, De Klerk (1984) found that 1:4 men employed 'full-time' earned R17 in cash a month. Monthly cash earnings ranged from R5 to R100 and the average wage was R33. He gives an average total wage of R150 per month, of which cash represents only a quarter (De Klerk, 1984:21). Yet it has to be borne in mind that he considers his findings to be above the true average. State estimates put average wages at R85 per month, of which 40 percent was in cash, i.e., R34. And this latter figure is almost identical to that given by De Klerk for cash incomes.[4]

In the *Northern Transvaal*, the wages of men working on cattle ranches near Louis Trichardt (Harries, 1984:6) 'could reach' R35 plus an 80 kg bag of mealies a month (1984). But wages of around R20 or so, plus mealie meal, were not unusual either (Hugo, 1984:11; Farm Labour Project, 1982). On the Sapekoe tea estates near Elim hospital, wages were apparently much better (relatively speaking). Men were said to be earning R60 a month plus a production-linked bonus of 25 kgs mealie meal every fortnight. They worked six days a week and had a so-called 'weekend holiday each month' (Harries, 1984:7). On farms in the Letaba district, however, the more usual wage was R37-R40 a month (Smit and Herbst, 1983:15).

In the *Eastern Transvaal*, conditions were little different. In 1980 on the farms in the Malelane-Komatipoort region, described as 'one of the most important and productive irrigation regions in South Africa', workers employed 'full-time' were earning an average wage of R33 cash on a 220-hour month. Those on farms producing squash and cucumbers, however, earned 20 percent less on average, i.e.,

R26.60 per month (Brotherton, 1980).

But whilst wages seemed to average around R40 a month (De Klerk, 1984:21) in 1983/4, the range they covered was extreme. In the Middleburg district, Seleoane (1984) found that wages ranged from nil to R50 and R60 a month (see also Hugo, 1984:11). One worker, after 30 years on the job, reported a monthly cash wage of a mere R25. In interviews with farm worker families in Piet Retief district, where labour tenancy was abolished only around 1980, it was found that men were working twelve months a year at wages of R10 a month for half the year and R20 a month for the other half. Rations were sugar, mealie meal and potatoes, and they were allowed to keep a maximum of five cattle. They also had a patch on which to grow vegetables (Farm Labour Project, 1982, para 1.4.1.1).

Finally, regarding unskilled wages for men employed 'full-time', in *Natal*, a 1975 study of mean cash wages by farming types in the province revealed the following range:

Table 6.2
Mean cash wages paid by farm type in Natal, 1975 (R/month)

Type	'Full-time' Skilled	'Full-time' Unskilled	'Part-time'
Sugar	46.35	29.51	15.73
Wattle/timber	36.68	22.55	12.34
Sheep/beef	27.18	14.77	8.69
Dairy	26.43	17.02	9.07
Pigs/poultry	32.46	21.90	10.51
Crops	18.95	13.49	11.12
Horiculture	24.08	16.63	9.43
Other	27.22	18.87	11.26
Mean	**29.91**	**18.51**	**11.09**

Source: Standish, 1976:2

Whilst cash wages averaged just under R19 a month for unskilled 'full-time' workers, they dropped to as low as R13.50. Indeed, more than two-thirds of the farms paid less than R25 a month. The lowest paid workers were to be found on crop farms (R13.50) and the highest paid unskilled work available for men in the area was on the sugar estates. A survey of farm workers in the area of Hluhluwe/Mtubatuba (1982) found a similar differential pattern in pay practices. Whilst wages had risen nominally to an average of R33 or so a month, workers employed to weed and plant in the cane fields earned an average of R31.50. Their wages differed little from those employed to plant and harvest in the pineapple fields (R27.50) or to trim and clear timber (R28.33). But those employed to irrigate, harvest and load cane earned R44 — R45 a month, i.e., an average 27 percent more.[5]

Taking differences within the province into consideration, again an extensive range in pay practices was evident. The northern district, where labour tenancy was still being practised in 1980, displayed similar extremes to those found in

Piet Retief, for example. In Babanango district, wages of R10 a month were described as 'the norm' although some workers were getting less or no pay. Workers on Elandslaagte farms were also earning R10, and in Vryheid cash wages averaged R10 — R20 during 'the six months on'. In Weenen labour tenants were getting R4 — R16 per month for their six months, and 'full-timers' — those working on the farm the year round — were being paid R12 — R20 per month.[6]

Even within these districts wages ranged considerably. In a study of 44 households of evicted farm workers in November 1980, it was found that eleven adult 'full-time' workers earned an average of R13.91 in cash, ranging from R5 — R34 per month, and this excludes those who earned nothing. Seven men in Muden worked 'full-time' for rations only, that is, half a bag of mealie meal per man (AFRA, 1980-84: Reel III).

Cash wages for unskilled men working 'full-time' on the farms in all these regions express common features. First, they tend to gravitate around a norm. In the early 1980s this was R25 — R45 per month for all regions bar the Western Cape, where wages of R20 — R35 a week were common. Second, cash wages range widely in all regions, dropping to very low levels. These variations, it would seem, are largely shaped by the type of farming practised. But they also reflect the degree of labour intensity that characterises the different branches of production and the extent to which they have been reorganised in the course of restructuring. Whilst the lowest rates of pay for unskilled 'full-time' employment are likely to be found on farms and in branches which are labour intensive, this is not necessarily the case as the evidence for cattle farming (low labour intensity) and sugar cane (high labour intensity) reveals. What the evidence presented above also clearly shows is that Coloured farm workers in 'full-time' employment in the Western Cape earn substantially more than their African counterparts in the rest of the country. What they are paid a week, African unskilled 'full-time' farm workers in general average per month.

Women in unskilled 'full-time' work
In the case of women in 'full-time' employment there is much less information available. Nevertheless, from the little that exists a clear picture emerges of their structural position in the workforce. The highest proportion of women farm workers recognised as being in 'full-time' employment are found in the *Western Cape*. Women working in the Langkloof Valley — some 45 percent of the 'full-time' workforce — earned R9 for a 40 hour week, or 22.5 cents an hour (Bekker et al., 1982:18). They were unlikely to be paid a food ration and, if they were, it invariably would be less than that paid to men. But even if they were allocated the equivalent calculated for men, their weekly wage would total only R12.45 or 31 cents an hour. Comparing cash wage incomes, women unskilled 'full-time' workers in the Langkloof Valley earned 31 percent less than their male counterparts. In the Schoemanshoek area (Oudtshoorn) women were earning a cash wage of R6.50 — R8.50 a week, i.e., 56 percent of men's wages on the farms there (Buirski, 1984:5). In general, in 1981 women 'full-time' workers employed in unskilled jobs on the farms of the Western Cape were earning an average of R12 per week (*Voice*, 1.4.81).

In the *Eastern Cape*, women employed 'full-time' in the Albany district in 1977 were earning R9.54 on average. This was 45 — 60 percent less than unskilled men (Antrobus, 1984:100). A similar yawning wage gap was found in a later study of one farm in the area. For the same 65-hour week as men, women's basic wages in the pineapple fields were R13.50 (1983), i.e., less than half of that paid to unskilled 'full-time' male workers (Manana, 1984:3).

In the *Transvaal* a woman working on a Highveld farm near Vereeniging was earning R4 a week (R16 a month) (1982) and no rations for a ten-hour day (*Sunday Express* 11.7.82). In the reserves of the Northern Transvaal, it was reported in one area that the 'chief' had given permission to a farmer from Brits (Western Transvaal) to recruit people in the area to work on his farm. They were employed for the whole year and came back only at Easter and Christmas. He only took women with passes (i.e., 16 years and over) and paid R30 a month plus rations (1983). 'The only women who will do this work are women with no other source of income; others will not do this work ... since it is too badly paid and the work is too hard' (James, 1983:53). On the Sapekoe tea plantation women were paid R40 a month (1984), one third less than male workers there (Harries, 1984:6).

Working in *Northern Natal* under labour tenancy conditions, for example, a figure of R10 — R15 (1980) was given as the average cash wage for women in the Vryheid area during their six-month stint (AFRA, 1980-84: Reel I). However, again this was far from universal. In fact, it is often hard to call the money paid to many of the women and children a wage. The 1980 survey of households evicted off Northern Natal farms found that four women, who formerly lived on farms in the Weenen district, had been paid R1 per month and a tobacco ration for their six-month compulsory stint. Wages for children ranged from a high of R10 for a boy working six months, to a low of R1 to a girl working over the same period (AFRA 1980-84: Reel III).

In short, women employed as 'full-time' workers in commercial agriculture are always paid lower cash wages than men. Since they also generally do not get payment in kind, or, when they do, it is also a fraction of that paid to men, their overall wage is even smaller than the disproportion in cash indicates. Nevertheless, it is gross enough. Unskilled women workers in 'full-time' employment earn wages ranging from 30 percent to as much as 60 percent less than men in the same jobs. In the early 1980s they were earning, on average, R10 — R20 (high) per month (or this per week in the Western Cape). It is probable that their wages have a tendency to gravitate around the very low average base, which means that they are less likely to range as widely as those for men. Again their wages in the Western Cape reflect regional particularities.

Skilled 'full-time' workers
The information on wages paid to 'full-time' workers whose skills are recognised is also very limited, and the material is complicated. Not only are there differences between regions and even between farms, but also the classification 'skilled' is very broad. It ranges from semi-skilled occupations, such as tractor drivers, to skilled jobs such as mechanics, heavy machinery operators and builders; from first-line management, for example team leaders, to foremen and supervisors. Sometimes

this hierarchy is very stratified; at other times no occupational distinction is made within the category and several jobs are rolled into one, to be done by the same person. So, for example, a trek worker from Beaufort West (Western Cape) in 1983:

> My father is a regular farm worker. He's been nine years on the farm where he is now. He gets R69 a week. He gets more than other men. He's the old man of the farm. He works with machinery and that sort of thing (Schmidt, 1984:43).

At best, the figures provide pointers to the kinds of pay levels reached within this classification.

In the Western Cape, a 1976 survey of workers in the Elgin district revealed average wages for skilled workers of R61 per month (Petersen, 1976: Table 3). These ranged from R35 — R57 per month for semi-skilled operatives such as pruners and tractor drivers to R80 — R100 for foremen and skilled operators. The highest wages reached R200 per month and these were paid to 'key men' such a top-line sprayers, artisans and supervisors — but pay for them also ranged widely, dropping to as low as R100. On farms in Citrusdal and Vredendal (Theron, 1976: Appendices), a mechanic (one found in the survey) and the foremen were earning R2.10 a day (R46.20 on a 22-day month). Four years later (1980) in the Langkloof Valley, average cash wages paid to skilled workers — mostly tractor and lorry drivers and *baasboys* (foremen) — had nominally increased to R60 — R80 per month (Bekker et al., 1982:18). In Oudtshoorn in 1983/4 the top cash wage for skilled workers was between R102 and R140 per month (Buirski, 1984:5).

In 1977, tractor drivers working on farms in the Albany district (Eastern Cape) earned an average monthly cash wage of R19.31 and top-paid *indunas* (foremen) were being paid R20.20 per month (Antrobus, 1984:100).

In the Transvaal, wages for skilled work ranged widely. In Young's study of an Anglo-American farm pay scales were as follows:

Table 6.3
1976 pay scales on a company farm in the Transvaal — (Rands per month)

Job Group	New Min. Wage	New Max. Wage	Old Ave. Wage	New Ave. Wage	Classification	Race	Job Title	Slope of pay curve
A	28.50	42.75	27.00	31.00	Unskilled	Black	Labourer (1&2)	1.5
B1	42.75	56.00	33.00	44.00	Semi-skilled	black	tractor, truck, combine driver, clerk	1.5
B3	73.40	96.20	83.00	96.00		black	*induna* 1	1.5
B1	134.00	174.00			clerical	white	telephonist	1.5
B2	175.00	234.00			clerical	white	typist	1.5
B3	235.00	310.00			clerical	white	bookkeeper	1.5
C1	311.00	465.00			junior manager & skilled	white section manager	senior book/keeper	1.5
C2	466.00	699.00			skilled	white	unit manager	1.5

Source: Young, 1979: 18, Table 4.

In the Eastern Transvaal, in 1976, a study of three farms revealed that 'boss boys' (African foremen) were being paid wages ranging from a low R45 (dairy) to R60 (citrus) and a high of R80 (tobacco, tomato, beef) per month (Godet, 1976). On the huge Zebediela citrus estates artisans were earning an average of R140 a month in 1977 (*Financial Mail* 26 July 1977). Tractor drivers on farms in the Malelane-Komatipoort area could expect to earn R52 cash working an average 260-hour month (i.e., 11.82 hours a day x 5.5 days a week) in 1980 (Brotherton, 1980). In Middleburg, a milking machine operator was earning R100 in 1984 for a 256-hour month and after ten years' service (Seleoane, 1984:9). In the Letaba district in the north of the province, average wages for skilled workers in the 1983 survey were as in Table 6.4.

Table 6.4
Average cash monthly wages of skilled farm workers in Letaba District, 1983 — (Rands)

Clerk	150.00
Foreman	70.00
Lorry Driver	176.50
Tractor Driver	66.70
Semi-skilled operator	60.00

Source: Smit and Herbst, 1983:59

In other words, the highest paid workers — clerks and drivers of heavy goods vehicles — earned between R150 — R177 cash a month. But the majority of semi-skilled and skilled workers (55 percent of the sample) earned less than half that a month, i.e. between R60 — R80 in 1983.

In Natal (see Table 6.2) monthly cash wages paid to skilled workers in 1975 averaged R30 but, in fact, apart from skilled workers on the sugar estates, two-thirds were earning less than R37. Seven years later (1982), a survey of workers in the Hluhluwe/Mtubatuba area revealed average cash wages ranging from R67 — R102. The median wage for the skilled workers surveyed was just R88 a month.

Table 6.5
Average monthly wages for skilled workers in Hluhluwe/Mtubatuba (Northern Natal) — 1982 (Rands)

Supervisors (*Indunas*)	102.33
Cutting/loading timber	101.08
Tractor drivers	75.78
Mechanical work	66.40

Source: Daphne, 1982:5 (from Table 2).

These figures do not reflect the full range of skilled wages in the region. Research in the northern districts in 1980 (AFRA, 1980-84: Reel I) revealed that the top wage on a farm in Babanango district was R18 cash a month (paid to a mechanic). In the Weenen district, an *induna* was being paid R34 per month plus a 50 kg bag of mealies.

In the OFS in 1983/4, tractor drivers on the farms around Clarens averaged monthly cash wages of R120 (Welwyn, 1984).

Whilst the implications of wages paid to skilled workers will be looked at in more detail below, what these figures show is that the highest earners in the sector are those who are paid for their skills. Often skilled workers earn double or more than unskilled men workers. And their wages are qualitatively higher than those paid to women in 'full-time' unskilled work.

At the same time, as has been pointed out (Standish, 1976), their wages also express the greatest range and the least uniformity. This reflects the generally ambivalent stance adopted by employers, who recognise the need to pay for skills but who are unwilling to do so meaningfully. This means that, although relative to all other farm workers, their wages are the highest and the best, when compared with skilled workers doing the same or similar jobs in all other sectors, farm wages are again amongst the lowest.

Wages of workers in 'part-time' employment

Wages paid to workers employed 'part-time' reveal the opposite end of the pay scale in the sector. Indeed, they demonstrate just how low pay can go and still be termed a wage.

Problems of definition

Before we examine these wages, certain aspects of 'part-time' employment need to be looked at. Again there are problems of classification. The ambiguity of definition between the various forms of labour falling within this general category poses problems similar to those raised earlier with respect to migrant and 'casual' workers and 'full-time' employment. This affects migrant workers, some of whom are employed 'full-time' and some of whom work seasonally. But it also affects 'seasonal' and so-called 'casual' work. The division between these two groups is far from clear. On the one hand, seasonal work is increasingly done by casualised labour, workers who are hired out by the day. On the other hand, so-called 'casual' work may entail employment sustained over a period as long as or even longer than 'a season'. The problem is further compounded by the fact that seasons are being shortened and the demand for labour flattened through the reorganisation of production. This, in turn, leads to a concentration of employment, especially for 'part-time' workers resident on the farms who are employed seasonally and 'casually'. In addition, these aspects are complicated by the gender and age characteristics of the 'part-time' workforce, as well as by the residential location of the workers. In short, differences in pay between these forms are as much related to the type of employment, as to the characteristics of the labour force.

There are also the different methods of payment for 'part-time', which affect wages, and which have to be taken into consideration. Equally, pay differences may simply arise because of the cumulative effect of more sustained employment. Finally, all these aspects are made worse by ambiguities in reporting pay levels. There is, in fact, no easy way to unravel this web, nor any point, given the present data base, in attempting to distinguish any groups within the category 'part-time'. Furthermore, since employers tend to calculate 'part-time' pay rates by the day, it is proposed to use this as a basis to describe wage levels for agricultural workers employed under the broad classification 'part-time'.

Women, men and children in 'part-time' employment

As already indicated, pay policy often differentiates between workers according to sex and age, invariably to the advantage of adult men. When it does not, wages are usually dragged down to the lowest level for which wage labour can be obtained. There are also skilled workers who are employed 'part-time' and these are always adult men. Such work is generally confined to sheep shearing, fencing, construction and specialist contracting work, when these jobs are not included in the work routine of workers employed 'full-time'. Apart from shearers, there is very little information on the wages paid to workers for intermittent skilled work. Antrobus (1984:100) refers to 'machine boys' contracted from outside to service the combines during the harvest. They were paid R1 a day plus half a bottle of brandy in 1977. Indeed, it is likely that these workers are paid the 'going rate' for male 'part-time' workers in the particular region, but it does depend on the skill involved and the scarcity of such workers. With respect to sheep shearers, the information available tends to concentrate on pay levels in the Western Cape. In Hanover district, for example (Archer and Meyer, 1984:7,11), 70 percent of sheep shearers were earning an average monthly income of R50 in 1983/4. Only 30 percent earned R150. They could expect to be employed for about seven months in any one year. In the Rietbron area, the going rate per sheep was 17 percent lower (i.e., 5 cents), giving a daily average income of R6 — R9 (Wentzel, 1984:85).

Moving from skilled to general 'part-time' employment, the most striking regional difference is to be found in the Western Cape where the Coloured labour preference policy is practised. The going rate for casual employment was given as R4 a day for men in 1983/4. Thus a worker whose last job had just finished and who lived a life 'on the trek' (moving from job to job with his family) reported that 'my last job lasted one month and 14 days. It paid R4 a day. Everyone pays R4 a day.' He had earned about R144 and expected that finding a new place (and job) would take a week to 14 days. Until then he had to live with his wife and infant children on the road, sleeping under the donkey cart (Schmidt, 1984:44).

On the fruit farms, harvest work is done mostly by women and children, and this is reflected in the lower rates of pay. In the Elgin district, the mean basic rate for pickers and packers in 1976 was R2.05 a day (Levy, 1976). Eight years later, in the 1983/4 picking season on farms in the Schoemanshoek area (Oudtshoorn district) workers were only earning an average of R3 — R4 cash per day. This meant that working from December to mid-January they could earn between R90 and R120 (Buirski, 1984:6).

In the rest of the country, cash wage rates for 'part-time' work — whether it was done by men or women, adults or children, workers resident on the farms or in the reserves — were everywhere lower. Women employed 'part-time' on mixed production farms in the Albany district (Eastern Cape) in 1977 earned average wages of R5.21 a month. The average daily cash going rate in the area was given as: women — 36 cents, youths — 32/4 cents and children — 32 cents (Antrobus, 1984:100). At the Tyefu irrigation project in the Ciskei bantustan, wages were even more appalling. In 1983 carrot and brussels sprout pickers were paid 20 cents per crate picked. They could perhaps fill two of these vast crates per day, giving them a daily income of 40 cents (Grahamstown Rural Committee, 1983).

In the north of the province in 1982 'farmers came into the area with trucks to pick up women and children ... paying R1 for a ten to twelve hour day' of digging, weeding, sorting nuts, etc. The only men taking up such jobs were described as those who were desperate (SPP, 1983: Vol.3,134). But there is no doubt that it was out of the same desperation that women or children were driven to accept hard labour for such wages.

In the Transvaal, conditions were much the same. Working in the Malelane-Komatipoort district in 1980 'casual' workers could expect to earn, at best, an average of R1.30 per day in June — the peak month for casualised employment in the area (Brotherton, 1980:245; Schneider, 1984:6). Workers who were picked up from Dzumeri village in the Gazankulu 'homeland' and taken in open lorries to the farms around Maferane, Bonn and Burgersdorp, for example, earned wages of between R1.20 and R1.40 a day in 1983/4. They left home each morning at 5.30 a.m. and returned each night at 7p.m. (Harries, 1984:6). For those labouring on the tomato farms around Moketsi (between Tzaneen and Louis Trichardt) basic pay in 1983 was given as R1.60 a day for women and R2 for men (R30 and R44 a month respectively). Many workers tended to stay on the farm during the period of their employment as the work day was too long, no transport was available and their homes were too far away for them to commute daily.[8]

On commercial agricultural enterprises in the reserves themselves, wages dropped even lower. Most of these farms are solely or partially owned by the parastatal CED (Corporation for Economic Development). Its stated and much-publicised policy is 'to encourage labour-intensive products, methods and systems' (*Survey*, 1984:374). But what the authorities omit to mention is the crucial question of pay, revealed in practice to be exceedingly low (as already witnessed at the Tyefu irrigation farm in the Ciskei). On the sisal plantation of Gazankulu, for instance, women were earning from 90 cents to one rand a day in 1982 (Harries, 1984.6). On all its cotton projects in the Transvaal reserves (and this probably holds true for projects in other reserves), the rate of pay (1982) was set up at 5 cents/kg picked. Workers picked on average 14 — 20 kgs a day, earning between 70 cents and one rand for their labours (James, 1983:22). The cotton picking season lasted a month, giving them a maximum of R26 working six days a week. Whilst women gleaning *agter die masjien* (behind the machine) in the Eastern Transvaal were earning one rand a day in 1983/4 (Seleoane, 1984:22), in the Western Transvaal rates for 'part-time' work seemed to be higher. Seasonal workers resident on the farms were earning an average daily wage of R1.54 in 1981 on the maize harvest. According to De Klerk's findings, seasonal workers who were paid in kind earned as much as 2.5 times more if they were reaping, and 42 percent more than those paid cash for gleaning. Casualised workers lifting groundnuts in the area averaged a daily wage of R1.79 although as many as one-third earned between only R1 and R1.60 (De Klerk, 1984:26). Employment on the groundnut harvest lasted between three and six weeks, giving an income ranging from a low of R18 to an average high of R64.80 for the season.

In Natal, for example, in 1979 aged women were working on a cotton farm near Muden in the north for 60 cents for a 9½ hour working day (*Echo*, 8 November 1979). Three years later, in 1982, the going rate for adult workers recruited from the Sahlumbe settlement on the banks of the Tugela was still 60 cents a day. Children were being paid between 20 and 50 cents per day, or a bucket of reject potatoes, or whatever the crop being harvested (SPP, 1983: Vol.4:321). 'Casual' workers from the Hluhluwe/Mtubatuba area reported taking home wages averaging R1.35 per day in 1982 (Daphne, 1982:5).

In short, apart from the Western Cape, wages for casualised employment in commercial agriculture ranged from around R1 to R1.80 per day in the first few years of the 1980s. They dropped a few cents a day for quite a large number of workers (albeit a minority) and rose to the dizzy heights of R2 or thereabouts for very few.

Computed into monthly rates, these figures give hypothetical incomes ranging from R5 to R100 a month in 1982/3 on the basis of 25 days worked. Whatever the figure arrived at, all estimations based on monthly calculations will be upwardly distorting. After all, the very notion of 'part-time' employment, and therefore income, presumes that work is irregular and unsustained. For some this might mean working for several months, whereas for most it often only means having a job for weeks or days at a stretch. In between, inestimable periods pass when workers are unemployed. A monthly figure therefore represents the best possible income, rather than anything workers in 'part-time' employment are likely to receive. The experiences of Dombie Khumalo's adult daughter reflect the reality of working conditions and income for 'casual' labour: 'My eldest girl is about 18 years old. Sometimes she can get temporary jobs on nearby farms. In January she earned R10 and in February R14' (James, 1983).

The dynamics of super-exploiting farm workers

As revealing as this portrait of wages in commercial agriculture is, it does not expose the full depth of the South African reality. On the one hand, there are patterns and trends about wages which are discernible and need to be drawn out. On the other, and in order to answer the primary question 'How low is low?', this evidence has to be looked at diachronically and in relation to employment in other sectors of the South African political economy. In this way, a fuller picture can be drawn of the meaning of low wages and the impact of restructuring on them.

Patterns and trends in wage levels
The above description is essentially a synchronic look at pay levels in the sector in the years around 1980. Although the information is not comprehensive, it never-

theless reveals certain patterns and trends. In general, the highest paid workers
in the sector are men who are employed 'full-time' and whose skills are recognised.
The lowest wages in the sector are paid to women and children who are employed
'part-time' as unskilled labour. The gap in wages between these extremes is great.
It is likely to remain so, as long as farmers are able to meet most of their labour
needs through the particular combination of a physically divided and extensively
migrantised and casualised labour force, drawn from large and growing pools of
unemployed workers who are unorganised.

These extremes are somewhat qualified by the fact that often there is not a
qualitative difference in wage rates between the various categories. This is particularly the case between unskilled and skilled men in 'full-time' employment.
Also, in so far as the differences between unskilled 'full-time' workers and some
of those in 'part-time' employment are concerned, frequently it is the cumulative
effect of employment, rather than the rate of pay, which makes for the differentiation in wage levels.

Wages tend to range widely within categories of employment as well. The extent
of the range differs, however, according to whether workers work 'full-time' or
'part-time', and/or in skilled or unskilled jobs. The greatest uniformity in pay levels
is evident in the wages of the lowest paid workers, i.e., those in 'part-time' employment, and the least in wages for the highest paid group, i.e., skilled 'full-time'
workers. In general, the forces generating standardisation tend to lead to uniformity around the lowest common denominator. Farmers set the wage rates they
pay according to 'the going rate' in their locality. Lastly, the question of wage
differences within the sector needs to be seen in the context of the generally low
level of pay that the best wage represents. In other words, the qualitative
significance of these differences centres not on whether farm workers are poor,
but on how poor they are. Even in poverty, there is little equality.

Sex and age

With respect to sex and age, it is clear that within any particular category of employment, they have a direct and negative bearing on wage levels. Being a woman
or a child, almost without exception serves to depress a worker's wage. In the
category 'skilled' — be it in 'full-time' or 'part-time' employment — on the whole
only the labour of men is acknowledged in pay. This is so, despite the fact that
there are instances of female skilled workers, such as women chain sawyers on
the timber plantations and 'dairy maids', women working with milking machinery.
By ignoring their skills because they are women, and/or because of the form of
employment — as so-called 'part-time' workers — farmers are able to lower their
labour costs. Even when their skills are acknowledged, the value attributed to their
labour is reduced because they are women.

When it comes to 'full-time' unskilled employment, all speculation ceases. Here
the evidence is clear-cut and overwhelming. Being a woman can and does reduce
a worker's wage by as much as 60 percent. Age, too, serves as a device to lower
wages. Although it is hard to generalise, it would seem that being a male youth
(in the Albany district, for example) is as bad, if not worse than being an adult
woman in 'full-time' employment in so far as wages are concerned. The one

important difference, however, is that in a longer-term perspective the prospects for boys are better. They grow up and become men, and thus can grow out of the particular form of oppression. Women never can. Women remain women.

In so far as 'part-time' employment is concerned, skills and gender both (and especially in combination) tend to put men at a relative advantage in terms of pay. Age, too, has a negative effect on 'part-time' workers' wage levels. This particularly affects the pay of women who make up the majority of the 'part-time' workforce. The extensive exploitation of cheaper child labour drags their already low wages down further. It even removes them completely from the work situation as they battle in unequal and unfair competition. Their very existence then becomes solely dependent on the income from the labour of their children, and the burden of being breadwinners for the family is thereby transferred to the shoulders of the children.

Regional differences

The political geography of the South African countryside appears to be the primary determinant of regional differences in pay levels. The geographical divisions that policy practices have created rest upon African national oppression and the creation and maintenance of the reserves.

The most significant of these regional differences exists in the districts of the Western Cape, where the Coloured labour preference policy applies. This policy arises from the twin needs of white minority domination, namely cheap black labour and the restriction of the presence of the African majority in most parts of the country, as well as from the particular historical and social conditions in the Cape. Average wages for Coloured farm workers there are higher than in any other part of the country where Coloureds are employed on the farms and they are universally higher than wages earned by African farm workers anywhere.

This development does not stem from the fact that farmers prefer to pay Coloured workers higher wages because of the colour of their skin. Although higher wages have become associated with racial differentiation, the pressures forcing up wages on the farms in the Western Cape stem primarily from the restricted labour market that this policy has created. Although wages for Coloured workers are universally higher than those paid to Africans, relative to employment outside the sector, they are very low. So farmers have tried to stem the drift of workers from the countryside by raising wages, albeit very reluctantly.

This is not the full story, however. If it were, it would be reasonable to expect that the extent of the reorganisation of production and the reduction of the labour force on commercial agricultural enterprises in the region would be the most advanced in the sector. Yet this is not the case. Farmers in the Western Cape have been able to counter the upward pressure on wages that the Coloured labour preference policy generates through cheap labour. Despite the restriction of some avenues to cheap labour that this policy implies, there have been others which both the policy and objective conditions have opened up. In so far as paid labour is concerned, they have extensively employed African male migrant workers, a labour form which presumes cheap labour. Additionally, they have replaced Coloured male 'full-time' farm workers with the cheaper labour of Coloured women, thus ending the pattern of 'full-time' employment as the historical preserve of men.

The feminisation of the 'full-time' farm workforce is most advanced in the Western Cape, a direct outcome of the particular conditions expressing African national oppression in the region, i.e., the Coloured labour preference policy.

The wage levels of Coloured women farm workers closely approximate those of African male farm workers employed 'full-time'. So that for them when it comes to pay, conditions are little better than for African men employed as 'full-time' unskilled labourers.

When it comes to comparing the positions of Coloured and African women workers on the farms, however, then their relative advantage is restored. Not only are more Coloured women working 'full-time', but as 'part-time' workers their wage rates are twice and even three times as high as those of African 'part-time' women workers. Farmers in the region have also made extensive use of prison labour schemes — institutionalised, forced, unpaid labour.

But whilst the advantages of the Coloured labour preference policy for Coloured workers in general are clear, the weight of their significance cannot be judged in relation to the low wage earned by African farm workers only. They have equally to be assessed in relation to employment in other sectors and, more importantly, the cost of living. The low wage levels of Coloured farm workers have led to extensive and endemic poverty on the farms in these districts (SPP, 1983: Vol.4,317).

Whilst the regional specifics of the Western Cape represent the best of generally bad wage conditions that restructuring has generated in commercial agriculture, the other regional differences stemming from the political geography of the South African countryside exposes the very worst conditions that are to be found in the sector. From the evidence on 'part-time' wages, the lowest wage rates are found on commercial agricultural enterprises inside the 'homelands' themselves. Here, in the midst of mass and concentrated unemployment, wage levels drop to next to nothing, especially for 'casual' and seasonal workers. And, because of the extent of local unemployment, the casualisation of labour on these enterprises is likely to be most extreme. This finding is consistent with developments in other sectors where the lowest wages and the worst conditions of employment are always found within the reserves.

Proximity to them is also likely to depress wage levels on the farms, but this aspect should not be treated too schematically or categorically as is the wont in recent literature.[9] This is because, on the one hand, this effect is not restricted to the reserves. Rising unemployment in the ghettoes of so-called 'white' towns is creating a growing reserve of black labour which white farmers can draw on. This is partly an outcome of restructuring in the sector, and partly of the general structural unemployment that characterises the South African political economy. This means that lower than average wage rates are not necessarily only to be found on farms close to the bantustans.

On the other hand, the downward effect on workers' wages exerted by large concentrations of workers in the bantustans is not contained geographically. The changing and declining demand for labour, rising unemployment and the migrant labour system have all combined to influence wage rates in commercial agriculture throughout the South African countryside. So, for example, farmers can and do travel long distances to pick up workers who have been made migrant and whose employment has been made casual by the restructuring process. Likewise, workers can and do travel long distances to try to find jobs. Thus, the significance of the physical proximity of commercial agricultural enterprises to the reserves has to be qualified somewhat when considering the forces acting to lower wages in any particular area. The consequences of the political geography stretch beyond physical boundaries.

Briefly then, looking at wage levels at a particular juncture, the primary instrument in the restructuring process which has acted to keep wages low has been the reorganisation of the division of labour in conditions of African national oppression. Both the migrantisation and casualisation of the labour force and the replacement of men by women and children have been central to this process. In combination, these represent the cheapest form of labour in commercial agriculture. Their extensive exploitation has not only acted to make 'part-' and even 'full-time' labour cheap; it has also served to hold down the wages of all workers. From this evidence on wage levels, it is clear that the capitalisation and reorganisation of the production process in commercial agriculture in conditions of national oppression and social exploitation have perpetuated a cheap labour base.

Super-exploitation: the relative and absolute decline in wages
In reality, restructuring has even more far-reaching consequences for pay levels in the sector than just keeping wages low. With the exception of workers paid for their skills, a diachronic examination of pay in commercial agriculture reveals that wages for black workers have declined both relatively and absolutely. This deterioration is manifest even in official statistics, as the following examples illustrate.

A comparison of average monthly earnings of black and white 'employees' prepared by the Quail Commission (Quail Report, 1980: para.145) from official statistics not only exposes the extent of the pay gap between black and white workers in the sector and in the political economy as a whole, but also shows a twofold relative decline in African farm worker wages. In other words, African wages in commercial agriculture have deteriorated both as a proportion of white 'employees' average monthly earnings in the sector, and as a proportion of African earnings in other sectors of the economy. Whereas in 1960 African average monthly earnings on the farms equalled 4.3 percent of those earned by whites, in 1975 this proportion had declined to 4.2 percent. In 1970, the figure stood at an even lower 3.8 percent. In this same period African average earnings in 'non-farm' sectors had risen from 15.2 to 20.8 percent of white earnings.

The relative decline compared to African wage levels in other sectors is also revealed in a study of cash incomes of farm workers in Natal. Here it was shown that, whereas African wages on the mines rose by an average 8.4 percent per annum between 1965 and 1975, those for unskilled workers on Natal farms at best increased by 3.8 percent a year. This finding, however, was qualified not only by the fact that mine workers' wages began at a much higher rate but, perhaps more importantly, by the author's own doubts as to the accuracy of the calculation on farm workers' pay. He argued that, if the category 'mixed/other' was excluded from the wage comparisons (as it upwardly distorted average figures and was likely to be in error), average monthly cash wages for unskilled farm workers in Natal declined by 6.14 percent over the decade.[10]

In short, wages on the farms for unskilled workers showed both a relative and an absolute decline.

This is confirmed by more recent analysis. In her study of employment in the district of George, Levatan (1984:56) writes on the basis of official statistics that:

> The changes in agricultural wages over the 1970s show a rise in average regular earnings of African and Coloured workers up until 1975 and 1976 respectively, in real terms at 1975 constant prices. But real wages by 1978 had declined to 1975 levels for Coloured workers and below 1976 for African workers.

Whereas at constant 1975 prices Coloured farm workers earned on average R49.95 a month in 1976 and Africans R42.08, by 1978 their wages had dropped to R45.92 and R41.73 respectively. The decline of Coloured wages actually was faster than that for Africans employed in the district, probably a consequence of the rapid feminisation of the Coloured workforce over this period. Levatan found that real wages continued to deteriorate over the next five years (1977-82). Thus, 'in one major privately-owned sawmill all women earned R21 a week in 1982 as against R16 per week in 1979, representing a decline in real terms of 14.2 percent' (Levatan, 1984:59).

In a comparative study of conditions in Albany district between 1957 and 1977, average cash wages had increased by a sum of R93.42 to total a grand *annual* wage of R182.52 in 1976 (at 1975 constant prices). But, as the author points out, if rations and other payments in kind were excluded, 'labourers are on average worse off than they were in 1956 (Antrobus, 1984:257). This absolute decline is not confined to 'full-time' workers. A daily wage rate for 'part-time' work which remains constant over several years, in conditions of inflation means that real wage rates have declined. The nominal rate of 60 cents a day reported in Natal in 1979, 1980 and 1982, for instance, had a real value of only 38 cents by 1982.[11]

But the decline in wages is likely to be even sharper than these figures suggest, because of two hidden elements. One is the deterioration and withdrawal of payments in kind, while the other is the fact that the cost of living in the countryside is higher. Whilst the decline in non-cash wage forms is far harder to measure, it is apparent that the switch to a cash-based wage system has not been paralleled by a compensatory increase in cash payments. On the contrary, farmers have reduced wages precisely by cutting payments in kind. So, whilst many workers initially welcomed the shift to cash wages, their experiences soon led them to the unavoidable conclusion that it represented a change for the worse. In 1974 a worker on a company-owned farm explained: 'I had horses and cattle ... we were paid R1 a month (cash) and 100 *treë* of mielies standing in the field (i.e. 60-70 bags) per annum. This is the fourth year earning cash. I see no progress ...' (Young, 1979:10).

This deterioration in wage levels applies not only to unskilled workers employed 'full-time' but also to those working 'part-time'. De Klerk's finding (1984:28) that seasonal workers paid in kind earned as much as 40 to 50 percent more than seasonal workers paid in cash expresses precisely the implications of a change away from non-cash to cash payments in conditions of intensive labour exploitation. Without exaggerating the conversion value of payments in kind — often these are very limited — whereas daily cash earnings for 'casual' workers on a north-eastern Transvaal company farm averaged between 40 and 65 cents (1976), the value of the company's ten kg bucket of vegetables was given by management as 70-100 cents (Young, 1979:53, Table 21; 73).

The dominant principle guiding pay practices on the part of farmers is not the form of payment, but rather the value of its content, especially under restructured conditions. In other words, 'the wage represents a cost to the farmer which he will attempt to minimise' (Levy, 1976). The primary force underlying the change to a cash-based wage system has been the drive to reduce labour costs. When this is not possible they do not hesitate to pay 'casual' workers *in natura* — reject tomatoes, rotten fruit and even reeds.

With regard to the *higher cost of living* in the countryside, it must be recalled that the value of a cash wage lies in the goods it can purchase. In South Africa, the rate of inflation and its effect on the cost of living is calculated with an urban bias and on the presumption of goods being bought at the best possible price. Whilst the probability that workers in urban areas are likely to make such purchases is low, in the rural areas of South Africa the possibility of buying cheaply barely exists. The purchases of workers in commercial agriculture are confined almost solely to goods bought at rural traders' and farm shops. All the evidence (e.g., James, 1983; Yawitch, 1982; SPP, 1983; Carnegie Commission, 1984) points to the fact that prices of staple goods in these stores are consistently higher. Declining wages therefore mean that farm workers have less money and are able to purchase even fewer of their basic necessities than workers in urban areas. Furthermore, the effects of inflation are more strongly felt in the rural areas than in the towns, given the costs of fuel and transport, and the combination of higher prices and lower wages.

Forces acting to lower wages in commercial agriculture
What then are the forces acting to drag down wages in commercial agriculture below their historically low level? Central to this evident deterioration in black farm workers' wages in commercial agriculture are changes in the predominant labour forms and the reorganisation of the division of labour in the sector which the restructuring process has brought about (Chapters Three and Four above). It is the combination of cheap (often coerced) labour and unpaid, forced labour that both keeps wages low and pulls them down even lower.

Paid cheap labour
In so far as paid labour forms are concerned, wages have not only been held down by them, but have actually been further reduced by the physical division and the transformation of a substantial part of the workforce into casual and migrant workers, a process coupled with the feminisation of the workforce, and the extensive exploitation of the labour of children.

Even the wages of skilled workers have been affected by the process although they are the only group of workers in commercial agriculture whose wage levels have not actually deteriorated in the course of restructuring. Their wages have been held down by the generally low wage levels in the sector, so that most skilled workers have gained little relief from the struggle for subsistence. Furthermore, relative to workers in other sectors, wages in commercial agriculture are generally lower than for work requiring similar skills in the rest of the political economy.

Forced unpaid labour: Last, but by no means of least significance to pay levels for workers in the sector, restructuring continues to presume the 'employment' of a substantial minority of workers whose labour is completely unpaid. The base of this no-wage labour is institutionalised with at least 90,000 men (1980) having been channelled through various prison labour schemes into forced labour on the farms (Cook, 1982:30).

Non-institutionalised, forced, unwaged labour is also widespread. As shown in Chapter Four, it particularly affects women and children whose position in the social structure is exploited to compel them to labour unpaid on the farms. Although its extent is unknown, intermittent reports uncover and reaffirm its existence with regular monotony.[12] Thus, forced unpaid labour of black workers, whose condition is integral to the restructuring process, has served along with cheap waged labour to depress wages even further. Starvation is the depth to which wage levels can sink in commercial agriculture.

This chapter has shown that restructuring has not only meant that wage levels have been maintained at a universally low rate for all workers in commercial agriculture, but that for the majority — the 'unskilled' — wages have declined relatively and absolutely. This deterioration directly stems from changes in and the nature of the labour forms in the sector. It is also a consequence of the forms and methods of payment which characterise pay practices. As the evidence on wages so graphically shows, restructuring represents nothing less than an extension and intensification of exploitation — the super-exploitation of black workers in commercial agriculture.

Super-exploitation carries with it very far-reaching implications for workers (and capital, for that matter). It has a direct bearing on all aspects of social relations in the sector. Whilst these have not been analysed here, the inescapable conclusion is that it leads to conditions of generalised and rising poverty and widespread indebtedness. Coupled with the related aspects of control and coercion, these remain the twin scourges of existence for workers in commercial agriculture. It is not incidental that people labouring in the sector experience a lifetime of poverty, hunger and even starvation. Indeed the complete breakdown in the capacity of social relations to generate physical reproduction — i.e., malnutrition and abnutrition — usually associated with the reserves, is also common amongst the men, women and children working and living on the farms. It is a condition of farm employment. At Baragwanath hospital (Johannesburg), for instance, where in 1980 the children's ward was admitting an average of five cases of malnutrition a day, 'it is common knowledge ... that when a malnourished child comes in, it is likely that he has been living on the farms' (*Sunday Express*, 2 May 1982). This experience is repeated in many hospitals in various parts of the country and is not confined to children. In 1969, the then superintendent of the Batlaharos Mission Hospital in the Kuruman reserve (Northern Cape) reported that the winter months of July, August and

September were the worst. This was so because, in addition to the 'usual' health problems to be found in the area, women who had been working seasonally on the maize harvest in the Western Transvaal returned at that time. He said they came back 'in a horrifying condition', suffering from a range of nutrition and poverty-related diseases, including pellagra. In fact, admissions into the hospital increased by about one third when people returned from the farms (*Rand Daily Mail*, 1 November 1979; Desmond, 1972:109). As hard as these conditions were, they have manifestly deteriorated both on the farms and in the reserves in the period since this report.

This endemic condition of impoverishment is made the more gross by the inevitable state of indebtedness that it places workers in. Poverty wages condemn them to an endless round of 'owing the farmer', living off the 'magnanimity' of (or struggling in the absence of) his credits, being bound to him because he refuses to pay a living wage and does everything to ensure that most of what he 'pays' never leaves or comes directly back to his pocket. At worst, it circulates within the local farming and trading establishment. Payment forms aggravate indebtedness, [13] but the change to a cash-based wage system has brought little or no relief since it is the level of pay which is at the heart of the matter. The rude reality, as so many workers are painfully aware, is that 'all their pennies' go back to the farmer.

For the vast majority of farm workers, these social relations hold out no prospect of relief from a working life of grinding poverty. Indeed, most workers in commercial agriculture are made poorer by their labours on the farms. It is most usually a sentence to labour in slave-like conditions for less than slave 'wages', a sentence to super-exploitation. Surely it is no surprise that most workers do everything in their power to avoid it.

Notes:

1. In fact, it is not known what is included in 'in-kind' payments. In the Summary Report of Agricultural and Pastoral Production, 1936/37 to 1938/39, and 1946/47 to 1953/54, reference is made to

    the value of goods earned in the form of rations by way of mealies, meal, slaughter animals, meat, fish, milk, wine, bread, coffee, sugar and other goods such as tobacco, clothes, shoes etc. The real value of free housing is, however, excluded.

    But as Simkins (1984:13) points out, subsequent census reports are silent on their assumptions.
2. I leave aside 'domestic' since this aspect of employment on the farms has not been dealt with at all in this analysis.
3. The figures used will concentrate on the most recent ones available, and as such fall at the end of the period which is being considered in this text.
4. Without being too sceptical, this is not particularly surprising since the source of information is essentially the same — white farmer responses.
5. Daphne, 1982:5. He gives no indication of the sex of the respondents.
6. AFRA 1980-1984: Microfilm Reel I — Field trip, July 1980.
7. An average cash wage of R154 for semi-skilled operators drawn from the surrounding reserves seems disproportionately high and distorts the average wage quite significantly. It is likely to be due to sampling error, and therefore the lower wage of R60 is taken to be more reflective of average wages paid to semi-skilled workers.

188 Modernising Super-Exploitation

8. Some workers are in fact known to travel as much as 113 km daily from the reserves to the farms where they formerly lived. The people from Itsoteng, for example, travel by bus every day to Lichtenburg, Ventersburg and Koster (Farm Labour Project, 1982:para 1.4).

9. See papers presented at the Second Carnegie Inquiry into Poverty and Development in South Africa in 1984, for example.

10. Mining is itself an historically notorious low wage sector in the South African political economy (Standish, 1976:9).

11. Taking 60 cents in 1979 as 100, and the annual increase of the Consumer Price Index at an average 14 percent.

12. The *Rand Daily Mail* (18 March 1985), for example, reported that women who worked on a Doornkop farm were paying the farmer in labour in return for a place to live. He paid them nothing for their work, and as a consequence they were forced to live by prostitution.

13. Eugene Roelofse, Ombudsman of the South African Council of Churches, for instance, in exposing conditions on the farms in 1979, argued that 'the system of paying in cash and in kind binds the worker to the farmer from the cradle to the grave' (*Daily News*, 2 May 1979), and he was especially referring to conditions on the maize harvest. Yet indebtedness is endemic and characteristic throughout the sector and applies for all forms of payment.

Conclusion

In the introduction to this study, I posed a number of questions about the consequences of the restructuring process for farm workers in South African commercial agriculture. It is now possible to answer them and to identify the most important consequences. Clearly they have been profound but, in general terms, it is obvious that the shift to capital-intensive production as part of the restructuring process has led to a much more intensive level of exploitation of the labour force. This is evidenced by changes in the size, forms and composition of the agrarian workforce, as well as in a reorganisation of the labour process itself. In specific terms, the most important effects have been these:

1. A relative and absolute decline in the number of workers employed in the commercial farming sector. This decline has come about as part of the physical reorganisation of the division of labour in the sector which, in turn, has brought about a substantial change in the dominant labour forms on the farms. The most dramatic of these changes has been the suppression of labour tenancy and the expulsion of surplus labour from the farms and their relocation to the reserves. This has produced a drastic reduction in the size of the resident workforce on the farms and a substantial expansion in the use of migrant labour. What has happened, therefore, has been that the stabilisation of the on-farm core has gone hand in hand with the destabilisation of the lives of the majority of farm workers who, no longer able to live on the farms, have been forced into becoming migrants.

This extensive migrantisation of labour has formed a key part of the process of casualising employment in the sector with 'full-time' jobs being broken down into 'part-time' work, which, in turn, has led to the replacement of male workers by women and children. Even though they may often work excessively long hours for a substantial part of the year, the casualisation of the work process has transformed them into a so-called 'part-time' workforce. Black women and children also constitute the bottom of the pyramid of oppression in South Africa with colour, nationality, age and gender oppression combining to make their labour the cheapest and the most controllable in the South African social formation. Whether they still have jobs on the farm, or have been made redundant, the majority of farm workers have been relocated off white-owned farmland to be drawn on only when needed by white farmers. The relocation of labour to the reserves has brought commercial agriculture into line with that of the other sectors of the political economy. Together, these changes have constituted a key component of the regime's policy of African national oppression.

2. Production relations on South Africa's farms have continued to be based on a system of forced labour, ensuring thereby the survival of the most backward forms of social and economic relations in this sector. However, as a consequence

of the restructuring process, farmers have been able to complement direct coercion with indirect compulsion. Whilst they have been able to continue exploiting the forced labour of black prisoners and the bound labour of 'full-time' workers' families, they have also been able to make use of indirectly compelled labour, i.e., black men, women and children who, having been crammed into barren and remote places without the basic essentials of life and the means of subsistence, are forced by hunger and poverty to offer their labour under the harshest of terms. We see therefore that capitalist exploitation in conditions of African national oppression has generated structural unemployment while the generalised condition of malnutrition and hunger has constituted the indirect force compelling workers back on to the farms, often on even more unfavourable terms than before.

3. Reorganisation of the division of labour has led to the emergence of a more differentiated and hierarchically ordered farm labour force. In general, Coloured farm workers have continued to be better placed than Africans but their relative advantage has been undercut by the more extensive and systematic exploitation of cheaper labour forms — African, migrant, forced, female, child, etc. Likewise, that tiny minority of mostly male workers whose skills have been acknowledged enjoy a very limited relative advantage over the grossly disadvantaged majority of farm workers. This is because when comparisons are made with workers in other sectors, or when their position is looked at in relation to meeting the necessary conditions of social existence for themselves and their dependants, it becomes clear that their relative advantages are negated by their comparative absolute disadvantage.

4. The full implications of the decades of restructuring becomes most apparent through an analysis of wage levels. This makes it clear that the changed labour forms and the reorganisation and the division of labour in the sector have been central to keeping the labour base cheap. Far from being incidental to the process, the perpetuation of cheap labour (in fact, making it even cheaper) has been a driving force behind the shift to capital-intensive production. Since the late 1930s there has been a relative and absolute decline in the wages of farm workers in South Africa. Only the minority at the top of the labour hierarchy — skilled men and Coloured men — have not suffered an absolute decline, but neither have their wage levels risen. Their so-called 'advantage' rests on the fact that their labour is not as cheap as that of the majority of the workforce, but it is cheap none the less. For agricultural workers, restructuring and the consequent decline in their wages has meant a deterioration of their social conditions and an intensification of their exploitation.

The unavoidable general conclusion, therefore, is that restructuring has modernised super-exploitation on the farms of South Africa. It has not transformed social relations in the sector; it has modernised them, reshaping them without altering the terms of oppression and exploitation on which they have been built. It is a process which has brought social relations in commercial agriculture into line with changes in capital and white-minority domination in the political economy as a whole. It has also produced new contradictions. Investigation has shown that the consequences of restructuring for capital have not been the same as those for labour.

While progressive for the former, the opposite has been the case for labour. Restructuring has meant a more intensive and systematic exploitation of their labour power.

The framework and finding of this study carry many implications. They challenge many of the assumptions commonly held about South African commercial agriculture. At a general theoretical level, they question the usefulness of notions like 'backward' and 'progressive' commercial farming. These categories, which are value-loaded in favour of the most advanced sections of capital, confuse issues because they presume that the general unevenness of development between branches and between enterprises within the sector stems from fundamentally different ways of organising production, rather than being a natural outcome of the development of capitalist relations.

This confusion cannot be separated from a general mystification about the South African social formation and about agricultural relations in particular, i.e., that there are 'two agricultures' — one practised inside the bantustans and the other outside them. Solutions, like that of Simkins,[1] which propose that 'perhaps it would be best to distinguish three agricultures in South Africa which shade into one another', do not get to the heart of relations and therefore only serve to add to their mystification. This study has shown that commercial, and even petty, production has developed on the same basis inside the reserves as outside them, namely, on a system of colonial capitalist exploitation and oppression. The fact that the intensity of exploitation and oppression is uneven, and is often even greater in the reserves than in the rest of the countryside is not an outcome of a different mode of production, but rather reflects their position and function in the political economy as a whole.

At a political and organisational level, the fact that restructuring has served only to modernise the conditions of super-exploitation throws grave doubts on any suggestion that the structural reorganisation of relations in commercial agriculture can offer relief from or solutions to the general crisis it is gripped by. For farm workers, re-arranging the terms of exploitation and oppression has only offered superficial solutions to their very profound grievances, and then only for a minority. For farmers, restructuring has generated a grievous debt crisis, with gross production being outstripped by the sector's debt burden since the mid-1980s. As a result, 1,208 farmers' estates were sequestrated in the period 1984-87 and a further 3,000 faced sequestration at the beginning of 1988 (*Daily Dispatch,* 14 January 1988). Mass impoverishment and unemployment has continued to grow while the state has continued to subsidise the sector to produce for the domestic market at inflated prices, and for export at a loss.

Restructuring is therefore not the answer. The only way to overcome the contradictions of colonial capitalist relations and to end super-exploitation in commercial agriculture in South Africa is to destroy them. It is not enough to reform them, they have to be fundamentally transformed. This transformation of relations in agriculture cannot be separated from the process of transformation of the whole political economy. This is not only because a revolution in the whole social formation is needed to begin the process in agriculture, but also because the land and agrarian questions affect the whole society and not just those who work the land. Redistribution of the land is as much a national question as it is a social one. It demands that, at the same time as political and economic solutions are found to the problems of land hunger generated by African national oppression, conditions have to be created to end the social exploitation of workers on the farms. Equally, agriculture does not only have to produce enough to meet the needs of those who live and work on the land; it also has to meet the food needs of the majority of the population who have left or will leave the land permanently. And these needs are closely tied up with the demands that manufacture places on the sector. Commercial agriculture is also an important foreign currency earner. Production therefore has to be organised on a scale and in a manner which is adequate to all these tasks.

These often-competing demands are never easily reconciled and it is precisely this fact that makes agrarian transformation a complex, difficult and necessarily protracted process. What this work has aimed to establish is the starting point from which the process of transformation has to begin. Whilst further research will explore in detail the possible options and implications open to a liberated South Africa, some preliminary pointers can be drawn from this study:

● First, agrarian transformation requires changes in both land ownership and production relations on the land.

● Second, the demand and need for land and agrarian reform comes from different social forces. As this study has shown, the majority of people in the countryside with a direct interest and stake in agricultural production are farm workers, dispossessed peasants and sections of the mass unemployed in urban ghettoes or dislocated in the reserves. Their needs and demands differ from those of the petit-bourgeoisie, medium and large capitalist farmers, and their counterparts in the towns. The direction and course the agrarian transformation process will take will depend on whose needs and demands are met which, in turn, will be determined by the struggles waged now and during the national democratic revolution. The better farm workers, dispossessed peasants and the unemployed are organised, the more able will they be to present and defend their interests.

● Third, the state will have a key role to play in setting in motion agrarian transformation in a newly liberated, democratic South Africa. But the problems before it will be very difficult and often contradictory. Its legacy will be a grossly distorted production system built on four factors — massive subsidies to white farmers to keep them on the land, the organisation of production for export, the super-exploitation and gross impoverishment of the farm labour force, and mass unemployment. In this respect, commercial agriculture in South Africa shows many of the typical features of agricultural production in developing countries. How will the state reconcile the many different, and often competing, interests in the sector? Should the framework and orientation of production be sustained whilst changing the national composition of ownership and access to land? How will it be possible to redress the problems of mass unemployment and super-exploitation then? How can the pressures to export agricultural goods as a foreign exchange earner be reconciled with directing and expanding food production for domestic consumption? Who should subsidise whom? Should the countryside continue to subsidise the towns, or is it not possible and necessary to reverse the relation so that the urban areas subsidise and support the rural? Also, what measures need to be taken to break the syndrome where the poor and labouring masses subsidise a rich, élite and landed minority?

The questions are many and relatively easy to pose. The concrete solutions to be found will be complex, difficult and even contradictory to judge by the experience of others. They will be shaped not only by conditions within the sector, but equally by conditions in the political economy as a whole, as well as by the position of South Africa in the international division of labour. But whatever the solutions the national democratic revolution finds, the strength of the newly democratic state's agrarian policy will depend on its knowledge of relations in the countryside and the level of rural mobilisation. This demands organisation and research.

Notes

1. Simkins (1984: Paper No.25), for example, in 'questioning the thesis of two sharply divided agricultures' (i.e., one practised in the bantustans and the other on so-called white farms) argues that: 'perhaps it would be best to distinguish three agricultures in South Africa which shade into one another:
    (a) progressive capitalist agriculture where a cash wage is most highly developed;
    (b) backward capitalist agriculture in which there is a constant tendency for officially discouraged forms to emerge: labour tenancy, sharecropping and rent farming arising from high African/white population ratios as the reserves are approached;
    (c) reserve agriculture in which the wage form is virtually absent.

Postscript

As this study was completed in the early 1980s, there is a need to consider briefly whether any recent developments have produced any substantial changes for South Africa's farm workers. Has, for example, the abolition of the pass laws improved their lot? In April 1986, Parliament passed the Abolition of Influx Control Act. Consequently, for the first time in modern South African history, Africans were no longer condemned by law to labour on farms. In practice, however, this reform has produced little real change for African farm workers as other legislation and administrative practices have been used to control and limit their access to urban areas: these have included a restrictive housing policy, tough anti-squatting legislation applicable to both urban and rural areas, and the making of access to urban areas conditional on employment at a time of acute structural and cyclical unemployment. What has happened is that the administrative technique of using seemingly non-political factors (housing and employment), long used to restrict Coloured farm workers' access to towns, have been extended to Africans. The reality is that the pass laws have simply been replaced by other controls with the general effect being one of 'granting freedom to move but no freedom to stop moving'.

In so far as restructuring in the sector is concerned, the pass law 'reform', in combination with new anti-squatting legislation has been entirely consistent with the trend to substitute labour for capital and to expel the 'surplus' workers, characteristic of the second phase.

The past decade has brought no change to the legal status of farm (and domestic) workers. They are still denied protection under the Labour Relations Act (1956), the Basic Conditions of Employment Act (1983), the Machinery and Occupational Safety Act (1983), the Workmen's Compensation Act (1937) and the Unemployment Insurance Act (1937). With the passage of the amended Labour Relations Act in 1988, which has severely curtailed trade-union activity, the prospects of farm workers being granted their rights as workers have become bleaker. Indeed, in 1988, Greyling Wentzel, the Minister of Agriculture, was categorical that black trade unions would not work on South African farms because 'they were not established for this'. To date, the Report of the 1982 National Manpower Commission into possible measures to regulate conditions of employment of farm and domestic workers has not been published. Although completed in 1984, it is unlikely ever to see the light of day because even limited recommendations to establish basic conditions of work would prove too politically volatile for the ruling National Party given the potential support for the Conservative Party amongst white farmers. The acting Manpower Minister, Eli Louw, stated as much when he told Parliament that 'the Report concerned served as advice to the Minister and was not meant for publication' (*Weekly Mail*, 10 March 1989).

The crisis of the 1980s suggests that the general deterioration of conditions in commercial agriculture has continued unabated to the political, social and economic detriment of black farm workers.

April, 1989

Select Bibliography

Articles, Books and Pamphlets

Association for Rural Advancement (AFRA) *Fact Sheets 1980-84*, Natal.

AFRA (1984), *Memorandum*, Natal.

Aires, A. (1976) 'The changing patterns of labour relationships in the Sundays River Valley of the eastern Cape', Paper No.31, Farm Labour Conference, SALDRU, Cape Town.

Anon (1939) *Farm Labour in the Orange Free State*, SAIRR, Johannesburg.

Anti-Slavery Society (1983), *Child Labour in South Africa*, London.

Antrobus, G.G. (1976) 'Farm Labour in the Eastern Cape 1950-73), Paper No.20, Farm Labour Conference, SALDRU, Cape Town.

— (1984) 'South African farm wages and working conditions with special reference to the Albany district, 1975-77', Unpub. PhD thesis, Rhodes University, Grahamstown.

Archer, S. and Meyer, E. (1984),'Hanover: a profile of poverty on the Eiselen line', Paper No.34, Conference of the Second Carnegie Inquiry into Poverty and Development in Southern Africa, SALDRU, Cape Town.

Barrett, J. et al (1985) *South African Women on the Move*, CIIR and Zed Books, London.

Beinart, W. (1982) *The Political Economy of Pondoland, 1860-1930*, Cambridge University Press, Cambridge.

Bekker, S.B. et. al (1982) 'Langkloof farmers practices and attitudes regarding Coloured and black farm workers', Development Studies Working Paper No.7, Rhodes University, Grahamstown.

Benjamin, P. (1984) 'Workers on white-owned farms', in *Removals and the Law*, transcript of a workshop held in Grahamstown, 1982.

Blaine, M.H. (1954) 'Induced Volunteer Farm Labour', unpub. mimeo, Institute of Commonwealth Studies, London.

Bird, A. (1983) 'Organising women workers', *South Africa Labour Bulletin* 10,8, Johannesburg.

Bohning, W.R. (ed.) (1981) *Black Migration to South Africa: a selection of policy-oriented research*, ILO, Geneva.

La Borde, R.M. (1980) 'The development and application of work standards and methods in harvesting bark and timber of black wattle', unpub. PhD thesis, UNISA, Pretoria.

Bromberger, N. (1984) 'Technical change and the destruction of farm employment', Paper No.273, Conference of the Second Carnegie Inquiry into Poverty and Development in Southern Africa, SALRDU, Cape Town.

Brotherton, I.A. (1980) 'Optimum organisation of developed irrigation farms in the Malelane-Komatipoort region, unpub. MSc thesis, University of Pretoria, Pretoria.

Budlender, D. (1984) 'Agriculture and technology: four case studies', Paper No.23, Conference of the Second Carnegie Inquiry into Poverty and Development in Southern Africa, SALRDU, Cape Town.

— (1984a) 'Mechanisation and labour on white farms: a statistical analysis', Paper No.26, Conference of the Second Carnegie Inquiry into Poverty and Development in Southern Africa, SALDRU, Cape Town.

Buirski, P. (1984) 'Poverty in Oudtshoorn: Some Impressions', Paper No.37, Conference of the Second Carnegie Inquiry into Poverty and Development in Southern Africa, SALDRU, Cape Town.

Bundy, C. (1979) *The Rise and Fall of the South African Peasantry*, Heinemann, London.

Clarke, D.G. (1977) 'Foreign African Labour Supply in South Africa', DSRG Working Paper No.1, University of Pretoria, South Africa.

Cook, A. *Akin to Slavery: Prison Labour in South Africa*, IDAF, London.
Daphne, P. (1982) 'A Preliminary Survey of Farm Workers in the Mtubatuba/Hluhluwe Area', Centre of Research and Documentation, University of Zululand, Natal.
Darrington, Dr and Mrs (1976) 'Maintaining a Stable Labour Force on a Fruit Farm in the Northern Boland', Farm Labour Conference, SALDRU, Cape Town.
Davenport, T.R.J. and Hunt, K.S. (eds.) (1974) *The Right to the Land*, David Philip, Cape Town.
Davies, R.H. (1979) *Capital, State and the White Working Class in South Africa: 1900-60,* Harvester Press, Brighton.
Desmond, C. (1971) *The Discarded People: an account of African resettlement in South Africa*, Penguin Books, London.
Evans, A.R. (1976) 'Farm Labour in the Viljoenskroon District — OFS', Paper No.41, Farm Labour Conference, SALDRU, Cape Town.
Farm Labour Project (1982) 'Submission to the Manpower Commission of Inquiry into Farm Labour, unpub. mimeo, South Africa.
First, R. (1959) *The Farm Labour Scandal*, New Age Publications, South Africa.
Godet, R. (1976) 'Farming in the Eastern Transvaal', Paper No.36, Farm Labour Conference, SALDRU, Cape Town.
Graaff, D. (1976) 'Farming in the Hex River Valley', Paper No.42, Farm Labour Conference, SALDRU, Cape Town.
Harris, J. et. al. (1982) *South Africa, A Land Divided*, Black Sash, Johannesburg.
Haysom, H. (1984) 'Law and Order in the Eastern Transvaal', in *Lawyers for Human Rights*, South Africa.
Hendrie, D. (1977) 'Agricultural statistics, a need for reform', in Wilson, F. et al, *Farm Labour in South Africa,* David Philip, Cape Town.
Hendrie, D. and Kooy, A. (1976) 'Some Employment Patterns in South African Agriculture', Paper No.49, Farm Labour Conference, SALDRU, Cape Town.
Hobart-Houghton, D. (1964) *The South African Economy* Oxford University Press, Cape Town.
Horner, D. and Van Wyk, G. (1984) 'Quiet desperation: the poverty of Calitzdorp', Paper No.36 Conference of the Second Carnegie Inquiry into Poverty and Development in Southern Africa, SALDRU, Cape Town.
James, D. (1983) *The Road from Doornkop — a case study of removals and resistance*, SAIRR, Johannesburg.
Jones, B.M. (1985) *Land Tenure in South Africa: Past, Present and Future* University of Natal Press, Pietermaritzburg.
Keegan, T.J. (1981) 'The transformation of agrarian society and economy in industrialising South Africa', unpub. PhD thesis, London.
De Klerk, M. (1983) 'Maize farming technology and employment', in *South African Labour Bulletin* 1, 2, Johannesburg.
— (1984) 'Mechanising farming: implications for employment, incomes and population distribution', Paper No.27, Conference of the Second Carnegie Inquiry into Poverty and Development in Southern Africa, SALDRU, Cape Town.
— (1984a) 'The incomes of farm workers and their families: a study of maize farms', Paper No.28, Conference of the Second Carnegie Inquiry into Poverty and Development in Southern Africa, SALDRU, Cape Town.
Kooy, A. (1976) 'Farm labour in the Karoo', Paper No.45, Farm Labour Conference, SALDRU, Cape Town.
— (1976) 'Notes on sheep shearers', Paper No.46, Farm Labour Conference, SALDRU, Cape Town.
Lacey, M. (1981) *Working for Boroko*, Ravan, Johannesburg.
Levatan, L. (1984) 'Structural changes in the George economy: underemployment and unskilled labour as conditions of impoverishment', Paper No.39, Conference of the Second Carnegie Inquiry into Poverty and Development in Southern Africa, SALDRU, Cape Town.
Levy, B. (1976) 'The seasonal labour market in agriculture — an empirical study', Paper No.33, Farm Labour Conference, SALDRU, Cape Town.
Lipton, M. (1977) 'South Africa: two agricultures?' in Wilson, F. et al (1977) *Farm Labour in South Africa*, David Philip, Cape Town.

Manona, C.W. (1984) 'Migration from the farms to the towns and its implications for urban adaptation', Paper No.30, Conference of the Second Carnegie Inquiry into Poverty and Development in Southern Africa, SALDRU, Cape Town.

Mare, G. (1980) *African Population Relocation in South Africa*, SAIRR, Johannesburg.

Maree, J. (1976) 'Farm Labour in the Dealesville District — OFS', Paper No.47, Farm Labour Conference, SALDRU, Cape Town.

Marks, S. and Atmore, A. (eds.) (1980) *Economy and Society in Pre-industrial South Africa*, Longman, London.

Marks, S. and Rathbone, R. (eds.) (1982) *Industrialisation and Social Change in South Africa*, Longman, London.

Marx, K. (1973) *Das Kapital,* Deitzverlag, Berlin.

McI. Daniel J.B. (1984) 'Man land relationships in the Eastern Cape', Paper No.144, Conference of the Second Carnegie Inquiry into Poverty and Development in Southern Africa, SALDRU, Cape Town.

Meer, Y.S. et al (1980) *Documents on Indentured Labour: Natal 1851-1917,* Institute of Black Research, Durban.

Moolman, J.H. and Smit, P. (1975) 'South Africa's rural black population', in *The Conditions of the Black Worker — Foreign Investment in South Africa and Namibia*, University of Pretoria, Pretoria.

Morris, M. (1977) *Apartheid, Agriculture and the State: the farm labour question*, SALDRU Working Paper No.8, SALDRU, Cape Town.

Myburgh, A.J. (1976) 'The role of the state in agriculture', Paper No.19, Farm Labour Conference, SALDRU, Cape Town.

Nasson, W. (1984) 'Bitter Harvest: farm schooling for black South Africans', Paper No.37, Conference of the Second Carnegie Inquiry into Poverty and Development in Southern Africa, SALDRU, Cape Town.

Nattrass, J. (1981) *The South African Economy: its growth and change*, Oxford University Press, London.

Nel, F.J. (1985) *Guidelines for Manpower Management in Agriculture*, SAAU, Pretoria.

NUSAS (1983) *South Africa's Bantustans: The Pillars of Apartheid*, Johannesburg.

Petersen, A.J. (1976) 'Changes in farm labour in the Elgin district', Paper No.51, SALDRU, Cape Town.

Plaatje, Sol. T (1981) *Native Life in South Africa*, Ravan, Johannesburg.

Potgieter, J.F. (1976) 'Labour problems appertaining to a large sugar estate in Natal', Paper No.2, Farm Labour Conference, SALDRU, Cape Town.

Roberts, M. (1959) *Labour in the Farm Economy,* SAIRR, Johannesburg.

—   (1959) 'The laws relating to farm labour', in *African Farm Labour, a Survey*, SAIRR, Johannesburg.

SAIRR, *Race Relations News*, Johannesburg.

Schneider, C. (1984) 'Microstudies in Gazankulu: a study of eight villages in two districts of Gazankulu', Paper No.66, Conference of the Second Carnegie Inquiry into Poverty and Development in Southern Africa, SALDRU, Cape Town.

Schmidt, D. (1984) 'Beaufort West has many windmills', Paper No.35, Conference of the Second Carnegie Inquiry into Poverty and Development in Southern Africa, SALDRU, Cape Town.

Schroder, D.T. (1979), 'Factors Influencing Changes in Farm Size', upub. MSc thesis, University of Pretoria.

Seleoane, M.L. (1984) 'Conditions on eight farms in Middleburg, Eastern Transvaal', Paper No.29, Conference of the Second Carnegie Inquiry into Poverty and Development in Southern Africa, SALDRU, Cape Town.

Simkins, C. (1981) 'Agricultural production in the African reserves of South Africa', in *The Journal of Southern African Studies*, 7,2, South Africa.

—   (1984) 'African population, employment and income on farms outside the reserves: 1923-69', Paper No.25, Conference of the Second Carnegie Inquiry into Poverty and Development in Southern Africa, SALDRU, Cape Town.

Simons, H.J. and R.G. (1969), *Class and Colour in South Africa: 1850-1950,* Penguin Books, London.

Smit, P.T. and Herbst, D. (1983) 'Provision and Stability of Labour in the Agricultural Sector — a small scale study in the Letaba district', Paper No. MM100, HSRC, Pretoria.

Smith, R.H. (1941) 'Native Life in Natal', in *The South African Journal of Economics*, IX, 1941, South Africa.

South African Agricultural Union, *Annual Reports, 1978, 1980, 1981, 1983/4*, South Africa.

South African Communist Party (1981) *South African Communists Speak 1921-81*, Inkululeko Publications, London.

SAIRR, *Annual Survey of Race Relations in South Africa*, Johannesburg.

Stadler, A.W. (1976) 'Agricultural policies and agrarian politics: a note on the Marais-Du Plessis Commission on Agriculture', Paper No.15, Farm Labour Conference, SALDRU, Cape Town.

Surplus People's Project Reports (1983) 'Forced Removals in South Africa', Vols.1-5, Cape Town.

Suzman, H. and Kahn, S. (1947) *New Lines in Native Policy*, SAIRR, Johannesburg.

Theron, J. (1976) 'Farm Labour in the Citrusdal Valley', Paper No.22, Farm Labour Conference, SALDRU, Cape Town.

UN Unit on Apartheid (1976), *Land Tenure Conditions in South Africa*, Report No.36/76, New York.

Van der Vliet, E. and Bromberger, N. (1976) 'Notes on farm labour in the Albany district', Paper No.50, Farm Labour Conference, SALDRU, Cape Town.

Walwyn, C. (1984) 'Survey of aspects of rural poverty in Clarens and the surrounding areas and of certain aspects in the black townships of Bethlehem and Harrismith', Paper No.41, Conference of the Second Carnegie Inquiry into Poverty and Development in Southern Africa, SALDRU, Cape Town.

Walker, C. (1982) *Women and Resistance in South Africa*, Onyx, London.

Wentzel, W. (1984) 'Hard times in the Karoo: case studies and statistical profiles from five peri-urban residential areas', Paper No.38, Conference of the Second Carnegie Inquiry into Poverty and Development in Southern Africa, SALDRU, Cape Town.

Wilson, F, et al (eds.) *Farm Labour in South Africa*, David Philip, Cape Town.

Wilson F. (1972) *Migrant Labour in South Africa*, SACC/SPROCAS, Johannesburg.

— (1972) *Labour in the South African Gold Mines 1911-69*, Cambridge University Press, United Kingdom.

Wolpe, H. (1972) 'Capitalism and cheap labour power in South Africa: from segregation to apartheid', in *Economy and Society*, 1,1, 1972, London.

Yawitch, J. (1981) *Betterment: The Myth of Homeland Agriculture*, SAIRR, Johannesburg.

Young, R.G. (1979) *Labour in the Transvaal Agri-business: a study of two farms*, SALDRU, Cape Town.

Official documents

Central Statistical Services, *Abstract of Agricultural Census (1980)*, Pretoria.

Marais, M.D. (Chairman) (1968) *Interim Report of the Commission of Inquiry into Agriculture*, Pretoria.

Quail, G. (Chairman), (1980) *Commission of Inquiry into Independence for the Ciskei*, Pretoria.

Report of the Bantu Affairs Commissioner 1961, Rp 72/1962, Pretoria.

Report of the Department of Native Affairs 1945-47, U.G. No.14, 1949, Pretoria.

Report of the Department of Native Affairs for 1952/3, U.G. No.48, 1955, Pretoria.

Report of the Proceedings of the Native Representative Council, 1944, U.G. No.16, 1944, Pretoria.

Riekert, P.J. (Chairman) (1976) *Report on Legislation Affecting the Utilisation of Manpower*, Rp.32/1979, Pretoria.

Theron, E. (Chairman) (1976) *Report of the Commission of Inquiry into Matters Relating to the Coloured Population Group*, Pretoria.

Du Toit, F.J. (Chairman) (1960), *Report of the Commission of Inquiry into European Occupancy of Rural Areas*, Pretoria.

Index